THE FABULOUS GEORGE LEWIS BAND

"Your Daddy, Lorenzo Tio jr. taught most of the New Orleans clarinet players, didn't he?"

"Yeah, pretty much"

"But he didn't teach George Lewis. I know that"

"Oh no, God taught George Lewis to play"

Rose Tio, 2009

George Lewis at the time of the "Jazz Information" recording – 1942

THE FABULOUS GEORGE LEWIS BAND

"The Inside Story"

BARRY MARTYN

with

NICK GAGLIANO

Burgundy Street Press
New Orleans

ACKNOWLEDGEMENTS
The author wishes to thank the following;

The Historic New Orleans Collection: Alfred Lemon

William Ransom Hogan Archive of New Orleans Jazz, Tulane University:

Bruce Raeburn, Curator and Lynn Abbott, Assistant Curator

The National Park Service

The Tulane University Archives: Ann Case

Bill Huntington

Samuel Charters

Page Van Vorst

Mike Hazeldine

A very special thanks to Barry Price; he knows why

Burgundy Street Press
3621 Burgundy Street, New Orleans, La. 70117 U.S.A.
2010 Burgundy Street Press – New Orleans

First printing April 2010
Printed in the United States of America by Wendel Printing, New Orleans, Louisiana
Distributed by Louisiana University State Press

Library of Congress Cataloging-in-Publication Data

Barry Martyn 1941 -
The Fabulous George Lewis Band

Biography: p
1. George Lewis 1900-1968
2. Jazz musician – United States

Library of Congress No. 2009943021
ISBN 978-0-8071-3698-0

The paper in this book meets the guidelines for permanence and durability of the Committee on Production Guidelines for book longevity of the Council on Library Resources

Contents

Foreward: George Lewis and Friends
    by Bruce Boyd Raeburn 7

1 The seeds are sown 9

2 'Let's form a Jazz Club' 25

3 The men in the band 43

4 The 'Look' article and the El Morroco 61

5 The college tours 74

6 Change of management 102

7 The teachers in the band 112

8 George Lewis' genealogy 120

9 Recordings and broadcasts 136

Book CD: George Lewis Band in Ohio 152

Photographic acknowledgements:

Photographs on pages 2, 20 and 66 are reproduced courtesy of The William Russell Collection, Hogan Jazz Archive, Tulane University, New Orleans

Photographs on pages 26, 32, 120 and 122 are reproduced courtesy of the Ralston Crawford Collection of Jazz Photography, Hogan Jazz Archives, Tulane University, New Orleans

Photographs on pages 64, 112, 114 and 145 are reproduced courtesy of the University Archives, Howard-Tilton Memorial Library, Tulane University, New Orleans

The photo on page 132 was by Barbara Reid courtesy of the University Archives, Howard-Tilton Memorial Library, Tulane University, New Orleans and the photograph on page 118 was by Ann Charters.

All other photographs are from the collections of Nick Gagliano and Barry Martyn.

Jim Robinson, Joe Watkins, Elmer Talbert, George Lewis, Alton Purnell, Lawrence Marrero and Alcide "Slow Drag" Pavageau at Ciro's Patio – December 13, 1950

Jim Robinson, Charlie Hamilton, Elmer Talbert, Avery "Kid" Howard, Joe Watkins, George Lewis, Alcide "Slow Drag" Pavageau and Lawrence Marrero – Regal Beer program WTPS Radio.

GEORGE LEWIS AND FRIENDS

If the clarinetist George Lewis (born George Joseph Francois Louis Zenon in 1900) had not been recommended as Big Eye Louis Nelson's replacement for trumpeter Bunk Johnson's debut recording session in 1942 (organized by "hot" record collectors Bill Russell, Eugene Williams, and a contingent of Californians led by Jazz Man record shop proprietor Dave Stuart), it is doubtful that anyone outside of New Orleans would recognize his name today. In all probability, he would have worked himself to death on the riverfront as a stevedore who played a little music on the side. His association with Bunk Johnson changed all that. Although hopes for entering the entertainment world mainstream that accompanied the resuscitation of Johnson's career during the so-called New Orleans Revival were never fully realized for the leader or his sidemen at the time, the failed Bunk experiment did succeed in demonstrating the renewal of interest in "traditional" New Orleans jazz among a new generation of jazz aficionados in the 1940s, and it gained exposure for the small coterie of pioneers that were still committed to the practice of a community-based, "authentic" New Orleans-style jazz at home.

George Lewis returned to New Orleans in 1946 from his New York sojourn with Johnson profoundly disappointed because Bunk's "evil" behavior (some of which derived from alcoholism, the rest from egotism) had destroyed any sense of camaraderie among the musicians, despite the best efforts of "managers" Eugene Williams and Bill Russell to keep the peace, and it had seemingly cost him his chance for the "big time." Bunk's view that "reading" musicians (such as himself) were superior to the organically intuitive sidemen who supported him, "ear" players like Lewis, trombonist Jim Robinson, and bassist Alcide "Slow Drag" Pavageau, created dissension within the band and confounded his handlers, who defined authenticity in New Orleans jazz as the very antithesis of Eurocentric musical literacy and score-driven performance. Eventually, Lewis returned to a catch-as-catch-can schedule of "one-nighters" in local neighborhood bars that was familiar to him but offered little more than the musical equivalent of sharecropping for someone who had ambitions toward international recognition—a goal that was not unreasonable, given his talent, and one that he ultimately achieved. The story of how that reversal of fortune transpired, told from an insider's perspective, animates the pages that follow. George Lewis's deliverance from the doldrums and consequent celebrity is a fascinating tale of unlikely associations and friendships, spanning an international cast of characters and revealing how the power and beauty of jazz could be effectively harnessed as an antidote to segregation and as a force for positive social change, creating mutual sympathy among people of diverse backgrounds.

This book is a dialogue between two individuals who probably would never have met had it not been for their shared interest in George Lewis and his music. Nick Gagliano was the son of an Italian grocer in New Orleans's Seventh Ward, a multi-cultural and racially diverse community that nevertheless conformed to the strictures of racial segregation that governed social relations in the city during the 1940s. Gagliano served in the U.S. Navy during World War II, where he gained his first exposure to jazz, then returned to Tulane University to study engineering after his discharge. He later studied law at Loyola University, which became his primary, life-long occupation. Along the way, beginning on Mardi Gras Day 1947, when he heard members of the George Lewis band for the first time, almost inadvertently, New Orleans jazz changed his life forever – although it took a while for this transformation to become apparent. Gagliano's matriculation as George Lewis's representative and "manager" in 1949 required only minimal qualifications as outlined for him by the clarinetist: he should be white, literate, sufficiently personable, and willing to work on behalf of black musicians. Nick's decision to take the assignment inaugurated a voyage of self-discovery that is revealed in these pages, a "coming of age" saga in which the boundaries separating business and friendship were sometimes confused between the precocious Good Samaritan and his charges, a group of African-American musicians some thirty to forty-five years his elder. They needed his assistance to find work that was commensurate with their talents and musical orientation. He was entranced with their dignity and the majesty of their music. Gagliano took his work seriously, and he proved to be equal to the task--it was largely through his efforts that George Lewis built a stable foundation for success and celebrity on his own terms, leading to international touring in the long run, but starting with society jobs and concerts for members of the New Orleans Jazz Club, steady employment on Bourbon Street at the El Morocco, and a feature story in *Look* magazine in June 1950. In time, well after the management of Lewis's career had passed to others, Gagliano provided legal services to the clarinetist, and this book includes a number of revelations deriving from legal documents that have hitherto remained unpublished.

Serving as Gagliano's amanuensis and adding his own unique take on George Lewis is Barry Martyn, a London-born drummer who has worked with New Orleans musicians (including Lewis, Robinson, Pavageau, and other members of the band, such as Alton Purnell) in various locations for nearly fifty years. Martyn's experience and knowledge of New Orleans-style jazz (developed more fully in his memoir, *Walking with Legends*, LSU Press, edited by Mick Burns) provides an effective threshold for Gagliano's trip down memory lane, and the counterpoint of exuberant exchange is often as entertaining as the content itself as the pair compares notes from respective vantage points. The drummer's contributions have the additional benefit of offering an outsider's perspective on the peculiar attitudes about race that curtailed the liberty of black jazz musicians (and, in truth, all African Americans) in the United States in the pre-Civil Rights era. To meaningfully embrace traditional New Orleans jazz at this time meant fraternizing across the color line, which was fraught with risk at every turn: Gagliano did his best to avoid out-and-out confrontation on this issue, preferring to work within the system as much as possible, but Martyn suffered from no such compunctions. Their discussion of race, including insights into how black musicians such as George Lewis sought and achieved dignity as artists despite the obstacles that racism placed in their way, comprises a fascinating thematic thread that runs through the entire discourse, and it is one of the primary reasons this book is important.

But there are other reasons as well. Most people will be less surprised to learn that the renowned filmmaker Stanley Kubrick began his career as a photographer for *Look* magazine than they will be astonished to discover that he was also a competent traditional jazz drummer. Like his counterpart Woody Allen, his interest in New Orleans jazz rested squarely on his love of George Lewis's playing. Indeed, as an international icon of traditional New Orleans jazz, Lewis eventually eclipsed Bunk Johnson as a focal point of the New Orleans Revival because he made himself accessible by touring broadly, first within the United States (thanks to Nick), and then, by the late 1950s, internationally, with trips to England, Denmark, Sweden, and Japan. And, it should be noted, the world also came to him. He became a featured attraction at Preservation Hall in the French Quarter from 1961 until his death late in 1968, a shrine to traditional jazz that continues to serve the interests of jazz lovers from around the world to this day. One can state without exaggeration (and with no disrespect to Allen and Sandra Jaffe, the proprietors) that the Hall was an edifice that George Lewis helped to build in a major way. Yet, ultimately, it is the music that tells us the most about who George Lewis was and why he is important, and the concerts that Nick Gagliano set up for George Lewis and his Ragtime Band at Miami University in Oxford, Ohio, in the 1950s are all currently available on the American Music label (in nine volumes), thanks to the production efforts of Barry Martyn. In actuality, Nick and Barry were a team before the idea of this book was even born, and we can thank George Lewis for that, as I am sure they do.

With two full biographies already published on George Lewis, one might be tempted to view this volume as the last word on the subject, but I doubt that that will be the case. As long as George Lewis's music continues to excite and edify listeners, there will always be something new to say about his legacy. This book occupies a unique niche within the existing literature: it provides an intimate portrait of three friends, comprising an entirely new approach to Lewis's life story, but it also sets the record straight on a number of important issues relating to business and his personal life. And, perhaps most importantly, it demonstrates the enduring magnetism of a musician whose idiosyncratic combination of lyrical majesty on his instrument and innate modesty as a performer captured the hearts and minds of jazz lovers the world over, compelling recognition of the power of music to define the human condition for all who experience it, regardless of social circumstances. One can imagine no better basis for friendship than that.

Bruce Boyd Raeburn

Chapter 1

"The seeds are sown"

Gagliano : I'll tell you, my first beginnings of recognition of the ultimate group that became the George Lewis Band started when I went out on Mardi Gras Day of 1947. I had been in the service in World War II. I was discharged in July of 1946. So then in 1946, I was still in the service when Mardi Gras was on in New Orleans if, in fact, it was on. Mardi Gras is an annual event in New Orleans, usually in February or March, and is the Tuesday before Ash Wednesday, the beginning of Lent. It was suspended for about two years during World War II. I don't know. But anyway, 1947 Mardi Gras was my first Mardi Gras after I had returned from service, I was by myself and I had decided that I was going to devote the day to simply following the truck parades and listening to the bands, whatever bands they had on them, not so much the marching bands, but the bands that were playing for the individual trucks. In 1947, the so-called official float parades were staged by the Rex organization, then solely composed of the white New Orleans upper social class, and the Zulu organization then solely composed of middle class blacks and whose parade was in some respects a parody of the Rex parade. Each of these parades would consist of from fifteen to twenty mid-morning on fashionable St. Charles Avenue and then onto Canal Street and ultimately disbanded after about three to four hours of parading; Zulu was more flexible in its starting time and place, but would always fall in behind the Rex parade somewhere along St. Charles Avenue. The truck parade would fall in behind the Rex and Zulu parades, and would be composed of over 100 decorated truck floats, which were primarily 18 wheelers with a flat bed trainer; each truck would have its own theme, and would have from fifteen to thirty masked members in the trailer. Music was, and still is, a major component of these parades, with college, high school and military marching bands, and the traditional black brass bands, that would play throughout the year, usually for black social and fraternal organizations, and at funerals. Many of the truck floats would have their own small musical groups, both white or black. Usually they would be maybe anywhere from three to four people at the most.

Well, I happened to come across two trucks, one in front of the other, and they had two combos on them. My recollection is that one combo seemed to be reasonably well dressed, sort of sedate in a way for Mardi Gras, and then the other one was sort of bedraggled and, you know, down home, I mean real – no pretention. As I'm listening to these two groups, I'm immediately taken with the raggedy group, and I just listened to them. This was a cutting contest.

Martyn : Were they white bands? Black bands?

Gagliano : No, these were black –

Martyn : Both of them?

Gagliano : As I recall, I became enthralled with the trumpet player in the raggedy group. I had no idea who he was and no idea who the other guys were. At this time, my knowledge of New Orleans jazz was almost nil. I was taken with this trumpet player and the way he sort of ran that other band into submission, so to speak. You know, a real cutter. Okay, so this was Mardi Gras, which would be February, 18th, 1947.

I'm not sure when it happened, but there was an article that appeared in *Down Beat* magazine. Now, I had started to read *Down Beat* as a sort of introduction to some of my northern friends in the service, and I'm reading – there's an article in *Down Beat* about the New Orleans jazz scene, and my recollection is that this article was written by some guy from Australia. Okay? And he's writing about the George Lewis Jazz Band playing at Manny's Tavern, and this would be 1947.

So when I read this article, two things happened to me. First of all, I decided I'm going to go out and hear who this guy, George Lewis, is. And here's a guy from Australia coming to New Orleans, writing about George Lewis. So I decided to go out to Manny's and I'm immediately struck by the trumpet player who was the guy I heard on the truck.

And that was my introduction to Elmer Talbert. He was playing trumpet. He was George's trumpet player at this period in George's band.

Martyn : But the band on the truck wasn't a George Lewis band.

Gagliano : I don't think George could have been on that truck, because it seems to me that he would have stood out.

Manny's Tavern, Benefit and St. Roch – 2009

But Elmer stood out. Maybe my tastes were not refined enough to recognize anything else. So I'm saying, "Holy cow. This is the guy that was on the truck." And I heard the band with George. This is the first time I heard George Lewis, first time I heard Lawrence Marrero, Slow Drag (Alcide Pavageau). And Jim Robinson wasn't – what they used was they had a drummer, and it probably was Joe Watkins. I'm not sure. I think it was. Slow Drag, Lawrence Marrero. So they used three rhythms and a trumpet and a clarinet, and that's all that Manny's could handle.

Martyn : Manny's was on Benefit and St. Roch, correct?

Gagliano : Benefit and St. Roch.

Martyn : What's the area that you call that? Back of town?

Gagliano : I'd say today it's part of the Upper Ninth Ward. It's primarily a black area. Back then it was probably more integrated. Manny's was operated by some Italian fellow. I don't even remember his name, but I don't think he had any appreciation of the music. I don't know how George Lewis got back there. I never did find out. But Manny's Tavern became, from that article and subsequent things, Manny's Tavern became a sort of a code word for New Orleans jazz around the world, wouldn't you say?

Martyn : Yes, absolutely.

Gagliano : You were aware of it in England at some point in time?

Martyn : Yes, yes, yes, from the *Look* article.

Gagliano : I probably went with a couple of my buddies from Tulane. Remember, at this particular moment in my life, I'm in my senior year of engineering school at Tulane. So a couple of us would go out there and listen to George, and we kept going back. Of course, George, I think, recognized us as regulars, and we would talk to him and stuff.

Martyn : How many people would be in there when you would go?

Gagliano : Shoot. Maybe, at the most, thirty or forty people. The place ain't that big. It was for dancing primarily, those that wanted to dance, and then people would sit around drinking beer. I mean there was no great excitement about the music that I can recall. But you've got to understand the situation in New Orleans. This was pretty much taken for granted.

Let me back off just a wee bit, because I think it's important. When I'm growing up, I was born on the corner of Frenchmen and Rampart Street at the 1000 block. Now, you know 500 block and 600 block of Frenchmen is the big musical area in New Orleans right now. But back then, it was nothing – a neighborhood department store, fabric shop. It was strictly, you know, mom-and-pop operations. My father had a mom-and-pop grocery store. That's how I grew up. Our neighborhood was, as all neighborhoods downtown were, integrated. The pattern was that the black families would live in the middle of the block. More often than not, they lived in what used to be the slave quarters.

Martyn : Why did they go to the middle of the block? What was the significance of that?

Gagliano : I don't know. That's the way it's – hey, I may be wrong, but that's my recollection.

Martyn : That's interesting.

10

Gagliano : Well, the corners seemed to be dominated by stores of some sort. And then you'd get nice residences, and as you'd go down the line – I don't know that there would be any difference in quality, but the black families seemed to, in my opinion, seemed to live in the middle of the block. That's our neighborhood. Across the street from my daddy's grocery store, it was the Ace Bakery. It's still there. It's still a bakery. It's now

Gagliano Family Grocery Store – 2009

Binder's. When my daddy got bigger with his little grocery store, he was able to go across the street to 1001 Frenchmen. You go over there now, it's there. It's Rosetta's Praline Shop.

Okay, so what I'm getting at is I'm growing up in this typical low class, poor neighborhood. We were not considered poor simply because we had a grocery store. With the Depression, we had food, and we were probably financially a little bit a cut above everybody else in the neighborhood.

Now, my exposure to jazz was minimal. I had a consciousness of the black parades, but never had any desire to listen to them or what have you. So what happens? I'm growing up in this situation, and you wouldn't remember this, but Prohibition ended. I think it was in 1933. And as soon as Prohibition ended, my father added a little bar in the back of his grocery, and one of the things he eventually put in the bar was a jukebox. Okay? So one of the things I used to be interested in was when the guy comes, you know, to pick up the money out of the jukebox and maybe takes some of the records out, put new stuff in, I would just wonder what he was doing.

Now, at that time I became particularly aware of Artie Shaw. You remember his "Summit Ridge Drive"? That was very popular in the thirties, got a lot of play. Another guy that I was taken up with was Fats Waller. Those were on these old records on the jukebox. That was my musical exposure. New Orleans music as a whatever it was meant nothing to me at that time.

Now I go into the service in 1944, and I'm now tossed into all sorts of interplay with guys from New York, Chicago, all around, blacks and whites. And somebody, I don't know who it was, but I must have been ready to hear some good music, okay, and the thing that started me off, strangely enough, on jazz was Bunny Berigan. Somehow I was introduced to Bunny Berigan by some of my northern friends. I didn't know anything about Bunny Berigan. Well, found out he was a trumpet player, and at that time he had a pretty popular number called "I Can't Get Started With You."

Well, that became my mantra, and so now I'm listening to Bunny Berigan. Next thing I know, some other guy is telling me about the Duke Ellington in his Jungle Band era, and I took to that. So my introduction to jazz, broad jazz, was in the service, and that was the germ. And somehow or other, I learned about *Down Beat*

Nick Gagliano

magazine and I started to read about the musicians.

So I was in the navy for two years, '44 to '46, and then I came home in '46. And when I got home I started to read *Down Beat*, and then this article appears. And two things, I went to see George Lewis and I wrote a letter to *Down Beat* I said, "Why the hell are you using an Australian person to come in and write about the New Orleans jazz scene? You ought to have somebody here local."

So they took me up on it and they said, "You want to be the correspondent?" I'm a college student and in my senior year at Tulane University.

Martyn : Did you get paid?

Gagliano : No. No. They sent me a press pass. I went out and bought me a Speed Graphic miniature press camera, and I would tote my press pass and my camera and go to all of these things.

Martyn : Well, when you went to Manny's, let me just ask you a couple of questions about that. Did you have to pay to get in? I mean did anybody pay to get in?

Gagliano : No, no. No having to pay. You just went in there and you ordered a beer. I think they probably had a hat down there. It was somewhat traditional in New Orleans that the jazz bands playing in neighborhood bars and lounges, such as Manny's Tavern, Luthjens, etc., would place a hat on the floor right in front of the band for monetary tips from the audience, particularly when making song requests, to supplement the meager pay that the bands would receive from the operator of the bar or lounge. You know, I put money in a hat. I don't remember paying anything. I guess they expected you to drink and stuff. That was my other problem; I didn't drink.

Martyn : Well, what was the audience? It must have been just a white audience, huh?

Gagliano : Oh yeah. Well, remember now, we were in segregation. We were in strict segregation at that point, so Manny's was a white place with a black band. This was typical. All of the bands that were playing at these neighborhood joints were always black fellows. Occasionally I went to Luthjens. I remember going out to Luthjens and seeing Big Eye Louis Nelson and people like that. As I began to become aware of New Orleans and New Orleans jazz, then I began to have a sort of a historic interest in the guys that were still around.

Martyn : Well, George and the band, what did they do? Did they play sets? Like they played for forty minutes and then take off?

Gagliano : No. Man, they didn't have anywhere to go. They just played there all night, as far as I remember. Oh, they'd probably take a break and get something to drink. I noticed at that time there was some aura about George having had an alcohol problem years before and that he was sort of on the wagon. I seem to think that Lawrence Marrero was sort of his conscience in this and keeping him from drinking, and my recollection is he wasn't drinking at this time.

Martyn : What did the people – what dances did they dance to the band? Waltzes, fox trots and that kind of stuff?

Gagliano : Anything. Yes, anything. Whatever the band – yes, it wasn't all jazz standards, you know. They were doing a lot of the contemporary stuff. "Over the Waves." That kind of stuff. I guess "Corinna, Corinna" would be an adaptation of a pop song.

Martyn : Did they take requests too?

Gagliano : Oh yeah. Well, I assume so, but I never made any requests that I remember.

I mean because this would normally happen at a neighborhood joint. But you know, you don't go up there and say, "Okay, here," flip them five dollars and say, "Here, play this." No, that didn't happen. You'd go up there and say, "Hey, George, can you do this?"

Martyn : Did the people know him by name?

Gagliano : Some of them did. Yeah, some of them did. Once that article appeared in *Down Beat*, you know, more – I guess. Now, if you go back to the resurgence in New Orleans, it began around – when Bill Russell came down here with his group? My recollection is that Bill Russell and his group put out these American music records somewhere, and these are things that they recorded on wire recorders (Presto recorders) or whatever they had at the time. They were doing it in George Lewis' kitchen, and these records eventually were disseminated, so George had a small following when I first met George, this was after the Bunk period. Now, here I am – well, the Bunk period was what, 1945?

12

Martyn : Forty-two really they started. 1946 was his last recording with George.

Gagliano : I'm in the service and I'm oblivious to all of that. I know nothing at all about – and when I find out retroactively that George – once I met George and got to be one of his fans, so to speak, then I begin to understand and hear about his story. You've also got to understand, George at that time lived in the 1800 block of Dauphine Street. That's four blocks from my house. You walked two blocks down – well, you go – I'm on North Rampart and Frenchmen. You walk toward Esplanade and the first you come to Burgundy. Then you come to Dauphine. Then you come to Royal. So to go to George's house from my house, I'd walk two blocks along Frenchmen, turn right and go another block, and he would be in that next block.

This would be in August of 1947. Now, remember, my consciousness of George Lewis would be February or March, and I'm now going on weekends to listen to him play.

Martyn : How old would George have been then?

Gagliano : George would have been forty-seven. Drag would have been, like, about sixty-five.

Martyn : And how old were you in '47?

Gagliano : I was twenty-one.

Martyn : So George was more than twice your age.

Gagliano : Yes, at that time. I think Elmer would have been probably around George's age too. The problem with Elmer was he died very early.

Okay, so now we're in the month of August of 1947, getting ready to go back to my senior year at Tulane engineering school. I am a member of the Tulane Newman Club. The Newman Club was the Catholic students' organization for all the campuses in the United States. So you had Newman Clubs at every one of the universities. Tulane had a Newman Club.

Martyn : What religion was George?

Gagliano : Well, I found out ultimately that his mother was a staunch Catholic. I would think George, by the time – when I saw George, he was married to Jeanette, and I got the impression they were either Baptist or whatever, but I never did probe that at the time.

So me and a group of my fellow Newman Club students are preparing to have a party to welcome new students for the new school year, naturally, to try to encourage them to join the Newman Club.

Martyn : What was the Newman Club exactly then?

Gagliano : I'm saying the Newman Club is an official outreach organization of the Catholic church where they would — this would be like a mini-parish. You've got, you know, Catholic churches or geographic centers. Each neighborhood would have a Catholic church, and many neighborhoods would have three Catholic churches in the same block because they were ethnic. So you might have an Italian church, a French church, and an Irish church. I happened to grow up in my neighborhood with an Irish church, so my Catholic priest was from Ireland. You go up the road, you go to Holy Trinity, it was a German church. You go across St. Claude onto Marais and there was Annunciation Church. I don't remember what they were. But this is why you had this proliferation of churches.

My wife's situation was unique. Her neighborhood was the Irish camp. In a two-block area, there was a French church, a German church, and an Irish church. Now, the German church, St. Mary's, is now a cultural center. Across the street from it, it's still operational, and then the French church was knocked down years ago. Okay, so the Catholic Church has outposts, so to speak, on college campuses. The Newman Club is the official name of those outposts. They were usually staffed by one priest who did this part-time. He would do that as part of his duties, if there was a Catholic parish in that particular neighborhood, conceivably he would have a secondary ministry at the Newman Club. And the Tulane Newman Club, the headquarters – the priest was stationed at Ursuline College, which is on State Street and still there, a beautiful building, it's now just a high school, but they have a priest residence there. So what they did was they combined the priest resident at Ursuline College with Tulane and they made him the chaplain for the Newman Club.

So I'm in this club. We are preparing for the new year. Normally, we would have a dance, a little party and dance, probably to records, and that would be normal. So I said to some of the guys that were going with me to Manny's on weekends, I said, "Hey, why don't we see what it might cost to have George Lewis bring his group up to play for the Newman Club party." And they looked at me and said, "You must be a little bit off." I said, "No, no, no. Think about it. Probably these kids have never heard anything like this, and, secondarily, they're going to be initially repulsed by it. But eventually they might learn to like it, and this would be something different."

Now, think about this. With people along out there in all the hinterlands dying to see and hear George Lewis in person, here we are talking about bringing him in over our – then he said, "Well, what about the Ursuline nuns?" Because we were going to have to do this at the gymnasium of Ursuline School. "Well, they might have a problem with that." I said, "We'll have to rely on – well, first of all, we've got to talk to Father Malcolm Strassel the priest. See if he'll go along with it."

Martyn : Which would have been the biggest problem, that it was a jazz band or that it was a colored band?

Gagliano : That really didn't have a hierarchy. Yeah, I would think the concept of having a black band play was probably one of our concerns. The type of music was more of a concern. And so the group finally said, "Well, let's take a shot at it." We talked to the priest, and he said, "No, go ahead. Be all right. I can get the nuns to agree, it would be just a two-hour thing. We'll have a live band. Think it would be all right." I said, "Fine." So then they tell me, "Well, why don't you go ahead, talk to George Lewis and see if we can make a deal with him."

Well, I remember talking to him about it at Manny's on one of the weekends and I tell him what we're thinking, and he said, "Well, why don't we talk about it next week during the day."

Martyn : Were you talking to him in the intermission.

Gagliano : Yes, probably. I said, "George, we're thinking about having a little party. Think you guys might like to play for it? You know, it's something to do with Tulane University." He said, "I'll talk to you about it." I said, "Say, look, why don't we meet next week, George. Where do you live?" Either I asked him or he asked me. I said, "I live on Frenchmen and Rampart," and he said, "Oh, I live on Dauphine." I said, "Oh, okay. Would you mind coming over to my father's grocery store and we'll meet, talk over there?" He said, "Sure."

So he came over and I talked with him. He probably met my father. I don't know. I don't know. My daddy was sort of a liberal conservative. He had black customers, so he was used to dealing with black people. My mother used black ladies to do her laundry. So we were friendly, you know, we had relationships. I don't want you to think that we were integrationist, because that's not what it was.

Martyn : Well, was there any integration that was proposed at that time?

Gagliano : The integration we had was normal living in a place, you know. You just had neighbors. You didn't socialize with them. They were basically – at that time they were the working class for the whites.

So we met at my house and we find out he's a neighbor. We sat down and talked about it. I said, "This is what we're going to have. It's going to be a party for students, eighteen years old, all boys and girls from around. Would you think you could get the group together would that work out for you?" He said, "Oh, yeah. We do that."

Martyn : Could you understand what he was saying? Could you understand his accent?

Gagliano : Oh, sure. Oh, yeah. I'm used to the vernacular. I mean I could speak it myself, even though, you know, now I have to be careful as a lawyer. Okay? But I can get down there and dig with the neighborhood.

So I said, "George, you know, we've got to scrape up the money for this. How much would it cost for maybe two hours?" My recollection was that he said, "About forty-two dollars." I asked him, "Will that will be for five people?" I wanted the same five as at Manny's.

Martyn : Did he say, "I'll bring the same five," or did you ask him to?

Gagliano : Oh yeah. Yes, yes, that was understood. Yes, right. I wanted him to bring his group. And I said, "This is going to be up at Ursuline High School, way uptown." He said, "Well, we get there." I had no idea how they got there, but they got there.

Martyn : When you say forty-two dollars, that was for the whole band?

Gagliano : The whole band for two hours.

Martyn : Jesus Christ. Imagine the George Lewis Band for forty-two dollars.

Gagliano : In 1947. Just to put it in perspective, when I graduated from Tulane, my first job paid me, like, about 4,800 dollars a year.

So George showed up, and the reaction was just what we thought. "What are you guys doing here and who is this?" I said, "Just cool it. Let's listen to them." So we got them up on the stage, set them up, and they did a little bit of squeaking and squawking, you know, tuning up. And then they started to play, and I would say about after the fifth or sixth tune, we had the group pretty much okay with it, and it came out okay. That's about the best I – that was the beginning of a little bit of my relationship with George, which was more than just a fan. That's just one incident. At that party, like, there's guys and gals there. They didn't know what to make of this group. No, I'm serious. They did not know what to make of the group. It took them three or four or five numbers for them to get up enough nerve, or whatever you want to call, to get up and dance to it. But this was typical New Orleans dance music. I mean neighborhood dance music. It wasn't the Armand Piron type of music. But this was meant for dancing, and these kids eventually got it because the band was rhythmic. It put down a solid beat.

Martyn : At the end of it, did they say, "Well, Nick, you really did us proud bringing this band,"

Gagliano : To the best of my recollection, I was relieved that I didn't get lynched.

Martyn : And what did George and them think of it? Were they happy?

Gagliano : I have no idea what he thought of it at that time. I really don't. I know I thanked him for coming, and he thanked me for everything, paid them all the money. I'm sure they must have got there with taxicabs. Hey, listen. I didn't haggle with George. I just said, "George, what would it take to bring your group for two hours?" And he said, "Forty-two dollars." That's what I remember. And I'm sure we were able to scrape up the forty-two dollars and were able to pay George at the end of it. And I thanked him. I said, "George, I think it went over pretty good."

Martyn : Was that the only band on it? Just the one band?

Gagliano : Yeah. And they played – I guess they probably took an intermission. Maybe they didn't. I don't know. But my clique, we were happy that it went the way it did. We knew it was going to be risky, but as far as we're concerned, it accomplished what we wanted to accomplish. It was something different. It introduced these kids to something many of them had never heard before, and I don't know what germ it set.

Martyn : Did they dance to the band?

Gagliano : It took a while.

Martyn : How did they dress on that job?

Gagliano : They would wear a coat and shirt.

Martyn : Neckties?

Gagliano : Probably. Probably. No, they were very proper. A lot has been said about George being very docile, and he was that, but this was a survival technique. Everything went fine. I thought it went good. By this time I'm telling George, "Hey, George, I'm the *Down Beat* correspondent for New Orleans." So I think I have a little credential.

Martyn : Did he know what *Down Beat* was?

Gagliano : I'm sure he did.

Martyn : I couldn't imagine him reading jazz magazines somehow, you know?

Gagliano : No, but they would know about it because – let's face it – they had a story written about George Lewis at Manny's in *Down Beat*.

Martyn: And George knew that story was in there?

Gagliano : He had to know it. I mean I don't know that he did, but I'm assuming that he knew. I can't envision him not knowing that his group has been mentioned in a national magazine. Now, at that time, I think I found out that Down Beat had been in operation for some years. I think it was monthly. At some point in time maybe it became weekly, but I don't remember that. So after that, now that I knew where George lives, he knows where I live, well, I'd go visit him and we'd chat. I met Jeannette. I remember his daughter Shirley.

Martyn : Did George live in a one-storey house, two-storey, or what?

Gagliano : It was a ground floor. I'm not sure – it was a single – I know it was in the backyard. It was not the front of the house that – you might have gone – went down the alley to get to what might have been maybe a two-or three-room apartment at the most. I don't even know whether they had indoor plumbing or what. But all I know is it was relatively primitive, but not unusual for poor black families. And I have to believe George and Jeannette, at that time, were among the poor black families.

Martyn : Okay. Did Jeannette know anything about his music? Did she go and listen to him play music?

Gagliano : I don't know that she went to listen. Keep in mind, you've got to understand that we're dealing with New Orleans segregation. This is one of the reasons why, in my tour of duty as the correspondent for the *Down Beat*, I had a hell of a time trying to figure out how to go to these black clubs, but I wasn't that interested in that kind of music anyway. But to give a balanced account of what music was happening in New Orleans, you almost had to do that. And I don't know. I'm sure you must have met – at some point in time in your life, you met George "Tex" Stephens.

Martyn : Oh, yeah.

Gagliano : Okay, well, Tex was a young black guy and he was on the radio at the time, and somehow he and I ran into each other, and when he found out I was a *Down Beat* correspondent, man, he took the meat quick and he tried to, "Come on, man. You gotta come with me over there to the Dewdrop Inn. I want you meet Mr. Frank Painia." I never did do that, and that I regret. I didn't really pursue it. But be that as it may. No, I don't recall ever having Jeannette hear George play, although it would not be out of .... well, you know, it's an interesting thing.

Martyn : Just coming back to what we were saying about Jeannette, did she ever hear George play? I guess she obviously did when they made the records in his kitchen.

Gagliano : Oh yeah. She would be there for that.

Martyn : Did you think George's band was an old-time style of music or did you think it was a current style?

Gagliano : At the time, I did. Yes.

Martyn : You thought it was an old-time style of music.

Gagliano : Yes, I did.

Martyn : Had you heard any of the Bunk Johnson records.

Gagliano : Not at this time. At some point in time, I remember buying the Victor album, and I have a feeling I did this after I met George and started to talk to him about things, and I found out then that he and a number of the guys were up in New York with Bunk Johnson. And they told me, in essence, that, "We really missed a great opportunity. Bunk was just – we couldn't work with Bunk." If you read the books about Bunk, it seems like he was a reading musician. I think that he looked down upon George and those guys who didn't read, for whatever reason, and yet he used them.

Martyn : Well, the most amazing thing was when you put Bunk, let's say – Alvin Alcorn's another good trumpet player, reader. Red Allen, another one. You put those guys with George and Jim, George and Jim had – I worked with both of them. They had such fabulous ears that you don't have to play not even a chorus for them to pick it up. And he would pick it up on his clarinet and Jim would pick it up on his trombone. They had great ears, you know. But there's always a natural scorn of non-readers by readers in the music business.

Gagliano : Oh, sure. I understood that, and I think that was part of whatever animosity, plus the fact that Bunk was an out-and-out alcoholic.

Martyn : Yeah, there's no question of that.

Gagliano : You know, he would go on toots, according to the boys and they said, "Man, Bunk Johnson ruined our chance in New York." That was their mindset when I met them. So I'm getting a lot of negative feedback about Bunk, and then that's when the first glimmer of a suggestion that maybe I might be able to work with the band. I remember specifically George telling me, he says, "You know, Nick," he said, "we were in New York when we had people coming all over the world coming to see us. We played at United Nations. We had played some sort of a big United Nations thing with Eleanor Roosevelt."

Martyn : Yes, Orson Welles organized that thing.

Gagliano : Yes, Orson. Then he says, "Man, we had New York by the tail, and Bunk ruined it." That's the way he put it. "He ruined it, and here we are back at home, struggling, trying to make ends meet."

Martyn : And this wasn't that long after.

Gagliano : About a year or year and a half.

Martyn : Yes, it was a year and a half, maybe two years.

Gagliano : And that disappointment was still very, very palpable.

Martyn : I didn't realize they talked about that when you knew them.

Gagliano : Oh yeah. That's how I got involved. George said, "Man, we need somebody to talk for us." He said, "If we ever get the chance again, I want to get a guy like you to be my go between."

Martyn : Why did he pick you?

Gagliano : Just because I was there. Well, no. I would say that I apparently have certain qualities. I'm not trying to blow my horn, okay, but I'm telling George, "Well, George, I don't know. Maybe I can help." You've got to understand my own situation. I go through engineering school. I'm among the top 10 percent of my class. I'm president of the Tulane engineering student body. So I've done a few things, at least in college. I had an offer when I graduated to go up to Schenectady, New York, to go into the G.E. training program, and I turned it down. I didn't want to leave town again. I didn't want to go up there by myself, so I stayed home and I got a job in construction.

So here I am. Now I'm working full-time as an estimator-project manager for a plumbing company. I am moonlighting on Friday and Saturday nights at Manny's, and I visit George Lewis and his wife at home occasionally, and we sit around and talk, and the talk eventually got around to New York and how Bunk blew the deal. George says, "If we ever get a chance again, we gotta have somebody that can talk for us." He said, "Somebody like you." I said, "George, I don't know nothing about this business." "That's all right" he said, "You know how to talk – You can write, and that's what this business is about."

Martyn : Well, when I met, well, the whole band, I met George in '57 in England, but I met the whole band in '59 when they all came. And I remember talking to Jim in the intermission, and they went to the local what they call pub, the barroom. And there was a couple of us plucked up the courage to ask Jim about Bunk, and he said, "Oh, I'm not gonna say nothing bad about that man." He said, "I'm not gonna say nothing bad about him, but I'll tell you this, if there is a hell, he's in it." He's not going to say nothing bad, but that's exactly what he said.

Gagliano : Well, there you go.

Martyn : Jim was kind of a crazy character.

Gagliano : Now, listen. Jim Robinson wasn't in this initial entourage – at Manny's. Jim came into the picture later.

Martyn : I'm sorry to cut you off, but I wanted to ask you a couple more things about Manny's. Then we can leave that.

Gagliano : Sure.

Martyn : It was white patrons only, men and women. Was there more men there than women?

Gagliano : I have no way of knowing, but I would say half and half.

Martyn: Did the people come like we're dressed or did they dress up?

Gagliano : Casual!

Martyn : They didn't dress up?

Gagliano : No.

Martyn : Because I played some of the dance halls, like the Harmony Inn, the Hope's Hall and Munsters.

Gagliano : But Manny's was not like that.

Martyn : The people used to come in neckties, the men in suits and the women would wear dresses. They were pretty dressed up.

Gagliano : Yes, but that's a social occasion when you talk about Hope's Hall. You're talking about – these are put on by what? Who would have arranged the affair at Hope's Hall? Stop and think about that. Usually, it would be some kind of a benevolent association or a lodge, and they would put on a dance. And this would be a big – this was meant to be a social event. Manny's is a neighborhood bar with a band. The band is incidental to the bar.

Martyn : When you went in, you went in the front.

Gagliano : I seem to remember you went in through a bar and then went into the back room. That's what I remember.

Martyn : Oh, okay. I went to Manny's, but years later. It was a laundry.

Gagliano : Well, it was a washateria.

Martyn : It was made out of cinderblocks.

Gagliano : Yeah. Cinderblock building.

Martyn : Did they have amplification, George and the band? Did they have a microphone?

Gagliano : They probably did, but they didn't need it. The place was that small. And George's band, the guys, they could fill that little room easy.

Martyn : Who would do the singing? Did they have singing?

Gagliano : Joe Watkins and Elmer Talbert. Elmer was really a real gruff type of blues shouter, so actually the singing was done by Elmer Talbert and Joe Watkins. Drag said nothing. George said very little. Elmer was sort of garrulous, had a gruff voice. Lawrence would be benevolent, sitting there plunking away. He didn't do a hell of a lot of talking.

Martyn : Did they announce the numbers?

Gagliano : Yeah, I guess once in a while they did, but I'm not sure about that.

Martyn : You don't remember who did that.

Gagliano : Probably George or maybe Joe, because Joe would have the mike more often than not. They had a mike. No doubt they had a mike, and I'm sure they used it for singing because otherwise you couldn't have heard the voice.

Martyn : Well, they stayed there quite a while, didn't they?

Gagliano : On and off, yes.

Martyn : Because a lot of the people that I've talked to through the years went to Manny's, none of them as early as you.

Gagliano : Well, if you look at my timeline, you will see that I ran across the band on weekends – I would say this started in the early part of, I'd say, April and May of '47. And then what would happen is, after April, May, then we had summer vacation for the school, and that opened up again end of August. So the band was playing at Manny's certainly in 1947, and they played at Manny's all the way through the period until 1952, when they opened at the El Morocco. Now, when the *Look* magazine article came out in 1950, it was in June of 1950, all of the pictures were at Manny's Tavern. So all the while, starting, let's say 1949 and '50, I'm saying that this is the beginning period of my management of the band, and this consisted of setting up debutante and fraternity dances, miscellaneous gigs, including the WTPS radio show. That was a weekly show. I remember traveling in a train, I think to Mobile, Alabama. We did a promotion for Regal Beer.

Martyn : Was there any times at Manny's where there would be another band because George had to go and play somewhere else?

Gagliano : Not that I'm aware of. Oh, well, you mean when George wasn't there? I'm sure they brought in somebody, because there were times when, for instance, in 1949, we were one of the first bands that were engaged by the Jazz Club to play at – so this would have been a weekend thing. George would have had to probably take the night off.

Martyn : Do you remember anybody sitting in at Manny's? Other musicians?

Gagliano : I don't remember.

Martyn : There was a group of young white musicians from out of town that kind of – I don't know if you would know their names, but Alden Ashforth was a clarinet player. Sam Charters, he was also a clarinet player. They came and they sat in at Manny's, but it was later. It wasn't these early years. It was later.

Gagliano : Just to put things into perspective, my relationship, my band relationship with George would have ended around 1955. I found out that by this time I entered law school in 1954. Now, it was one thing for me to handle the band's business when I'm working and I've got time at night and I've got time on weekends, okay.

Martyn : In your early dealings with him, before you sort of really took over the dealings for the band, you know, about the time of the party that you organized for him, did he have a business head at all, do you think?

Gagliano : No, never did. Not to me. George had a certain aura of dignity about himself. You know, he would be very soft-spoken. He would talk to you if you talked to him. He would speak calmly, sheepishly. He played the role of the subservient black. That's the way he was brought up. You've got to understand he was brought up in that period. His mother taught him, "George, you got your place in life and don't you go beyond that."

Martyn : How was his mother to get along with? Did you meet her many times?

Gagliano : Oh yeah. She was a wonderful old lady. I would visit her at her. I was appalled at how she had to live at her age. She lived in a walkup apartment and no bathroom facilities. She had to come downstairs to go to the outside. She had no heat other than a stove, little stove and what she cooked on. She was an enigma because she was brought up in genteel white society, French white society. She was able to speak French. She had taught herself how to read. She became a reader.

Martyn : Did she speak English to you ?

Gagliano : Of course.

Martyn : Spoke English.

Gagliano : Oh yeah. But she spoke French too. English was her – as far as I'm concerned – was her first language, but maybe, in the old days, French was. And that accounts for George's name, Joseph François.

Martyn : How old was she when you met her?

Gagliano : Alice? At least in her seventies.

Martyn : What did George call her?

Gagliano : He was very respectful. He and his momma, they were very close, although she always lived on her own for the most part.

Martyn : Why did she want to live on her own? What was the reason?

Gagliano : George had no room for anyone. The only time that George had room for her was when he finally was able to build that little house he bought over in Algiers.

Martyn : On D'Armas Street, yes.

Gagliano : On D'Armas.

Martyn : But George, when you went to his house, did he ever play any of his records? Did he have a phonograph ?

Gagliano : Never did. I don't ever recall, for instance, I don't ever recall having dinner with George or his wife or anything. I think in some respects we were both observing the traditional New Orleans way, which wouldn't apply to people like you from out of state, like Bill Russell. I had the misfortune of growing up in our particular society, and just like my family had reservations about what kind of interaction you would have with black people, the black people had the same concerns about interacting with the whites. It was a mutual thing.

Man, I remember the first time we went up to Miami [Ohio] when the guys were treated royally. Man, it was a culture shock to them. When we went onto the campus and then all of these people would fawn over them.

Martyn : Well, they told me that when they went to New York, they couldn't believe it how the people were.

Gagliano : That's right.

Martyn : Jim was telling me that they spent hours – I think it's in one of the books – they spent about forty minutes looking through the window of this cafeteria to see if there was any black people in there before they could go in. And then they said, "Look, Lawrence, there's a black guy sitting down there with another black guy, so it must be all right for us. We're going in." Can you imagine spending forty minutes out there?

Gagliano : I wasn't a flaming rebel in this regard. I was always on the side of the black people. When I was in school, when I was in law school, I sponsored getting into an organization where we would have the black students with us. I was always liberal in that respect. When it came down to the Jazz Club, I more or less identified myself with the black men. It's not that I didn't appreciate the white guys. I did.

Martyn : Were you aware of, like, oh, New Orleans – what do they call it – folkloric sort of things like the "Who killed the chief?" Did you know what all that was about?

Gagliano : Yes, that was an Italian thing. That was the establishment versus the Italian community. You know, the racial history of this area is just tremendous. Now, I like to think about my grandfather. My grandfather came over here in 1891, one month after the lynching of the Italians and the "who killa the chief". He didn't know anything about it, but he could have walked into a real donnybrook. My grandfather was born in a town called Sambuca in Sicily. Sambuca was and is a small farming village, with a stable population of between 8,000 to 9,000 inhabitants, most of whom were poor landless peasants, scratching out a meager living as tenant farmers. It is located about 50 miles south, south-west of Palermo, and about 10 miles from the southern Mediterranean coast. And he came over here in 1891. He would always talk to the family about Sambuca, where he was from. We all knew in the family about Sambuca. About 15 or 20 years ago, I'm doing something with some people at Tulane University and I learned, "Did you know that there is a book written about Sambuca?" I said, "You've got to be kidding?" I said, "A book written about Sambuca?" "Yeah," he said. He gave me the name of it. Sure enough, – there was a book with – the name of it is "Militants and Migrants" and it was a sociological study that was done by a professor who was then at a university in New Jersey and she was studying over a 50 year period probably. She was studying patterns of immigration and unrest in the area – that are in an area she called "Wheat towns." And it was about a couple of hundred of these Wheat towns in Sambuca. And she went to Sambuca to research all of that stuff their records. And she wrote this book. Well, after I found out about it, I found out also that, coincidentally, it was published by the Rutgers University Press. So, I call up the University Press and I get about a dozen of these books. "I'm going to distribute this to the family." You know, I get about a dozen and I read through the thing and I found out who the author was. It was a lady named Donna Mae Gabaccia of Garden State University. So, I find out — as I read this lady's book and she says "All the data that I that I have in writing this book was collected by me over a six month period in the town of Sambuca and I made records of all of the people who I thought immigrated from Sambuca." And she's saying in here that she was able to identify about 3,000 people who immigrated over that period. And then, in addition to that, she said, "I created some family cards which sort of tied together all of these different immigrants into what family they belong to." That's not much, but it — it was something. She had my grandfather's mother and father and all that stuff.

Martyn : Let me get back to "Who killed the Chief?"

Gagliano : The phrase "Who Killa the Chief" started out as a mean-spirited epithet against the New Orleans Italian-American community, and as the years went by turned into a more subtle of somewhat joking recognition of a person' Italian heritage. I first heard the phrase from one of the beloved religious brothers teaching at my high school in the late 1930's and coming from him I could not see or feel any sense of insult, but I had no idea what it meant and he didn't attempt to explain it. Many years later, as I became more aware of the racial and ethnic turmoil in New Orleans in the decades before and after the Civil War, I came to learn the details which gave rise to the phrase.

In 1890, at a time when he was reputedly investigating the activities of two gangs of stevedores (all Italians) on the Mississippi River docks, New Orleans Police Chief David Hennessey was fatally shot as he was returning home late at night, but he held on to life in the hospital for several days, during which he was questioned a number of times by the investigating officers, and he made no incriminating statements until the moment before his death, when he was reputed to say "the Dago's did it". On the basis of this statement, the police rounded up about 19 suspects, all Sicilian Italians, some previously respected business men with maritime interest, but most illiterate laborers working on the Mississippi docks.

All of the suspects were kept in the Orleans Parish jail, which was adjacent to Congo Square, until the trial held in state court in March 1891. All of the defendants were acquitted, and immediately thereafter and before the accused were released from jail, a mob of thousands of people, incited and led by business and social leaders, stormed the jail, and shot and hanged about 10 of those Sicilians. At the time, this was played up in the press as the first appearance in America of an Italian secret society, later to be identified as the Mafia or the Black Hand. It was in this dangerous environment that my grandfather, Nicolo Gagliano, unwittingly embarked just one month later, to work in the sugar cane fields surrounding New Orleans.

Martyn : It seems this town has always had prejudices directed against someone.

Gagliano : While the parallel is clear, I would not in any way suggest that the Italian prejudice was anywhere near that practiced against the blacks. Nevertheless, George and I were kindred spirits of a sort in this situation, but George and his family paid dearly all of his life for the oppression imposed upon him; I felt only a twinge of it in my social connections.

Martyn : Well, what did your father think of you socializing with black musicians? What did he think of it?

Gagliano : Very tolerant. As I told you, he had black customers. He didn't encourage anything and he didn't discourage me. He allowed me to do what I thought I should do. As a matter of fact, the band played for my mother and father's twenty-fifth wedding anniversary.

Martyn : Where was that at?

Gagliano : My understanding was we did it out at Jim's Plaza, someplace on Airline Highway. And Dick Allen, in later years, reminded me, "Man, that was a great session at your daddy and mother's twenty-fifth wedding anniversary." I said, "Were you there, Dick?" He said, "Sure. You invited me to come." I probably invited him and Bob Greenwood and those fellows.

Martyn : But Bob Greenwood, that's a funny character because I remember trying to talk to him and I couldn't get any sense out of him. He was – oh, man, he'd be drunk.

Gagliano : But he was an avid fan of George Lewis.

Martyn : I know he was, yes, yes, which is why I wanted to talk to him. Did you know Bob Greenwood in later years when he was around here?

Gagliano : No, no, no. I only knew him in the era that I was with the band starting in 1948. You've got to remember, Bob Greenwood was not a native to New Orleans. He came to New Orleans to go to Tulane University.

Martyn : What did he study?

Gagliano : Library science. And one of the things that I want to tell you about that I'm sure you know nothing about, but he had conceived the idea of having interviews, which would have been, say, the foundation of what the Hogan Archive ultimately became.

Martyn : The Ford Foundation?

Gagliano : He was trying to be the curator. I don't remember who the first curator was for Tulane.

Martyn : Bill Russell. Bill Russell was the first one. They founded it in '58, I think it was.

Gagliano : In '58.

Martyn : Bill Russell was the curator. Dick Allen was the assistant curator. It was just them two.

Gagliano : In Bob Greenwood's vertical file at the archive, there is an interesting series of letters, an exchange of letters between him and Bill Russell. Bill Russell, at this particular point in time, I think

Bob Greenwood

20

Bill Russell's only physical exposure to New Orleans was when he came down here with the other gentlemen to resurrect Bunk Johnson and to do those initial recordings.

Martyn : Well, by '56, he was living here.

Gagliano : Well, maybe so, but the era that I'm talking about now is, like, 1949 and 1950. That's when Bill Russell was living in Canton, Missouri. And before he came to New Orleans, he eventually moved from Canton to Chicago, and apparently came from Chicago to New Orleans. I'm not sure about that.

Martyn : I think that's right.

Gagliano : But in any event, there was a correspondence between Bob and Bill Russell, which began with Greenwood trying to get records from Bill Russell and particularly about George Lewis and the other guys. And then Bill would write back to him matter-of-factly, just, you know, says, "I can send you this," or, "I can't get you this." And he's doing this in his handwriting. Bob is doing his thing on the typewriter. So in any event, this goes on for a number of months, and then finally, when Bob seems to think that he and Bill are a little bit more than just a record collector and Bill being a provider, they really start a correspondence, and he starts feeding information to Bill about all of the old guys that are still playing down here that probably Bill doesn't know anything about, and that goes on and on. But I can tell you that there are letters in his file from 1949, 1950, where he's writing to Tulane, telling them about setting up an archive for jazz.

Martyn : It's funny how in this music, there's several people who've either imbibed, shall we say, over-anxiously, or they've gone completely nuts like Gene Williams and people like that, you know.

Gagliano : Now you understand why I never became part of that group of people that frequented the French Quarter and hung out at the clubs. That's why I'm saying to you that people like Bob Greenwood and Dick Allen were more tuned in on the jazz underground than I ever was. I was a typical Italian boy struggling with my family to get further along in life. My daddy had made the point that I was going to go to college, and I did, in fact start college on my own in '42, but had to go in the service. Spent two years in the service and came back in '46, and by this time the government had formulated the G.I. Bill, and that's why I was able to complete my Tulane education under the G.I. Bill. I was not at all into this itinerant lifestyle that you might have led. I'm in a much more traditional situation. My mother kept my nose clean. She wouldn't even let me go to Washington Square two blocks from my house. In my day, when I was a kid, my mom said, "No, you can't go over there. They got too many muggleheads." So I was basically a sort of sheltered child.

And you know, It's just not my lifestyle and I didn't want to run the risk of screwing my life up. Some of these guys came to New Orleans for the express purpose of hanging out. Now, they loved jazz, apparently, but they loved a lot of other things, you know, and booze was another one, and maybe drugs, all of that going on.

Martyn: Well, I must confess, when I first met Dick Allen, he said, "Man, you should come to the Bourbon House." You remember the Bourbon House?

Gagliano : Yeah, the building is still there.

Martyn : Yeah, and he said, "Oh, it all happens there." And I went there a couple times, and I thought, what all happens? There's nothing but a bunch of weirdos chitchatting about some of it's jazz they were talking about. But they had no intent whatsoever of going to – I started going to the musicians, calling them and saying, "Look, Mr." so-and-so. Paul Barnes, for instance. "I'm a jazz fan Mr. Barnes, would it be all right to come to your house?" "Why, sure." And I'd go round there and talk with him, and Alma would be there, his wife, and all that. But those people never seemed to – maybe it was the social scene that they wanted. They hung around the Bourbon House like it was a jazz archive.

Gagliano : Yeah, but not anything that was being produced for posterity. Their aspect of it was what's here and now. Let me ask you the question. You got fellows like Dick Allen; you got fellows like Bob Greenwood that know a lot about jazz, apparently love it, and George Lewis is down here on his cuffs, on his heels, and nobody apparently made a move to specifically work with George to get him going. Why was it me?

Martyn : Well, I don't know, but thank heaven it was you.

Gagliano : But you see, the compromise was I didn't hang out down there. I wasn't part of the network. For instance, when you talk about the Otto party. Here I am. I'm the ad hoc manager of the band at this time just starting out. Ain't nobody told me to come to the Otto party, and I didn't know nothing about it until later years I'm finding out that they had a great big old party down there in the Quarter and all of this music was recorded. And Bob Greenwood has acknowledged that the band didn't get paid for none of this.

Martyn : Oh, no. I know they didn't. Because I interviewed Herbert Otto. Herbert Otto, do you know him?

Gagliano : I never met him.

Martyn : Oh, okay. Well, you wouldn't believe what he does. He's a doctor of orgasm, sexual orgasm. That's what he does. He studies sexual orgasms in men, women, and chimpanzees, and God knows what, I suppose. I don't know.

Gagliano : He wrote a book on it or something?

Martyn : Yeah, he did write a book. He gave me the book. I mean, I'm a musician. What do I need a book on that for.

Gagliano : And did you learn anything?

Martyn : He could have better interviewed me. He'd have learned something. No, I didn't learn anything. But it is a nicely produced book, and the people take him very seriously, Dr. Herbert Otto, you know. And he's a nice guy. He's of German ancestry, I do believe. The GHB Foundation bought his tapes, which were, amongst others, the Herbert Otto party. But it was recorded in two sections, Bob Greenwood's and Otto's so one of them was on a better tape recorder than the other.

I think I made a deal with Bob Greenwood or somebody to do with Bob. So we bought the two tapes and then we took the best of each. One started with, let's say, the first number of the evening, and the other tape started with the tenth number of the evening. The one that started first cut off earlier, so we only got, say, twenty numbers on the tape, whereas the one who started at number ten got thirty numbers. So there was an extra. Bob Greenwood wasn't that hard to deal with because he recognized the importance of this stuff. I think maybe all of these people sort of recognized the importance of it. I don't know.

Gagliano : Oh, Bob did. Listen, let me tell you this. As I reflect on everything, I think that George would be very, very appreciative of what – and I am too – of what he did on behalf of George. He was, evidently, one of the underground guys that set up this thing with *Look* magazine, not having to set up *Look*, but changing their original concept. According to him, they were coming down here to do Papa Celestin and Sharkey Bonano.

Martyn : I didn't know George like you did, but I knew him in a different way. But he was totally uneducated, but he wasn't a fool. He was very aware of people and what they were doing. Because I've seen people come to George and tell him what they're going to do, bring him to Australia and all that. And he said, "Oh, ain't that nice. Yes, sir. Yes, sir. Thank you." And then they'd walk away and he says, "Bullshit artist." You know, he could see through people. I don't want to put words in anybody's mouth, but I think he saw in you the very thing that you were saying, "Why, was it me?" I think it was you because he could see that the rest of these people were hanging out night after night at places like the Bourbon House and the Alpine Cafe and places like that. They went the circuit from one place to the other place, you know. But, of course, nobody but nobody could foresee the Preservation Hall coming into existence.

Gagliano : Well, you know, I think you're right, because as I reflect back on it, it was George who initially planted the seed of me being his manager. And I remember telling George, "I don't know nothing about this business. I really don't." I said, "I don't see how I could be your manager."

And basically what I remember him saying, he says, "You can write a letter, can't you? You can talk on the telephone, can't you?" I said, "Yeah, I can do that." He said, "That's what we need."

Martyn : Do you think there was a reticence on his part to do it or do you think he needed a white mouthpiece? I hate to put it like that, but it saves a lot of time.

Gagliano : The racial aspect of it didn't occur to me at all.

Martyn : But did it occur to George?

Gagliano : I don't know what was in his mind – no, I would imagine that. To get something going he had to have somebody in the white community push for him. Because the black community did not – at this time, the broad black community did not embrace the old-time music. We were starting to get into the rhythm and blues and the soul music and all of that, and that's where the black community went with regard to music. George's brand of music was going to appeal to, I guess I would say, a more sophisticated set that was interested more in the history. The white people were probably more into the history of the black musician than was the black person. And again, I'm saying that not to denigrate anybody in the black community.

Martyn : No, but it's true.

Gagliano : I'm just facing up to the facts that existed at that time.

Martyn : It's true even now.

Gagliano : See, the people that were hiring jazz bands were basically white people.

Martyn : Well, I just got through looking – I do a little research the same as you've been doing and I was looking at a page out of Paul Barnes' diary, you know Paul Barnes, the clarinet player.

Gagliano : Yeah. I don't know that I remember him personally.

Martyn : Emile Barnes' brother. I was looking at a page out of his diary and it designated a dance for white or was it for Negro, they called them then, I guess? And there's about twelve dates listed in the South and how much they paid. Very interesting. Some of them are ridiculous. But out of that, ten of them for white audiences, two of them for Negro audiences.

Gagliano : They derived from the black community their income from parades, okay, from picnics and all of the things that the black fraternal and self-help organizations would have, and that was a source of business for them.

Martyn : Well, even when I came here, funerals didn't pay nothing much, but they did pay. They paid six dollars.

Gagliano : It was bread-and-butter money. But if you wanted to go play in a club or if you want to play high-society functions, had to be white, and that's the way it was. And besides that, the damn black community at the time was so downtrodden that they probably couldn't support their own music.

Martyn : Yeah, but would they have supported it? I don't know. I personally thought and observed to some extent that that period of music was sort of the last flaring of something that went before in maybe the twenties, let's say, you know. I mean, right now at Preservation Hall – they get rock-and-roll guitar players to bring a banjo and strum a banjo just because they're black and they're old, you know, or they get a wild alto player that copies Charlie Parker to bring a clarinet and play "old style". But it keeps the musicians working. But I think really, with bands like George's and even Papa Celestin's, they kind of provided people, white people, with some inkling of what went before. Well, if they were playing for black people, the black people didn't give a shit what went before. They didn't give a crap what was going on now, let alone what went before.

Gagliano : Yeah, you're right.

Martyn : I mean, black people that I've known, I've known very few that are interested in their own musical culture, you know. The younger fellows like. Michael White. He's about the only one who studies it, you know.

Gagliano : Oh, okay. Well, let's face it. Michael White's background is as a student. He's a professor. This is his life and so he would be likely to go back into the origins of the music that he seems to have espoused. Now, what is Michael White doing now? Now he's starting to make compositions that are sort of contemporary, but which are based upon, supposedly, the black experience. So, you know, the thing is, I came to the conclusion that you can't keep this art form in a completely static condition. It's just not going to work. So you've got to give the younger guys, I suppose, enough head to see their own thing. Remember this, that probably in their original day, this was a new music when it started out, and it had to develop. You know, the one thing that I was always afraid of – there's two things I was afraid of when I associated with George. Number one, I knew the guys were older, much older than me, and incidentally, this runs through a lot of things that Bob Greenwood did, the speculating on what was going to happen to jazz music when a George Lewis jazz member died. They speculated on that. Now, that's a horror that I was thinking about when I was there. But you know what the strange thing about this is? Why, with all of these guys who felt this strongly about George, it takes a guy like me to come in there and offer help?

Martyn : But how was it for you? I mean, it was strange for you to be around all these black people?

Gagliano : Well, of course it was strange for me.

Martyn : Well, how did it manifest its strangeness?

Gagliano : Well, you know, I don't know how I could articulate it. I think that my family tolerated it, but I also think my family looking at me, I was the first college graduate – no, the second college graduate in my extended family. I had gone successfully through college. I had spent two years in the navy away from home, and I came back at age twenty, immediately went back to school under the G.I. Bill. Before, my daddy was picking up the tab. I said, "When I'm coming back, Dad, you don't have to worry about it. It would be on the G.I. Bill." My Dad said, "Hey, that's a-good." And when I brought George Lewis around the family house to talk about bringing him to this party I wanted to do up at Tulane, my daddy didn't raise any eyebrows about it. My mother never did question me about it. They might have been a little bit uncomfortable about it because my parents, like all of the other people, they were into this segregation thing where the black had to know their place. Now, George was a consummate courteous, unconfrontational type of a black that would not create any kind of a threat to anybody or any white establishment. So how I perceived myself, I just went ahead and I wanted to help these guys. And I loved the music, and I realized that this music had a finite period of time and that we've got to do what we could to keep it alive. And I think that was probably the universal feeling in the members of the Jazz Club.

Martyn : Let me just back up a little here, what branch of the armed forces did you say you were in?

Gagliano : I was in the navy, in the radar program.

Martyn : Well, was that segregated?

23

Gagliano : Well, let's put it this way. From a practical point of view, it was segregated. I don't really remember any black friends from my navy experience. No, my integration in the navy was integration between South and North. Well, you know, you had all these southern boys being thrown in to these northern boys, but it was a good interchange, because in fact, as I indicated to you, this is what opened my eyes to music.

Martyn : Do you know what the mutiny, or whatever they wanted to call it, at Port Chicago was all about?

Gagliano : Port Chicago? No, I knew nothing about that.

Martyn : Oh, okay. Well, it was quite big at the time. It happened at the naval munitions base at Port Chicago on the San Francisco Bay. The colored seamen refused to load shells after there was a – I'm paraphrasing the whole thing to make it quicker, but there was an explosion which killed a good few sailors, white and black. Over two thirds were black, and the colored seamen refused to load the shells because they said why should they be doing it and the white ones weren't doing it, and if there was going to be another explosion, they'd be the only ones who died, not the white ones. It was a very big thing. It was an important thing.

Gagliano : You say this was a navy incident?

Martyn : Yeah, navy incident. It was '44, I'm pretty sure. I mean I'm not into naval history, but the reason I was asking that, because when I interviewed Wendell Eugene, who was also in the navy same time as you were, well, he's a Creole trombone player. He's not really black, but he's classified as black. He was in Port Chicago* when all this went down and he told me this fantastic story about it, which I could have never got. It has nothing to do with jazz, but it certainly was worth interviewing him about, because he was there, you know. And I just wondered if there was any segregation that you knew of in the navy.

Gagliano : I have no personal recollection of having any black friends in the navy, in my training program, and I don't know whether this is something I had read earlier or later, I got the impression that the navy had sort of relegated the blacks to the subservient class. On ships they would be like stewards, be in the kitchen, doing the laundry.

Martyn : Like the railroads.

Gagliano : But that's not necessarily something I experienced directly or was conscious of. This was something that I recall reading.

Martyn : Well, I guess George and them; they were too old for military service.

Gagliano : Oh, yeah. No, no, they were – as a matter of fact, George, having been born in 1900, I have a reference in my notes on the *Second Line,* in one of its 1950 issues, congratulated George on reaching fifty years old and suggesting that he looked very young for his years, and also characterized him and his band as one of the most popular and busiest in New Orleans at that time.

Martyn : Like Jim was in the army in the First World War, as I understand it. Drag, well I don't know what kind of army would have taken Drag for anything.

Gagliano : No

Martyn : But he seemed a lot older than he was. I mean he just acted old.

Gagliano : My understanding was that he was in his late sixties when I was beginning my stint with the band, and that would be in 1949. I think that Jim was just a little bit younger than Drag. Lawrence Marrero was – my guess is, if Drag would have been sixty-six, Lawrence would have been like sixty. Elmer Talbert was pretty much the same age as George would be, and then the youngest of the group, Joe Watkins was probably a couple of years younger than George, I think. Later there was Alton, and I would think that there was maybe ten to fifteen years' difference between Alton and George.

Martyn : I think Alton was born in 1911. I'm pretty sure because I had to get these visas.

Gagliano : 1911? So that would make him eleven years younger than George.

Martyn : Well, when you got down to George Lewis, if you're a publicist and trying to write about him, number one, he didn't have anything to say. You know man, he wasn't the world's best talker, was he? When you see those pictures of him on the docks, of course, you know his trucks and the bags of coffee are heavier than him.

Gagliano : I was in on the very end of that part of George's life on the docks. That stuff we were able to generate together made it unnecessary for him to go back on the river. I feel good about that. I'm satisfied that I justified George's whatever faith he had in me, asking me to do this.

24

Chapter 2

"LET'S FORM A JAZZ CLUB"

Martyn : You said George asked you or kind of leaned on you a bit to handle his stuff. I mean, did you ever imagine yourself as booking the band or anything like that?

Gagliano : No, I had no experience. I had no knowledge about things, this kind of thing. What happened was that I became fairly active in the Jazz Club. I just want you to understand that a lot of what led me ultimately to do what I did and what George invited me to do came from things that I did when I was in the Jazz Club, things that I learned while I was in the Jazz Club, things that I did while I'm on the board, the acquaintances that I made, the alliances. And I told you a little bit before about the black and white thing, and although that was unfortunate, but that's the way it was.

Martyn : When was the Jazz Club formed?

Gagliano : '48. It was formed at Orin Blackstone's record shop, opposite the De Soto Hotel. Because you see, before I became, quote, "George's manager," if you want to call it that, that was in 1949, and I joined the Jazz Club shortly after it was formed in 1948.

Martyn : Who formed it?

Gagliano : Well, Al Diket, Gilbert Erskine, Don Perry, and Johnny Wiggs.

Martyn : So Johnny Wiggs was a musician.

Gagliano : He was the only musician.

Martyn : Okay. Don Perry – what was he doing at the time?

Gagliano : He was in media. He was involved with recordings and stuff. Al Diket was a teacher, but a lover of jazz, and Gilbert Erskine was a young guy from Chicago who came down here and had some smarts. The story goes that the four of them were talking over at the '48 Mardi Gras and they decided, "Well, we're going to have to form the New Orleans Jazz Club to foster the interests of jazz." Johnny Wiggs was a student of jazz. Johnny Wiggs was really – his love was Bix Beiderbecke. He was a math teacher, but I think he may have also taught the band at the high school. I think it was at Warren Easton High School. I liked Johnny Wiggs. I liked to hear him play, and he became active in the club, but he was not a professional musician at the time. He was in the school system, and he didn't get real active in music until he retired.

They just said, "Let's form the Jazz Club." And somehow or other, the original hub of it was Orin Blackstone's Record Shop on Baronne Street. As I recall, right across the street from what was the DeSoto Hotel. On the Canal Street side of Poydras and almost on the corner of Poydras and Baronne. The hotel was right across the street. It's now the Le Pavillon Hotel. At that time it was the DeSoto Hotel. Orin's shop was directly across Barone Street from the hotel, and he had a back room where they had sessions. It was a room where all of these young guys would congregate. Guys would be coming in here from all over the United States, coming here looking for jazz, and they'd wind up in the back of Orin's shop. We all got to know each other. That's when Dick Allen came on the scene, sometime around in there. Most importantly, Orin had a renowned collection of old jazz records, which were played in the back room sessions, and was the author of an early jazz discography; there also was an old upright piano, which was occasionally used for the live jam sessions.

Martyn : Yes, '49 I think he came here. If you were a jazz fan who came in here from Chicago, where would you hear jazz in '48?

Gagliano : Luthjens was another one that was doing the same thing. There was a place called the Harmony Inn. There were a number of neighborhood joints with a bunch of black bands. It just so happened that I caught Manny's and I caught George Lewis, and I didn't see any – and it was later on that I began to explore and began to find out that a lot of these old musicians were still playing around, like DeDe Pierce and his wife. I remember specifically seeing Big Eye Louis Nelson and being totally disappointed in the playing. I certainly remember seeing Alphonse Picou with his turned-up bell on his clarinet, but that was in the context of playing with Papa Celestin. I would see Papa – I liked Papa Celestin – but they were nothing compared to George Lewis' stuff, in my opinion.

Dick Allen (front), Ernie Cagnolatti (with cap). John Joseph, Jim Robinson, Vernon Gilbert – c.1949

Jazz Club audience at the Parisian Room – 1949

Martyn : So was there any jazz on Bourbon Street?

Gagliano : No, it started with Papa Celestin at the Paddock Lounge and then with Sharkey Bonano at the 500 Club.

Martyn : So anyway, these four guys get together and they say, "Well, let's form a Jazz Club."

Gagliano : They formed the Jazz Club and their idea was to have a meeting every month and to have a jam session and to invite musicians to come and play. And all of this was started out in the context of the segregated society of New Orleans. Consequently, when these meetings were held in, say, like at some of the local hotels, it was all white musicians. Couldn't bring in the blacks. They smuggled them in once in a while. Okay. So this was the spawning place for the Assunto Brothers, Peter Fountain, Stanley Mendelson, Jack Delaney, George Girard. All of these guys were young teenagers when the Jazz Club was formed, and they would come to the meetings and they would sit in. And they were the renaissance. This became a place for Johnny Wiggs to be able to play, and then Emile Christian was discovered around town, Harry Shields, and they all got together. And that's when Sharkey put his band together with him, Harry Shields, Emile Christian. They had Roy Zimmerman on the piano, Monk Hazel on the drums.

Martyn : What was missing? The trombone?

Gagliano : Santo Pecora at first on the trombone and eventually Joe Rotis. That's what I remember. And then the Jazz Club decided – once it got going, they said, "You know, we ought to put on a concert on Sunday."

Martyn : Every week?

Gagliano : Not necessarily; the first concert featured Johnny Wiggs and his jazz group, and the second was held several weeks later with Sharkey Bonano and his Kings of Dixieland, and both were successful from the Jazz Club's viewpoint, with a marked increase in attendance for the second concert.

Martyn : Where was it? The place?

Gagliano : Royal Street, in the first 100 block of Royal.

Martyn : Oh, the Parisian Room.

Gagliano : At the Parisian Room.

Martyn : And how did Tony Almerico get into taking over.

Gagliano : Apparently he saw the monetary potential in weekly concerts, and took a lease on the Parisian Room, and ultimately eased the Jazz Club out. He started out with Sharkey, but eventually eased Sharkey out and took over the trumpet spot himself.

Martyn : Oh, he put them out.

Gagliano : In essence. Yeah, well, he began to promote it and he really – he just simply – eventually the Jazz Club sponsorship just pulled out because – Tony Almerico doesn't know how to play jazz. I mean, he was a dance-band guy. He was a gig-around-town, but he had connections with a lot of these jazz musicians had to play, not only play music and earn a living, they had to play with dance bands like Tony Mello. At this time you also had the resurrection of Irving Fazola that dug in on them, and they got a whole bunch of other – Charlie Cordella, all these white Italian guys. Not that Fazola was Italian. No, his real name was Presnopnick. But Sharkey Bonano, Santo Pecora, Charlie Cordella, a whole bunch of these guys were Italians, and then we had an Italian music tradition here.

Martyn : Joe Capraro, the banjo player Joe Capraro. He was Italian.

Gagliano : Yeah, we got a whole flock of them.

Martyn : Yeah. When did you join the Jazz Club?

Gagliano : Early on. It would have been shortly after it was organized.

Martyn : Well, did they send you out a flyer?

Gagliano : I don't remember. You've got to understand, I was one of those guys that would go back to Orin Blackstone's shop every now and then, and I would run into these guys and they would tell me, "Hey, we're forming a Jazz Club." I said, "Sure, I'll join." Just like that.

Martyn : Was it a membership to join it? Did you have to pay money to join?

Gagliano : Oh, yeah, you paid dues. Five dollars a year or something like that. Ten dollars a year at the most.

Martyn : Oh, so minimal, huh? Well, how about people like Myra Menville and Helen Arlt. Where did they come from?

Gagliano : Well, they all gravitated to Myra Menville, who was a beautiful lady. She was an upper-crust person but who was so damn down to earth, it was embarrassing. She would be considered, in her family and in her society, as a maverick, but she was a married woman, respectfully married to a doctor. She had two children at the time, and she had a lot of time on her hands. She adored Louis Armstrong, and so she had an affinity for the black musicians, as well as the whites. She went either way. But when the race idea came up, you had the typical white musician's response with, "These black guys, they can't even read music. What the hell are they? They can't read a score. They can't do this. They can't do that." You know, that was their platform and if you're from that school, you look down on these guys.

Martyn : Well, then, the segregation part of it too. I mean you can't.

Gagliano : And you had that, yes. We had to work around it.

Martyn : Yes, it's not just related to the music; it's related to the people. Most white musicians that I knew looked down on the black musicians for the simple reason they were black. There was a few of them that didn't. Raymond Burke. You remember Raymond Burke?

Gagliano : Sure, really well.

Martyn : Raymond didn't seem to care who he played with. Didn't make any difference to him. But there were some of them in there that – like one – I won't call his name, but I've heard him cussing "those damn niggers" and all that.

Gagliano : You had that.

Martyn : In later years, when he had the chance to join one of those bands.

Gagliano : You're not talking about Tony Parenti, are you?

Martyn : No, no, not Tony. That's a good guess. No, this is a local fellow. Just studied here. But anyway ....

Gagliano : That's all right. But Tony Parenti took George Lewis' place when he was ill.

Martyn: Yeah, I know that because I issued a CD of Tony with the band. But this guy, when he got the chance to play with – well, the chance – when they hired him to play with so-and-so's black bands, it was all different. He was saying, "Oh, how wonderful it was."

NEW ORLEANS JAZZ CLUB
IN CONJUNCTION WITH LOUISIANA CHAPTER OF
National Society For Crippled Children & Adults, Inc.

PRESENTS

1952 ANNUAL
FESTIVAL
Municipal Auditorium

Sunday, September 28th
8:15 P. M.

Tickets:
$2.50 - $2.00
$1.50 - $1.00
At Philip Werlein's

PROGRAM

SHARKEY'S KINGS OF DIXIELAND

GEORGE LEWIS' RAGTIME BAND

JOHNNY WIGGS' FESTIVAL BAND

PAUL BARBARIN'S JAZZ BAND

BUGLIN' SAM
LIZZIE MILES
PORK CHOPS & KIDNEY STEW
JOE DELANEY

Help Crippled Children

THERE WILL BE RESERVED SEATS FOR COLORED PATRONS

Gagliano : I want you to look at something.

Martyn : Okay. What have you got there?

Gagliano : This is what I found.

Martyn : Oh, fabulous. Well, look at that.

Gagliano : New Orleans Jazz Club. This is an advertising poster for the 1952 Annual Festival, Municipal Auditorium. "Sharkey Bonano, George Lewis, Johnny Wiggs, Paul Barbarin, Buglin' Sam, Lizzy Miles, Pork Chops and Kidney Stew. There will be ...."

Martyn : And Joe Delaney.

Gagliano : ".... reserved seats for colored patrons."

Martyn : Well, I'll be damned. "$2.50 to see it. Reserved seats for colored patrons." Well, it's quite amazing that they, at that time, let them in, you know.

Gagliano : And now let me say this to you. This thing is something I found over the weekend, and it tells me what my involvement was. And this is the sketch. Well, now I could tell you what happened. I was in charge of public relations for the Jazz Club at the time, and it was probably my job to coordinate all this stuff, to promote the concerts. I have no specific recollection of it, but why would I have this? Well, I did know that I was to handle publicity stuff for the Jazz Club.

Martyn : Was it a proper registered organization?

Gagliano : Yeah, it was a properly established organization. It had its federal number as a nonprofit. It had a functioning board of directors and officers, and it was that way for a long, long time.

Martyn : Who was the first president of it, do you know?

Gagliano : Well, my guess would be it was either Al Diket or Gilbert Erskine. The other two guys who were always thought of as the founders were Johnny Wiggs and Don Perry.

But I must tell you that the only guys who stayed with the Jazz Club for any length of time was Johnny Wiggs because, first of all, he was a musician, and Don Perry, as I recall, because he was involved in the technical aspect of recording and radio and television. So this was his thing. I'm not too sure how long Gilbert Erskine stayed around, because I know he left to go back to Chicago, and Al Diket sort of faded out. If you asked me, my guess would either be it could have been Diket, and then Myra Menville became involved. Harry Souchon, Doc Souchon, and a number of others.

Martyn : Well, where did you first meet the Souchons?

Gagliano : I would have to believe it would be in 1949. Probably at the Jazz Club. In 1949, I was working as an estimator and a project manager for a plumbing and heating firm in New Orleans. So it was a very, I would call it, a low exposure type of thing, and if I was to meet this group of people, I would have to meet them on a cultural level. The New Orleans Jazz Club became a very, very equalizing cultural medium where you had real blue-collar people, you had middle-class people, and you had the upper crust. I would think that the upper crust in terms of their particular place would be Harry Souchon, Doc Souchon, and Myra Menville. I remember also George Schmidt's mother. Jo Schmidt. I never did know George until much, much later. Jo Schmidt was very active in the Jazz Club for many years. And Harry Souchon, at the time and for a long time after that until his death, he was one of the strong members in a big downtown law firm, and his social credentials were impeccable. But he was not as deep into it as Doc was. His daughter became queen of Mardi Gras in 1948 or '49, I believe. I had a crush on her. Well, I mean like I had a crush on Mona Freeman or the movie star people. And I was very delighted to go to Doc's house a couple of times, but, man, I never saw – ain't nobody that was in taking part in any of the stuff that the Jazz Club was in.

Martyn : Wasn't his daughter's name Dolly Ann?

Gagliano : Dolly Ann Souchon.

Martyn : Was she married?

Gagliano : She married, unfortunately, one of her younger suitors, a fellow named John Parker. John Parker, later on in life, took up the banjo, among other things.

Martyn : Wait a minute. Isn't John Parker the son?

Gagliano : I would think that the John Parker you're thinking about is Dolly Ann's son.

Martyn : Yeah, yeah, yeah. He is. I know because I deal with him.

Gagliano : But her husband's name was John Parker. He was a socialite and he was in business. Something must have gone wrong with him, though. Don't know what it was, but ultimately it – I'm not too sure whether they divorced or whether he died as a young man, but at some point in time in his life, he began to fool around with the banjo, and I think that's where his son got it from. John Parker today, that is. He would be a young man maybe, maybe in his thirties. I would think, this is my guess, that he would be the son of Dolly Ann Souchon and John Parker. And of course, it's very likely that John Parker, being the son of Dolly, got his credentials to learn how to play the banjo is probably from Doc Souchon.

Martyn : Well, Dolly Ann married a guy that was a Norwegian.

Gagliano : That's the second marriage. Erik Johnsen.

Martyn : Okay, well I didn't even know that she married a John Parker. I thought John Parker the banjo player, the boy, was the son of the shipping magnate and Dolly Ann. And I'm thinking, well, how come his name is John Parker? Well, see you just solved all that. You don't like to ask somebody, "How come your name is different." Yeah, it is, yeah. But he's good on banjo and guitar and he's very nice to deal with. I've had several dealings with him. I wanted to reissue the Paradox recording of George and the band, and we paid John some money, which he doled out to his family, you know.

Gagliano : That's that session that Doc recorded with Elmer Talbert?

Martyn : That's right, yeah. And then the Six and Seven-Eighths Band ....

Gagliano : I remember that.

Martyn : We got some clearance. Sam Charters recorded it, but Sam paid him, but a nominal fee. So when we kind of put it out, we contacted John Parker and made the deal with him, you know. So actually, the New Orleans Jazz Club, was it formed when you joined it or were you one of the charter members kind of thing?

Gagliano : Oh, no. My guess is that I joined just as soon as it was organized, because I was sort of consorting with these fellows through Orin Blackstone's Record Shop. I can't remember my beginnings, but I think that's probably what it was. It was a very well-functioning organization for, my guess would be, at least twenty years, and it was able to have enough local credentials to be able to establish the Jazz Museum. By this time I'm now in law school or I've become a lawyer, and, of course, Myra, and I was working here hand in hand with Harry on doing little things for the Jazz Club.

Martyn : Now, Harry didn't play any instrument, did he?

Gagliano : I don't remember Harry ever playing any instrument, but he was a student of the music and he was really the mainstay of the Jazz Club's radio program. He had the records. He had the knowledge of the old musicians and stuff, and he would create the scripts. Well, you know, the thirty-minute shows that usually were on Sunday night. And then eventually Harry got to the point where he couldn't do it anymore, so then it became a bouncing ball between Myra and Doc Souchon and then Don Marquis came into it. I don't remember Marquis being in the Jazz Club when I was active in it. I would have to say that my activity in the Jazz Club pretty much waned by the time I got to be maybe five to six years into my law practice, which would have put it into the mid-sixties.

Martyn : What about Helen Arlt? What was she to do with that?

Gagliano : Oh, Helen was always – yeah, I'm sorry. She was one of the stalwarts. I knew Helen, now, privately from another source. Her family lived in the vicinity of the family where I was working, and somehow or other I got – I remember meeting her. She had a brother named Donald Arlt, and I think I met him maybe in engineering school. And eventually I got to meet Helen.

Martyn : Did she come from a rich family?

Gagliano : Oh, no. No. Helen was the longtime secretary to Crawford Ellis, who was the president and chairman of the board of Pan American Life Insurance. This is Doc Souchon's – I would say this was his business connection. He was the medical director for Pan American Life Insurance and I'm sure he must have been a major stockholder in it, and I'm sure that probably that was one of the major sources of his income.

Martyn : Where did Doc Souchon live?

Gagliano : He lived at 1313 Octavia Street. I say that, and now I'm beginning to think maybe it was Harry Souchon who lived on at 1821 Valence St. I know he lived uptown. His home, for instance, doesn't fit the stereotype of the old socialite Orleanian like the people who live along St. Charles Avenue, but very lovely home, but not pretentious.

Martyn : Was he a practicing surgeon?

Gagliano : In the years that I knew her, she was the executive secretary to the president of Pan American, and then when Mr. Ellis died and whoever took his spot, she carried on as the executive secretary for him, and I think she stayed into that until she probably retired. That's the only work connection that I knew about Helen.

Martyn : Do you know she sings? Did you know that?

Gagliano : Oh, no. I never heard that.

Martyn : You know, she's no Doris Day, but I mean she's good.

Gagliano : Well, this is something that developed over many years, apparently when she was traveling, I guess she's had to curtail some of her travel.

Martyn : Yeah, she is pretty frail now, but she's nice.

Gagliano : She was always one of my favorites in the Jazz Club. In later years I would see her, anytime I wanted to see her, I'd just go to Jazz Fest and you could see her there always.

Martyn: What about Fred Hatfield? You know anything about Fred?

Gagliano : I didn't know him too well, if at all. He became president of Jazz Club. I think this was in its waning years.

Martyn : Did the Jazz Club use George and the band because you were representing them?

Gagliano : No, no, I don't think that was it. I'm certain that that helped, but I don't think there was any real question once – well, the first jazz concert that the New Orleans Jazz Club put on was in 1949. The *Look* magazine article didn't come out until the following year, so that didn't have any effect on it. But many of the people in the Jazz Club knew and liked the George Lewis Band. Somehow or other, I became known as his primary spokesman, and so when the Pops Concert people got together with the board of the Jazz Club to talk about rescuing them financially – this is sort of a joke in my mind, you know, but that's all right. I mean basically what we did was we prolonged the season another four weeks with two concerts a week, and as I recall, this poster that you see, that I showed you, showed only four bands.

Martyn : And that was '52.

Gagliano : Yeah, that was '52. I don't know whether there was a progression downward by that time, but I would say that my relationship with George certainly helped. It was not the essential factor.

Martyn : Did he actually say to you, "Nick, I want you to manage my band's affairs"? How did that – the actual time, the place, the words? Who told who to what?

Gagliano : I can't even pinpoint a time. I can only point to a number of conversations that we had at different times, at different places, and where they told me about their resentment over the failure of the Bunk Johnson experiment, if you want to call it that, the feeling that they lost their golden opportunity, it was blown, and that they really wanted to have somebody to look after their interests and talk for them, and that was what they wanted. At some point in time, you know, I guess George said – by this time, he knows I'm a college graduate, so I'm, okay, I'm an engineer. So I've got to have some – he thinks I've got some smarts, okay? Well, he's generally right, and I suppose that I am a little bit beyond the typical engineer-technical type. I'm more of a people person, and eventually that's what took me out of engineering and put me into law. So maybe George Lewis recognized that talent in me early on, before I did, when he said, "Yeah," he said, "man, we gotta have somebody, somebody like you." And that's the way he put it, you know. "Somebody like you that can talk for us and look after us." And of course George was always looking for people to look after him.

Martyn : Let me just get one question here that I've been meaning to ask you. How many people were in the Jazz Club? I mean I've got no idea. Five hundred? Fifty?

Gagliano : This is a guess. I would think it had a couple of hundred local people, and then they began with their radio show on WWL. Then they began to tout memberships to people outside. In other words, "If you want to keep the music alive, if you want to help us in our efforts to preserve the music, join." And I have no idea how many people joined then.

Martyn : You just said, "if you want to keep the music alive." Let's go back to '49. Did you see that music was in danger of dying yourself?

Gagliano : Well, of course it was. As I mentioned earlier to you, I had this phobia. Wasn't too much longer after I met George and the guys and began to be friendly with them, and I'm looking at them and I'm saying, "Jesus, these guys play great music," and I'm looking at their ages. I said, "Well, Jesus, this isn't going to last that long." I don't know why I would even think that at the time.

Martyn : Was it not the general feeling of the rest of the Jazz Club people?

Gagliano : Well, that was the reason the Jazz Club came into existence, was to try to preserve it, because, as you know, the so-called history of the music was that by the late thirties and the early forties, it was dead. There was nothing going on. And the truth of the matter was that it was here underground in New Orleans playing in the neighborhood joints and playing in the parades and everything, but people didn't – this wasn't high profile. That's how I think sort of George became one of the, shall we say, pioneers associated with the revival.

Martyn : Let's go back to those years again. There seemed to be only one band that was – I don't know whether you would call it competition, but it was certainly in existence at the same time – Celestin. Now, what was the relationship between Celestin's band and George Lewis' band, and what was the relationship from the New Orleans Jazz Club towards those two bands?

Gagliano : Well, I can tell you that there was not any great relationship between the guys. They never did interact. We were competitors. We knew that we could not break Papa Celestin's hold on the social set, because Papa had been – well, I'll give you my own personal feeling. Papa was a very limited musician, at least to what I know. He didn't have much of a range on the trumpet, but I guess the true jazz player didn't need a big range. George's attitude would be that the trumpet would lay out the melody and don't do all these flourishes and this and that would be terrible. But basically, you know, Papa had the credentials to play that chair.

Papa Celestin had to do what he did in order to survive. You could call Papa whatever you want to call him, but he was a successful bandleader for that era. But even he wasn't playing very much in the thirties, from what I gather.

My recollection is that Papa Celestin, before he was discovered on Bourbon Street, Papa was doing most of the debutante parties, and the higher social classes always hired Papa Celestin's Band. That's why it was imperative for me to push George Lewis in that era to rely on Myra Menville. Myra was in that group and she would talk for – Myra was happy with Papa Celestin, but she knew that Papa Celestin's Band couldn't hold a torch to George Lewis. So she encouraged people to try us out, and that's how George put the band together.

Martyn : What did George think of Celestin's band? Did he ever say?

Gagliano : I don't know. George was never critical about any of the guys, as far as I knew. We simply looked at Papa Celestin as – I guess I looked at his band as being more archaic, less musically talented than the George Lewis Band.

Myra Menville

Like for instance, Bill Matthews on the trombone, you know? Like a machine gun. And I mean, you listen to Jim Robinson with his flowing – you know. And then, of course, George versus Picou, or George versus Brother Cornbread. Now, I could tell you this, George was very friendly with Cornbread, Brother Cornbread. He had nice things to say about him. He didn't have any problem.

Martyn : Did Celestin have management?

Gagliano : Oh, I don't know. No, I don't think so. I never knew anybody else that would have handled his business.

Martyn : I mean, I do know that, for instance, the club we work for now, the Recess Club.

It's a New Orleans men's club, you know, and we worked for them. But they had New Orleans bands working for them from the time of Celestin, their grandfathers. And they told me in conversations with them, "We just used to call Papa Celestin on the phone ourselves." Well, their fathers did, or the grandfathers, and say, "Papa, can you play?" So they said they didn't think he had management, not official management.

Gagliano : No, I don't think he did. I'm not aware of it. I didn't know Papa that well. In fact, I don't know that I've ever been formally introduced to him, but I enjoyed listening to him. I liked some of the things he did and he was a link. He was a link. And I guess that a lot of local jazz people felt the same way about Celestin as some of the jazz critics up north felt about Bunk Johnson when he tried to resurrect himself. You know, they sort of put him down. But Papa was who he was and he was a product of his time. He was a survivor and he entertained people. No doubt about it. He relied as much on his singing as he did on his trumpet playing.

Martyn : Yeah, yeah. That's for sure.

Gagliano : And I think what they knew Papa more for than anything else would be "Marie LaVeau" or numbers of that type. "Lil' Liza Jane."

Martyn : Oh, yeah. That was one of his big ones.

Gagliano : And he'd have to play that three or four times a night whenever he would get one of these social jobs, I would imagine.

Martyn : Well, what about the people at the New Orleans Jazz Club? How did they feel about this black-white thing, in general?

Gagliano : Well, as I seem to recall, and I think I might have mentioned this to you before, there was definitely a clique that favored the white musicians and there was a clique that sort of favored the black. And it never got to the point of Hatfield and McCoy. These guys, the white Dixieland guys, they don't know how to play ensemble.

Martyn : Was that a factor, playing ensemble?

Gagliano : In my opinion, that was the major difference between the white and black bands.

Martyn : Oh, I didn't realize that was thought about that early.

Gagliano : Oh, yeah, yeah. I did, because I got to the point where you're sitting there watching a white band and you're going to have an opening couple of choruses or whatever you call it, and then boom, trumpet, clarinet, trombone, blah, blah, blah. Sometimes it would get down to the drummer. Sometimes it would get down to the bass player, guitars. And then, boom, after all that's done, then you come back to have a closing ensemble. That was it.

George Lewis Jazz Band, they played together often, and at some point in time, they did solos, but that was just show business. But you take the band, whenever they're backing up a vocal, the instruments are behind that vocalist. Howard is playing behind and counterpoint and all that sort of stuff, and so I always – my personal unschooled attitude was that the black bands knew more about how to play ensemble and the white bands knew how to play mostly solo. I'm giving you what my impression was, my particular impression. I'm not a musician. I've never played – to my

32

dismay, I've never learned how to play an instrument. I mean the weird thing is, putting a little bit of my own twist on this if you listen to the Joe Oliver Band of 1923, it's much more ensemble than there is in the equivalent, let's say, of Johnny Miller, which was recorded in '24 here in New Orleans, a white band, you know. The Joe Oliver Band is practically all ensemble and Johnny Miller's band is all solos, even then. That's how I made the distinction between black music and white Dixieland. The prevalence of solos in white Dixieland was something that I'm not saying was bad, but it got to be sort of boring to me. Eventually, if you like music and you're going to like harmony and you're going to like all of the things weaving together, it's playing harmonically together is what turns me on. It was nineteen forty-nine. And it was that concert when the Jazz Club agreed to bring in George's band. That's when they talked to me. "Can George put together a band?" I said, "Sure he can."

Martyn : So they asked you.

Gagliano : Yes.

Martyn : And they would have the concerts outside?

Gagliano : Oh, yeah.

Martyn : Always outside?

Gagliano : Well, at that time because, as I told you, the Jazz Club came into the thing as an afterthought to the summer pops concerts. The summer pops people had a bad season in 1949. They were losing money. They had to pay for all the setup, the setup outside. You know, you had a stage, you had tables and chairs. A typical pops operation is that you have an informal setting, you can buy drinks. They had tables set up out there all around the square.

Martyn : Was it in the daytime or nighttime?

Gagliano : No, no. No, it was at night.

Martyn : So they had floodlights, too?

Gagliano : Yeah, and they had to string out all the lights, and then they had a sound system. They had to do all the infrastructure necessary to seat people comfortably, encourage them to buy drinks and listen to the music. Basically, the pops would start on the bandstand with maybe thirty or forty musicians, and this was the typical type of a summer, mild, light, classical music. Well, that particular summer, for whatever reason, maybe it was just general, maybe the people were getting tired of the – whatever it was, the summer pops was losing money, and they came to the Jazz Club and asked the Jazz Club if they would consider putting on some jazz concerts.

Martyn : That's a new twist.

Gagliano : Now, evidently, the pops season was over by the end of July, because the first program that the Jazz Club put on was in August of '49.

Martyn : Would George and them, when they appeared at those concerts, would they wear suits?

Gagliano : I think we probably got suits for that occasion and then that was going to be what they were going to wear wherever they wanted to. I mean, we weren't regimenting. I just made the recommendation to George, and he agreed that maybe this would be something that would be helpful to – because, you know, he was trying to sell his band to play for social parties and engagements.

Martyn : You think he was trying to sell his band or himself?

Gagliano : No, no. His band.

Martyn: Perhaps he'd seen enough of people doing things for themself with Bunk.

Gagliano : Probably so, but I think if he was going to go ahead and market his group to play for debutante parties, you can't go there all scruffy, you need to present an image of cleanliness and, you know, whatever. And we thought, rightly or wrongly, that one way we could enhance the physical image of the band was to dress the guys in a nice, not a zoot suit type, I mean, you know, a nice suit. I remember going up to the tailor's and get everybody measured up.

Martyn : Who was the tailor's? Joe Gemelli?

Gagliano : No, I remember Joe, but no, it wouldn't have been Joe Gemelli. I don't know that Joe was even in that business at that time.

Martyn : Oh, okay, because Joe once told me years later, he said, "Yeah, I made George Lewis' first band uniforms."

Gagliano : He may have. I just don't remember. And I could tell you it was a store. I mean, it was not somebody's back room. It was some kind of a small clothing store that made tailored outfits cheaply.

Martyn : Well, a lot of people told me through the years, people I've interviewed that you couldn't buy clothes at a white clothing store. They wouldn't let you try them on. You could buy them, but they wouldn't let you try them on.

Gagliano : That's true.

Martyn : Even shoes. They wouldn't let you try them on.

Gagliano : That's very true.

Martyn : So would they have tailor-made suits for a colored band? Probably not unless it was a colored store.

Gagliano : Probably was a colored store.

Martyn : I would have thought, because I remember Andy Blakeney, who played trumpet with me in Los Angeles, said, "Man, we couldn't even buy shoes. You had to go in there and you'd say, 'Give me size nine.'" All right. Another thing they all had band ties too, matching neckties.

Gagliano : Yeah. That was part of the uniform. That was a part of our marketing strategy. Elmer Talbert was a little bit taller than Jim Robinson. And I would say that Elmer was like six-two or six-three. He was a physical presence, I remember him when I first saw him on that carnival truck playing trumpet, I mean his physical appearance was impressive.

Martyn : I think he was a presser by trade. But noticeably here, George is wearing the same suit of clothes as the men.

Gagliano : Oh, yeah, there was no band leaders dress.

Martyn : Never to your knowledge, all the time you were with him, he never did any different?

Gagliano : There was never any distinction, other than the fact that he was the leader and everybody knew he was the leader. But there was no pretention about him dressing differently or being treated differently.

Martyn : And you never suggested it to him?

Gagliano : No. This was not about George Lewis specifically; this was his band.

Martyn : Who was the most unpredictable one in the band for you?

Gagliano : When you say unpredictable, you mean musically or ....

Martyn : Well, just – if I clarify, it will give you an idea to answer. Just unpredictable in any kind of way or shape or form.

Gagliano : I'd have to say it would be Kid Howard, both in terms of a little bit of his personality and the other was the physical problem he was having with his lip, plus Kid had a reputation for maybe drinking a little bit too much. The only thing I can remember about Jim, he would occasionally drink too much, but it looked like it didn't affect his playing.

Jim Robinson, Joe Watkins, Elmer Talbert, Alton Purnell, George Lewis,
Lawrence Marrero, Alcide "Slow Drag" Pavageau

Martyn : Yeah. I was laughing at the fact, Jim, when he was drunk, I could see he was drunk because I saw when he would drink. He didn't talk any different. He just talked that same nonsense.

Gagliano : Yeah, it didn't seem to affect him and it may be because the trombone – maybe it's unfair to pin this on Kid Howard, but the problem with the trumpet player is he's got to be able to play the melody. And I'm pretty sure this was George's insistence. You know, you play the damn melody. You've got to carry the line. The first concert that was played and was sponsored by the Jazz Club. It didn't mention a place. It mentioned that it was on a Sunday afternoon. And now, having thought about it, I do remember attending an early Jazz Club-sponsored concert at one of the smaller rooms at the Municipal Auditorium.

Martyn : On the top?

Gagliano : Yeah, maybe, like, on the second floor. This was one of the smaller rooms, and I remember one Sunday afternoon. And it's interesting, but the Jazz Club's *Second Line* mention this concert because it preceded the Parisian Room concerts. It mentioned a place and I'm thinking that it would have been at the Municipal Auditorium.

Martyn : Now, if George and them played these concerts, then they wear their uniforms.

Gagliano : Well, that's why we got the uniform. My recollection is when the band was finally selected to play. They decided that they were going to try to use seven bands and that there would be – since there were going to be eight concerts, then the eight concerts were over four weeks, one on Tuesday night, one on Friday night starting at, like, about at seven-thirty or eight o'clock. And it stated that they are going to try to get together seven bands and then the eighth concert would be the band that drew the most people, okay? So what they did was, they started off with Papa Celestin and he drew 1300 people, according to the records. And then when he came back, they said he played the sixth concert, and at this time there was rain threatening. They only drew 500. But apparently, Papa Celestin was then very popular in this city and he apparently drew the most people. George played fourth, and the only comment about that was it says that this was one of the more successful concerts in the series. Then finally they came down to the last two, and one of them was Paul Barbarin's new band, and they characterized him as the surprise of the series. At this point they didn't identify the personnel other than Paul Barbarin, and then they finished up the series with the Dukes of Dixieland.

Martyn : There was one New Orleans Jazz Club presentation, it was a Christmas party and George's band was hired. Now, I don't know whether it was once or twice or ten times they hired him for a Christmas party, but there's a trombone player that is not Jim Robinson, and he's never been identified properly. I asked Wendell Eugene, I said, "It sounds a bit like you." And he said, "No, that ain't me." I asked Frog Joseph and Frog said, "No, man, that's not me. I played better than that." They all came with this stuff and the nearest I could get – of course he's dead; I couldn't ask him – was Eddie Pierson. You remember on one job Eddie Pierson playing the trombone?

Gagliano : No. I don't remember any Christmas parties that George played for the Jazz Club. It wouldn't have been Bill Matthews?

Martyn : No, I know Bill's style. It's one of the more modern trombone players, but I don't think it's a white guy because I can't see it. But anyway, it's just a discographical thing, and nobody's been able to answer, including me.

Gagliano : I'll be happy to listen, but I don't think I can identify him.

Martyn : But look, getting back to the concerts, who was Mildred? You were telling me about her singing with the band at the Jazz Club Concerts.

Gagliano : Mildred was one of the four of five children that George had with his first wife, Emma, and she was identified as Mildred Zeno. In fact, this was probably – when I met her and George identified her as Mildred Zeno, this is probably the first time that I had ever heard the name Zeno associated with George, because I didn't know anything about his background at that time. So I don't know whether she would have been his oldest child, but I know that she was the one that he had a relationship with because she sang occasionally with the band. Now, she was not a member of the band; she would be like a guest.

Martyn : What would she sing? Pop songs? Gospel?

Gagliano : No, no, no. She would be probably singing whatever jazz tune or spiritual or whatever. I couldn't even begin to tell you what she did on the program, but I know she was on the program.

Martyn : Was she billed?

Gagliano : No, she wasn't billed at all. This was something that George would do. He says, "We're gonna play this number and my daughter, Mildred, will sing it."

Martyn : Oh, he would say it was his daughter?

Gagliano : He certainly identified her to me as his daughter.

Martyn : But other than that, you never saw George with any singers? He never brought any singers out there?

Gagliano : No, he never did. Although in later years Lizzie Miles worked with him. Not touring, but out at the Hangover Club, she had a little group with the intermissions, and she kind of sang with the band a couple of times.

Martyn : I know Lizzie – I used to correspond with her.

Gagliano : Lizzie was having a resurgence herself in this period. And I think she was a presence. Somehow or other she got some help from the Jazz Club.

Martyn : She was a very likable woman. I mean, she's never had much to say about anybody bad, and she loved George and the band and she liked Paul Barbarin's band. She liked everybody. Just a happy old lady, I'll put her down as. Well, she used to write to me in around '56, '57, '58, around that time. One of the things she said, she never did or couldn't or didn't want to say anything publicly in New Orleans, but she said, "Barry, since you live so far away from here and the likelihood of you coming here is not very big – now, but whatever. She said, "I just wanted to tell you I did a concert with a no-account ...." She never swore, but it was a "no-account bloop, bloop, bloop, bloop that the white people are trying to make into something great, which is hopeless. His name is Al Hirt. I doubt you'll ever hear of him." But that was Lizzie's opinion of Al Hirt.

Gagliano : But we all know and George always felt, that he wanted to have the full traditional lineup, and he went further than that when he occasionally would use two trumpets.

Martyn : Why did George use two trumpets?

Gagliano : I don't know the musical reason for it, but he seemed to like to have two trumpets. I really can't tell you. But with a talent like Percy Humphrey, it worked. I don't know that it would work with everybody.

Martyn : Well, I think that I told you the story that George told me about Elmer Talbert. I said, "Who's your favorite trumpet player?" And he said Coo Coo. He loved playing with Elmer Talbert.

Gagliano : That just happened to be his nickname, and I do remember he had a sort of a malformation of one of his eyes where it was sort of bulging out a little. But he was a big, tall guy and very strong, and one that you wouldn't want to mess with. But he played a straightforward horn, no great embellishment.

Martyn : Did you think at some point George felt he was further ahead than he was with Bunk or was catching up to what that period and that era did, or do you think he didn't think about it at all?

Gagliano : I really, from a viewpoint of the artistry of the music, I would think he felt that he progressed. I personally believe that George progressed from his Manny days, whether it be because of the variety of the music we were playing, maybe it was coming from the stimulus that the band got from the audience, maybe it became part of being accepted up there as a human being on a par with everybody and not being subjugated by, you know, the culture of the South. I had to believe that George's golden years were like '53, '54, but that's just a recollection. I could be wrong. Maybe there wasn't that much of a change. But I would think that you would see an improvement of the product if you're now playing consistently with seven pieces as against five pieces. You stop to think about how much depth and harmony is injected by the trombone or the piano, okay? And you go back to Manny's, and those two pieces were missing.

Martyn : And plus, they were all friends, too, you know. It was like playing with your friends all the time for them.

Gagliano : Exactly, and so, I mean, George always wanted to have at least the seven pieces, and so whenever we – like, I think the second year that George was on the program for the Jazz Club at Congo Square, that was when he first brought in two trumpets that I was aware of. And in this case, the implication is that he brought in Percy as a second trumpet to Elmer Talbert. I'm not too sure that Elmer did play that, but I guess he did. The first concert was '49, and I'm sure that was just Elmer. Second year, the notation in the *Second Line* is that George added Percy Humphrey, but didn't say "added to Elmer Talbert."

Martyn : And you don't think it was because Elmer Talbert was getting sick?

Gagliano : No. Well, he didn't tell me that, but maybe that was so.

Martyn : Well, I've heard suggestions that possibly people in the New Orleans Jazz Club tried to recreate the old Joe Oliver Band. Would you put any credence to that?

Gagliano : Which is possible. It's possible, but I don't know that the Jazz Club would have told George to do this. I think this would have – unless – let me put it this way. I don't remember any input from the Jazz Club people. "George, we want you to get two trumpets." I just don't remember that.

Martyn : How were those Jazz Club people? Their attitude to George and the band, was it benevolent? Were they sort

New Orleans 8-Concert Jazz Festival Musical And Financial Success

New Orleans—The August Jazz festival, staged by the New Orleans Jazz club and spotlighting the top two-beat jazz outfits in town, proved to be a profitable promotion for everyone but the Jazz club. Jazz itself profited by holding the musical limelight for the first time in many years.

And the management of the Summer Pop concerts was pulled out of a financial hole by the rental of its outdoor plant and a lion's share of the profits, while the bands were boosted by the publicity.

Profit and Loss

Also, a smart operator, the erstwhile paid manager of the Jazz festival, pocketed a healthy wad of green by promoting an encore concert that outdrew any of the others nearly two to one. But the Jazz club netted about $100 for its troubles.

All the different schools of New Orleans jazz were heard in the eight concert series, each concert being given over to one band. Traditional New Orleans music was blown by Oscar (Papa) Celestin's Tuxedo Jazz band and George Lewis' Ragtime Jazz band; Dixieland was offered by Sharkey Bonano's Kings of Dixieland and Leon Prima's combo; radio jazz and 'Cajun' tunes were the contributions of Pinky Vidacovich and his studio band, and funny hat jazz was the forte of the zany Phil Zito International City Jazz band.

Everyone Satisfied

Musically, everyone was satisfied by at least one of the outdoor bashes. Celestin and his boys proved that the old jazzmen could still blow with the younger fellows. Most noteworthy were the vocal offerings of Papa and pianist Octave Crosby, Bill Matthews' staccato-styled tromboning, and the fine drumming of Black Happy Goldston.

George Lewis' new band had his crowd doing flips as he revived old, seldom-heard marches, spirituals, and rags with a drive not often heard today. It was the largest band of them all, eight pieces: Elmer Talbert and Kid Howard, trumpets; Jim Robinson, trombone; Lawrence Marrero, banjo; Slow Drag Pavageau, bass; Charley Hamilton, piano; Joe Watkins, drums, and Lewis, clarinet.

Carefree Sharkey

Sharkey was his usual carefree self at the concerts and his veteran crew went through its paces as if they'd been through this sort of thing many times. And they have. Raymond Burke subbed for the ill Lester Bouchon, and it was his clarineting, especially in the lower register, that provided the high spots.

Zito's crew was a curious combination of young hornmen backed by a veteran rhythm section. George Girard, trumpet; Peter Fountain, clarinet, and Joe Rotis, trombone, all are young, eager, and very promising Dixielanders. They furnished all the clowning, doing not-so-subtle takeoffs on Sharkey's routines.

Jazz disc jockeys Roger Wolfe of WDSU and Ed Hart of WTPS split the emcee chores.

—Nick Gagliano

nnocents

Mercury Rising

New York—Mercury records hit such hot pay dirt with Frankie Laine's *Lucky Old Sun* and Vic Damone's *You're Breaking My Heart* that they had to make a deal with Victor to press 100,000 sides for them. Mercury's facilities couldn't keep up with the demand.

fickle crew, and soon we were listening to the Ray Noble records imported from England, followed by the Casa Loma era at Glen Island and the Essex House, and Hal Kemp, before the Dorsey Brothers and Benny Goodman came along to change the whole outlook. Our age group went

Nick Gagliano's review of the concert in Down Beat

of didn't have anything to do with them, they talked to you and you talked to them, or what the hell was their attitudes?

Gagliano : No, no. The inner core of the Jazz Club was very, very favorable to George, and if you were to read – like, for instance, when they were talking about the eight concert they made a point to say, "George Lewis' performance was one of the better." This could have been Myra Menville, okay?

Martyn : I mean, you had an education, so you could see for yourself, "If I do this right, I can go here or I can go there." But George could only just get up there, you know.

Gagliano : All right, I'll tell you again. One of the biggest jokes I used to have with my friends in college, you know, all during my early years, was that the only way I could get into a debutante party or other high-society event was as a manager of a black jazz band. And that's true, because being a downtown Italian kid, man, I had no chance to get involved in any of that.

Martyn : But even so, you had an education and you could probably figure out, "If I work hard, I can get to here." But as George knew, whatever he did, he's only going to get to here. He is never going to get to there, let alone past you know.

Gagliano : And I think this is the reason why George was happy to have me help him out, because I guess he realized or he recognized that I was able to do certain things that he couldn't do. Look, George had no earthly reason to get me as his manager on the basis of what I knew, because I didn't know anything about the business.

Martyn : How big do you think it was that "If a white man speaks for us, we'll get places"?

Gagliano : Oh, I think it helped. I think it helped in getting his bookings with the social set, even though I'm a downtown Italian kid. But at the same time, I was also a graduate of Tulane and I was elected the president of the Tulane engineering student body, and I was on the Tulane Student Council, which was the governing group for the whole school. So I had notoriety in the college set, but George wouldn't have known any of that. But the people that I had to deal with would have known some of that. The people at the Jazz Club knew that. They also knew that I was the New Orleans correspondent for *Down Beat* magazine.

Martyn : Would he have known what *Down Beat* was?

Gagliano : I would think George knew, certainly from the Bunk Johnson time. I would think so.

Martyn : If you hadn't have done what you did, do you think there would have been somebody else who would have done what you did for the band?

Gagliano : If I answer, in a way it might sound like I am the indispensable part of the story. I don't mean to say that, but I don't know who was on the horizon. I mean, you take the young guys at the time or all the people that were in Jazz Club, for instance. Dick Allen could have been – I mean, look how prominent he finally became in terms of the history of jazz. But nobody approached George in the sense like, well, we talked about, and maybe this was George's doing because maybe George didn't want one of these hang-alongs. I don't know. I don't know who would have done it, because there was no profit in it.

Besides, you know, I told George I'd help him. And if there was ever going to be an ultimate payoff, if George would have ever been taken up by one of the national booking agencies like Milt Gabler or those people, which I find as a very ridiculous thought because George would not have the kind of broad appeal to satisfy that kind of people.

Martyn : You mean Joe Glazer and those agencies?

Gagliano : Yeah, Joe. I tried writing to him. You've got to be a little bit naïve to think that they could do something with George on a national basis. Well, same with me today. I said, "Hey, I was the manager of the George Lewis Jazz Band." "Who was that?"

Martyn : And yet where is the name Nick Gagliano most associated with? You'll probably go down in the history books as being the manager of the George Lewis Band rather than being some legal eagle. But getting back to George and celebrities and all that. What did George think of bands like Sharkey and all those kind of bands, the white bands? Did he respect them?

Gagliano : He never did talk these down that I knew about. I think he realized that they were coming from a different perspective. They learned the music in a different way, I guess. Maybe he would have thought that they really didn't struggle the way he had struggled, but George was never judgmental about all of these guys. I mean he might have – I guess if you asked him, "What about bebop?" I guess he would have said, "Well, I don't know what that is. I don't understand what they're trying to do."

Martyn : One other thing I wanted to ask you. We were talking about band uniforms. This is a strange thing to harp on, but on the other hand they seem to have bought them pretty early on.

Monday Night

Dear Nick,

Here is the list of debutantes; there may be more later on. I have typed out (very badly) a sample letter; some of it might not meet with your approval but I thought very carefully and feel the letter ought to stand as it. I think I know the people concerned well enough to say that flowery phrases, details about where and when and with whom George has played, the qualities of his band should be completely OUT of the letter or kept to a minimum! The parents of the debs receive dozens of letters like this every day the rest of the winter, plugging bands, florists, dress shops, caterers, etc. and most of them get thrown away unopened! I've been guilty of the same thing, haven't YOU?

ALSO I've mentioned the Henican's who are well known, but naturally you'll leave that part in the letter TO the Henican's...you just MIGHT make an automatic slip-up and include it in the one letter you CAN'T. Is this the right one? JP or Ellis Henican? Check the initials.

The only reason I've included my name in this particular group of letters (I know you must be planning to send many more to business organizations, etc.) is because I honestly think the letter will be read before tossed aside; This gang know me or my family (and WHAT they'll think I've DESCENDED to, God only knows!) And I mentioned Piron because they all danced to his music at the country club for years, whether George ever played with him or not! And I made it Nicholas instead of Nick because they'll prefer it that way, babe but you'll always be Nick to me!

You take it over from here....plain paper, good typing, dignity! And cross your fingers!

Myra Menville

I thought if you sent the price list on a separate piece of paper, (printed, I hope?) it would be more convenient for them to put it aside in a desk or a memo book or date book or something...letters collect and get destroyed and any information in it is lost; looked for, shrugged off, and someone else gets the contract or assignment. Right?

1227 Webster St.,
NEW ORLEANS JAZZ CLUB
NEW ORLEANS 12, LA

Mr. Nick Gagliano,
6115 Canal Blvd.,
City

NEW ORLEANS JAZZ CLUB
439 Baronne St.   RAymond 2564
NEW ORLEANS 12, LA.

Oct. 1, 1949

Dear Mrs. Shober,

Mrs. John Menville, Secretary for the New Orleans Jazz Club, suggested I write you. I am the manager of George Lewis's Dixieland Jazz Band, and simply want to remind you and Mr. Shober of the wisdom of engaging an orchestra fairly early in the season for any parties you may be planning.

George Lewis's band is one of the outstanding colored bands in the country. It consists of eight men, all old-timers, each one well known in his special field; George himself, a fine clarinetist, is an Esquire Award winner, and has played with men like Bunk Johnson and the late Piron. His records are in great demand.

By way of recommendation, I would like to point out that this band has been selected to play at the Metairie Country Club on New Year's Eve, besides playing there for other occasions such as the Thursday Night Buffet dinners. George is also engaged to play for Mr. & Mrs. J.P. Henican's cocktail party this month, besides several other debutante parties. You can hear his band every Sunday afternoon on Station WTPS at three o'clock. I'm sure you would want not only the very best jazz played at your parties, and I know you accept Mrs. Menville's opinion of George's band.

Very sincerely,

Nicholas Gagliano
Nicholas Gagliano

typed { 6115 Canal Blvd.
New Orleans, La.

Draft letters by Myra Menvill (above) and Nick Gagliano (left) on plans to promote the band

39

Gagliano : They look like the suits that I had somehow talked the band into getting, and it had to do with their performance, as far as I can recall, he had them for the concert at Municipal Auditorium, which I characterize as the beginning of my formal relationship as manager for George Lewis.

Martyn : Did you get them that job?

Gagliano : Well, I was part of the planning committee for those sessions, and I told Myra Menville, I said, "Myra, you've got to get the George Lewis Jazz Band on. No question about it." And yeah, I had a little bit of a part to play, but I also told her, I told Myra, I said, "Myra, George wants me to help him out to manage the band." And I said, "We've decided that we're going to do this," after the decision was made that I would be his manager, come hell – for whatever reason.

And Myra, at that point, told me, says, "Gee, that's great, Nick." She says, "I'm going to try to help you guys out and put you in touch with all my social friends so that you could get a group of bookings for their parties," and whatever. We were playing just a series of dances, deb parties, fraternity parties.

Martyn : Would they use six pieces on these jobs, or seven pieces or five pieces?

Gagliano : Well, we were using seven pieces. The only time we didn't use the piano was when maybe the venue didn't have a piano. But for the most part, all these places had pianos, so my recollection is we used seven pieces.

Martyn : Well, when you joined the gang for doing their bookings, did you think you were booking essentially a five-piece band like they had at Manny's?

Gagliano : No. For the parties, we were insisting on a seven-piece band. You know, three horns and four rhythm.

Martyn : Did George insist on that?

Gagliano : Oh, no, it wasn't me. It was George. I think we all agreed on it, but George would have made that decision. It was just that having made that decision, then I had to implement it in pricing up his engagements.

Martyn : How did you price the engagements? Was there a union scale that you went by or just figured out what George would advise you?

Gagliano : I think they were in the union at the time. I think we had a work scale. I don't know that we ever got much beyond scale, not on a local level.

Martyn : So when you started doing them, their bookings, how did you operate? With a contract? With a union contract? Did you do up a contract? How did you operate? I'm not talking about out of town. I'm talking about strictly in town.

Gagliano : To tell you the truth, I don't remember using any contract. I thought it was word of mouth. I don't remember, you know. I don't recall ever – or maybe I did see the union contract. I pretty much relied upon George as to what the scale would be. The only thing I remember about that was that the formula was that you had to get scale as a minimum for each sideman and that you would have to charge double for leader. And that's all I remember about the union regulations. I was always concerned a little bit about these recordings. I can't tell you how religiously we observed the rules.

Martyn : Well, let me put this before you. Now, I don't know for sure then, but I would imagine if I do a contract for my band, all right, I'll get the employees. Say you were hiring us to play in there for in the ballroom. Okay, I'll bring a contract and you'll say, "Mr. Gagliano , would you sign this contract and give us a deposit?" And you sign the contract, but if I'm not the bandleader, if I'm the booking agent, the union requires you to have a booking agent's license. Was that the case then or was it something that never came up?

Gagliano : I didn't care about that. I never did have any kind of a license. I don't consider myself a booking agent. I was basically acting in a managerial help capacity for the band. No, I was never licensed to do anything. I was never called before the union. I don't recall the band ever having – during the time that I was with them, they never told me that they might have been hauled before the local to answer certain things. It just occurred to me, of course then the unions were segregated.

Martyn : So perhaps the black local didn't have any requirements, like a booking agent's license.

Gagliano : I would think that the black local was so much looser than the white.

Martyn : Yeah, well, it certainly was. I joined the black local, you know. For what reason? Well, I knew all the people in it, you know, and I wasn't trying to prove anything, but I just joined it. And oh, it was more fun. It was fun to be in that local. There's no fun to be in this damn thing.

Gagliano : And I think it was a much more informal following of the national, international rules.

Martyn : Well, they took themselves seriously, the black local, but I think they kind of looked at it – perhaps this is a bit wild, but they perhaps looked at it, "Well, we're true to ourselves more than we are to Yankees coming here and telling us how to run our business." Nobody ever said that to me, but I just felt like they would abide by what suited them to abide by.

Gagliano : I've got to tell you that I would be ultra surprised if, in the days in the thirties and the early forties when everybody was struggling to make a living and the only place that jazz was being played was at neighborhood bar rooms or restaurants – that's what Manny was – I would be overly surprised if there was an enforcement of minimum scale.

Martyn : Yeah, or even the hours, I wouldn't think.

Gagliano : Or the hours, you know, or this intermission thing. Those are work rules, and I don't think they paid any attention to those work rules at the time. I certainly was never indoctrinated into it. The guys didn't tell me, "This is what we've got to do. This is what we can't do." None of that.

Martyn : They never quoted any union stuff to you then, saying, "Nick, we've got to do this. We've got to do that"?

Gagliano : Not really. Somehow or other, I must have gotten the idea from George as to how much we had to charge, because now we were getting into more visible types of things, okay? Manny's was a neighborhood thing. I had nothing to do with Manny's, even after I became the so-called manager of the band.

Martyn : When I was attached to the National Parks Offices as New Orleans Jazz Commissioner, for what it was worth, but we used to advise them on things, and a guy came there. He was obviously trying to sell this book, which he'd, I think, gotten from George Augustine, a former president. But anyway, I don't know what, but it was the minutes of the local 496 from, let's say, 1940. It was very interesting.

Gagliano : Yeah, that would be interesting.

Martyn : I wish I'd have been able to copy it, but the guy wouldn't let me. Randy Mitchell, I think his name was. But anyway, he couldn't get any joy because we couldn't buy things. So I don't know what became of it, but I looked at it while he was talking, like this, and I got to this, the George Lewis Band. I wish I had made a copy. It said, "It was brought to the board's notice by brother Percy Humphrey, who was bringing up an inquiry against bandleader George Lewis, with whom he played".

"Brother Humphrey told us, 'When I play with George, he don't take intermissions like he's supposed to. He's supposed to take fifteen minutes' intermission, and sometimes he calls us back after ten or twelve minutes." I couldn't believe all this stuff going on between them. And then, "When brought before the board the inquiries of that board, Mr. Lewis said, 'What people don't understand, sometimes you have to do what the man's telling you to hold your job. That's why I go back sometimes." It was only about, like, two minutes or three minutes, but it was so funny.

Gagliano : Freddy Kohlman and all of them were commercial players. I mean, they were typical Bourbon Street players, all of them, you know. George was really the only one that really adhered to the old style.

Martyn : Well, maybe Celestin in a way.

Gagliano : Yeah, in a way. Yeah, I guess so. I guess so.

Martyn : I mean, a lot of people say Celestin was an old Uncle Tom. Whether he was or not, you couldn't ever say George was, because he never said anything. Although I have got pictures somewhere of George and them wearing some strange fezzes. You know what fezzes are? Like the Egyptians wear around their head. I can't imagine George featuring comedy routines or anything, but there's a couple of bands that got these things on. This is on the job, where Celestin, you might see him wearing any kind of crazy hats. You know what I mean? They were much more. He was an entertainer.

Gagliano : And music, to some extent, was incidental to his being an entertainer, and he did a hell of a job of it, you know. He had these signature numbers that he would sing, "Liza Jane" and "Marie Laveau." These were production numbers, so to speak. But that was his thing, and he was very popular with the social set and it made him a good living.

Martyn : But did the New Orleans people that were interested in, the Myra Menville's and Johnny Wiggs', the Don Perry's, did they see a difference between George Lewis' style of music and, like, Celestin or Freddy Kohlman?

Gagliano : Oh, yeah, absolutely. Celestin was sort of relegated to sort of a secondary status musically. George Lewis, to those people, was basically getting to be the apex of the old really New Orleans music, unadulterated. Not to say that Celestin's band had any less of a historical place in this whole thing. You know, Celestin was always considered to be one of the top jazz bands or orchestras. But nevertheless, so the point I'm making is all of the people that were involved in the New Orleans Jazz Club and the New Orleans jazz scene from Doc Souchon and Myra Menville to Don Perry, they realized that George was different – George's group was more instinctive, not based on reading music. Celestin, although maybe he would never realize he was playing, you now, read music, but he probably was. You know, after playing it forty, fifty years, you didn't need sheet music.

Martyn : Well, the thing is I guess Celestin – well, I don't guess; I know. Celestin, they first recorded, like, in 1925, I think it was, and consistently, '26, '27. They were recording for OKEH, Columbia. So they had kind of what you'd say was a name.

Gagliano : Absolutely.

Martyn: Whereas they'd always try to link George with a recording in 1924, with Lee Collins. But George said – I asked him about that and he said, "Well, I don't know." He said, "I don't honestly remember it, but ...." he said, "I don't think it would have been called the Imperial Serenaders.." He said, "Every time I recorded, except with Bunk, it was George Lewis and his band," you know. So I don't put a lot of stock in that. The first recorded example we've got of George

Gagliano : You mean in the Zulu parade?

Martyn : Yeah, but Celestin had been recording for Columbia, probably race records, what they used to call race records, sold mostly to a black audience. But I don't know who bought those records. But so Celestin had his made, whereas George hadn't quite made it yet.

Gagliano : Let me cite you an example. When the Jazz Club decided to put on – I don't know whether it was the first set or the second set of concerts, either in '49 or '50, probably was '49, maybe the first set, what they had decided to do, they were going to string out a four-week schedule. They were taking over the chairs, tables from the pops concerts. They were going to extend the season for four weeks. They were going to have two concerts a week, one on Tuesday and one on Friday at night, out in the open, Municipal Auditorium, Congo Square. They said they were going to line up seven bands, and whichever band drew the most people would play the last concert. Okay, so here I'm going through the thing, and Papa Celestin starts out. He had the first concert, and they made a big point of it that he drew 1,500 people.

Martyn : That's a lot of people in those days, isn't it? Yeah.

Gagliano : A lot of people. He drew 1,500 people. And then George's band played, I think in the fourth slot, which would put him on a Friday night, and apparently nobody approached Celestin.

Then later on in the program, and I don't know how this happened, but Celestin played again on I think it was the sixth concert. Well, by this time, they must have figured out who was going to be drawing the most, and nobody ever, apparently, came close to Papa Celestin's 1,500. George did well, but he didn't make 1,500.

So the sixth concert said, "It's going to be Papa Celestin, brought back by popular demand." And then after that they had the Basin Street Six and I think Paul Barbarin to close it out. So Papa Celestin then was, I would say, the most well-known and the most popular band among the citizenry of New Orleans and he drew the most people.

Martyn : Would he primarily play for white people?

Gagliano : For the most part, yeah. The whole social structure had to be white. He played, but I mean, for the most part, the deb parties and the Southern Yacht Club and the Patio Royal thing, all of those were white.

Martyn : Well, you remember we were talking about off tape about the banjo player John Chaffe? John had, for whatever reason, connections with all of those places that Celestin played, the Southern Yacht Club, all of them.

Gagliano : His family was from that social set.

Martyn : Right, and so when we started to play with John Chaffe, we would play all of those places that Celestin played you know, the New Orleans Country Club, the Southern Yacht Club, you know, all across New Orleans. And it was interesting to see the places. But George, I can't remember – apart from the El Morocco, then the Mardi Gras Lounge, and then they went away to college tours, you know, I don't remember George playing any of those social places.

Gagliano : Oh, he played them. That's what I was doing. That's what Myra Menville was helping me out with.

Martyn : At the Southern Yacht Club and the New Orleans Country Club?

Gagliano : Sure, yeah.

Martyn : I didn't realize George played them.

Gagliano : Oh, they played there for private parties.

Martyn : Yeah, okay. All right.

Gagliano : I'm sure we played the country clubs, Metairie Country Club. I'm sure we played New Orleans, but not necessarily for the club, but for people who were throwing parties at these places. I specifically remember one at the Patio Royal which was a deb party. The Patio Royal is where Brennan's Restaurant on Royal Street is right now. Right exactly opposite in the center of what you know as the Wildlife and Fisheries Office Building, what I now know as the Louisiana Supreme Court.

Chapter 3

"The Men in the Band"

Martyn : How organized a bandleader was George?

Gagliano : At that time the band was just basically at Manny's as I said. He was only playing with the five pieces. Always the same people. George was always the bandleader. You were always aware that he was the bandleader. George led the band with his eyes, in my opinion. You know, you could see him, while he's playing his horn, he's looking at somebody and they catch his glance. And then, of course, stomping off the numbers. But that's what I remember about it.

As I said earlier, I don't remember ever having attended any formal kind of a rehearsal. I don't doubt that they had informal rehearsals where – and you read about Dick Allen and all writing about the way they learned new numbers, about they'd get a record and they would sit around and listen to it. And, of course, I know Alton, on the piano, was a reading musician to some extent, and he could help out in that regard.

Martyn : Well, I think from the ones I knew; Drag – he wasn't any kind of musician as a technical musician. You know what I mean. I loved playing with him because he had fabulous timing and liveliness; George wasn't much of a musician, but he had a fantastic ear. This is me talking as a musician, not as a biographer. Jim was the same way, you know. Percy was pretty good a musician.

Gagliano : Well, Percy came from a family that, for instance his Grandfather taught music. His family tradition. The big difference here between George and Percy is Percy had a family tradition of musicians. His grandfather supposedly taught Jim Robinson down at the plantation. But George had no musical background in his family. Well, Lawrence came from a whole family of musicians. I would think that the only one in the band that had that kind of lineage would be Lawrence. Now, I'm not too sure about what Kid Howard had.

I think the only two guys in the band that had people in their background would have been Percy Humphrey and Lawrence. George was the first in his family to play music.

Martyn : Yeah, and obviously the last, too, come to think about it.

Gagliano : Yeah, that's right, as far as I know.

Martyn : I wonder what motivated him to do it. Was it because they loved to play music or was it an economical thing, or a bit of both, or what?

Gagliano : Oh, I'm sure it was both. First of all, I think they probably liked to play music together. They liked the sounds. And I think then, right next to that, it became an opportunity for them to play together and make some money on the side. I don't think anyone ever set out to make music their profession, other than George. He wanted to be a musician from the time he was ten years old, and hopefully he could make a living at it. That's one of the things that Alice told him, "You're not gonna make a living at it, son." But he didn't listen to her. And then when he started to bring home a couple of dollars, then Alice had to change her mind because, you know, nickels and dimes are what they would bring home, but when George started to bring home dollars, well, you know.

Martyn : Well, I remember Alton Purnell, who obviously I played with the most. He was in our band for nine years, you know, so I knew Alton more than any of them. I think Alton was not what you'd call a top-class piano player when he lived in Los Angeles, or certainly here or anything. But he was a good – he could skate through music. In other words, if you saw "The Skater's Waltz," let's say, he could pick it up, you know. He couldn't actually look at it and come on down with it, but chords –he could read any chords that you wrote for him. And my knowledge of him was that I think he played music the same as all of them, for economic reasons because of his family. I don't think any of them were determined to be musicians for the artistic reason. That's what I'm saying.

Gagliano : Well, you know, that is an interesting point. At what point in time did they realize that they were true folk artists that had to ply their art? I don't think they ever looked at it as art.

Martyn : No, I don't think hardly any New Orleans musicians do.

Gagliano : All of that sort of started when they hit those college tours, you know, and they saw the adulation that these

George Lewis with Lawrence Marrero in the background

44

people were bringing to them.

Martyn : Well, let me give you an example with Alton. With my band, the Legends of Jazz, it was an all black band except for me. And the trumpet player, Andy Blakeney was the one who took Louis Armstrong's place in King Oliver's band, so he was a first-class musician, you know. And one time, at rehearsal, he was criticizing Alton. "Alton," he says. He used to have a finger missing, and he'd always point with that finger that was missing. He said, "You ain't making that chord there. That chord's a D flat ninth, and you ain't making your chord correctly. And Alton said, "Man," he said, "you think you know everything about music. Let me tell you something. I've always played music for a living, man. You had to get a job working in a bank and doing this and doing that." Alton was very proud that he only ever played music for a living, and I think it meant a lot to him. But Alton could work solo, too, you know. He would work solo and sing. He has a beautiful singing voice. I loved his singing. He's my favorite singer ever, including Frank Sinatra, that would sound ridiculous, but he put so much feeling into his songs, you know. But he was really adamant about what it took to be a professional musician when he was talking to Andy about – yeah, I'll never forget that conversation. "Man, you worked in banks and you had to work for the school board. I never did nothing like that." He said, "I just played music."

Gagliano : I think he meant it in bragging. I don't know that he could have made a living in the thirties just playing music.

Martyn : Well, yeah, but he was born in 1911, so in the thirties he'd have been twenty plus; but whatever. I think Alton was the best musician in that band, looking at it from a technical aspect.

Gagliano : Well, yeah, from a musical point of view, a knowledge of music. And I will say this about Alton. When I listened to the band with or without the piano, I mean, the piano just gives it so much more richness than when the piano's not there, regardless of who it is, but as I listen, Alton playing in the band, I think he did drive the band. I thought he was a major player in the band.

Martyn : I think that most of the band thought Alton was a bit wild. He was younger than they.

Gagliano : Well, yeah, he was younger. The only thing I remember, you know, they just .... "Oh man, he's one of these young guys." But I didn't know Alton to be wild. I mean, I knew nothing about his background. At some point in time, I remember meeting his wife. I was impressed by her.

Martyn : Esther?

Gagliano : Yeah, as a nice person, and that's when I found out that he left her to go out to California, and got a little angry with him. Not that that made any difference.

Martyn : Oh, he'd have gone anyway. But he came from a musical family. His brother, Theodore, was an alto player. And somewhere it got away from me. I kick myself every time I think of it. I don't know where I got it, but I had a tape of George Lewis' band, and Theodore came and played alto with them. There was only one title, "Bourbon Street Parade," and it wasn't complete anyway. I don't know where the hell that tape went or on what the occasion was.

Gagliano : I've never met him. You mean Alton's brother? No, I never saw him around.

Martyn : Oh, I met him. I knew him – well, not as well as I knew Alton because Alton played in our band, but, I mean, I knew Theodore. They was brothers. Always, when there's two brothers, they're as different as chalk and cheese, generally. You'd never believe. Theodore was calm, collected, and Alton was a trifle volatile, to say the least, you know. I mean, I saw him once, he took his hat off, threw his hat on the floor and jumped on his hat.

Gagliano : I don't remember any of that going on.

Martyn : Oh, man, I remember it so well. I'd say, "Alton, calm yourself." I'd say, "You're gonna have a stroke, man. Calm yourself. It's not worth getting that upset about." But Theodore was completely calm, collected, never got excited. It's like Harold Dejan and his brother, the same thing. There's not many of those brothers – well, Louis and Paul Barbarin. They weren't quite as different as the Purnell brothers, but god. And then look at Percy and Willie and Earl. They were three completely different people, you know. Getting back to George, did he ever tell you who his main influences were in music? Did he ever discuss anything like that?

Gagliano : I guess what I remember about that was he was mostly talking about the trumpet players with whom he played. I think he always told me that, "Man, Buddy Petit was the best trumpet player that I ever played with." And then he mentioned Evan Thomas. Not Evan. He called him E-van. I don't remember him ever necessarily telling me about his peers, his clarinetists. I just don't remember.

Martyn : He told me once about Isadore Fritz.

Gagliano : Yes, I remember him talking about him and that he probably treated him as one of his sources. I don't know whether he mentioned Lorenzo Tio or certainly not Barney Bigard. I don't remember him talking about any of those guys. They were Creole people. I don't think George was privy to their society stuff. Oh yeah, as far as I knew. All during what I call the Manny's years, yeah. The only trumpet player that I knew was Elmer, and then, of course, as I got in closer with the band, and Elmer was beginning to have frail health and George had the problem, you know, of ultimately replacing Elmer.

Martyn : What was his trouble? What was the health problem?

Gagliano : I don't remember. Probably heart or lungs. And when you're talking about this, I'm wondering, here is Elmer Talbert, who was a pretty strong black man. There he is, he's in Flint Goodridge. I don't know the dynamics of all of that. I really don't. Incidentally, one of Bob Greenwood's letters is actually giving a physical description of all of the members in the band, and he identified Elmer Talbert and Herb Morand. He used a phrase that I guess I've heard before, and he used it affectionately, not in any bad way. But he said, "He was what people would call a "dark" Negro, dark, menacing."

Martyn : Menacing.

Gagliano : Well, you look at Elmer. You don't want to meet Elmer in a dark alley, let me put it that way.

Martyn : Yeah, I know exactly.

Gagliano : Elmer Talbert's last days at Flint Goodridge Hospital, where he was crying out for doctors or something. Actually, Myra Menville got into it because they knew that Myra's husband was a kidney specialist, and one of Elmer's problems, physically, was that his kidneys were shutting down. There was some conversation where Dr. Menville said he couldn't ethically go in there, ethically, and take over from the black doctor. Flint Goodridge was a private hospital up on Louisiana Avenue, right smack in the middle of the black community uptown. I'm not sure whether the building is still there or not, but that was the black hospital, aside from Charity. Now, if you ask me, I would have to think that Flint Goodridge was a private hospital. It might have had an affiliation with Dillard University, but I'm not sure about that.

Martyn : Well, how would, like, Elmer Talbert's family pay for him being in there?

Gagliano : I don't know, but he was there. It was, that everything on Elmer was shutting down. This was in 1950, and that was, you know, my first experience with mortality. And then the next close person who died was George's wife, and I had the misfortune of having to tell George that his wife died because George was playing in California at the time.

Martyn : Just for clarification, this was the first wife?

Gagliano : No, no. No, this was Jeanette. I never knew the first wife. I knew only of her. The only other of George's wives was his third wife, Valletta Gremillon, whom I remember meeting on only one occasion, at a train station in New Orleans, when George was either going to or returning from a road trip; she was there and George introduced her to me as his new wife, and of course I was somewhat surprised, and then I congratulated them; she seemed to me to be a very nice middle aged lady. This was obviously after Jeanette died, and I'm convinced that George married this lady to have somebody to help take care of Shirley and George's mother while George was on the road. He didn't tell me that, but that's what I think happened.

Martyn : Well, I remember, when I first came here, Charity Hospital was a terrible place to go. In the black ward, I went to see lots of musicians. Some of them died in there.

Gagliano : It was tough, yeah.

Martyn : I remember going to see, Papa Celestin's drummer, Christopher "Happy" Goldston. I took him a magazine that we published in England with a picture of him on the front cover. He burst into tears and he wouldn't stop crying, and he couldn't speak. He just saw his picture on the front and started crying and you couldn't stop him. I mean he just kept crying and crying, and we had to go – you know, we didn't want to leave him crying. I mean, he couldn't speak, so he couldn't tell us why he was crying. Just joy, I suppose, or recognition. I don't know what it was, but he just couldn't stop.

I remember that all the black people that got out of there would say about somebody dying in there, you would ask, "Well, what did he die of?" "Oh, external, man," or "internal." You know, there wasn't such a thing as breaking it down. It was just internal or external. External would be like a gunshot wound or something like stabbing, I suppose.

Gagliano : It could be a staph infection too.

Martyn : Yeah, I mean it could have been anything. And it was a horrible place to be. I mean, I do remember that.

Gagliano : In later years, though, it became much more renowned as a Trauma Center.

Martyn : Yeah, and of course, with the advent of, well, the whole segregation movement, that made it so much easier.

Gagliano : Yeah, well, you're talking about what—well, wait. When you start telling me you were visiting in New Orleans, what is this? In the sixties, seventies?

Martyn : January of '61.

Gagliano : Sixty-one. Yeah, well, civil rights hadn't kicked in yet, although we were in the midst of it kicking in, because the school integration thing happened in '60.

Martyn : Yeah, that was all going on just before I got here, and they had just taken the screens out of the buses before I got here, just about two weeks before. But I remember going to visit Joe Watkins, at 832 North Galvez and he was in such bad shape. No, Edna was still living.

Gagliano : She was still living?

Martyn : Trixie, the little dog, was still living too, yeah, but only just, you know. And Joe said, "Man." I said, "Well, can you walk? Can you do anything?" "Oh, yeah, man," he says, "it getting better every day." He says, "It gotta get better. I don't want to go to that damn Charity Hospital." He was scared stiff of going in there. He said, "If I check in there, I'll never check out." But the poor man, you could see—he actually did make a little comeback, but not for long, and then he died. I actually mentioned in my book that they couldn't get anybody to play for him, because there was no money to pay them, you know. There was no money to pay a band and nobody – but anyway, by then Edna had died and his little dog, Trixie, so he was all alone in the house. It was upstairs.

Gagliano : I visited him over there. He was above a little drugstore. My recollection is a small Pharmacy.

Martyn : Right, the bus stopped right there, right outside the door. But they dreaded going in. So in your opinion, was this Flint Goodridge as bad as Charity? Not as bad?

Gagliano : Oh, no. I don't think it had that kind of reputation, and it may very well be that Flint Goodridge was the hospital of choice for the Creole community, okay? You know, I told you that I thought maybe there was an affiliation between Flint Goodridge and Dillard University, and there was a network of black physicians who were operating Flint Goodridge. I have to believe that maybe Flint Goodridge was a step up from Charity and was supported maybe to a great extent by the Creole community. When I speak Creole, I'm talking about the light-colored blacks in New Orleans, you know, like Peter Bocage, Manuel Manetta. All those guys, A.J. Piron, they had their own society, and they, unfortunately, felt much more superior to the dark-skinned blacks.

Martyn : They still do, you know.

Gagliano : And when you're talking about this, I'm wondering, here is Elmer Talbert, who was a pretty strong black man. There he is, he's in Flint Goodridge. I don't know the dynamics of all of that. I really don't.

Martyn : Well, just recently we played Lorenzo Tio's daughter's ninetieth birthday. I told you we were going to play, and when I was interviewing her and another lady, "Cookie Gaspard", who is Corinne Gaspard, her name is. She was married to Charlie Gaspard, the alto player, Creole people. Well, Lorenzo Tio is definitely Creole people. And I said, "Let me ask you something, Miss Rose, Miss Cookie." I said, "In 1927, let's say, Louis Armstrong was at the height of his prowess, known all over the country. If you would have brought him home on a date to meet your family, what would have happened?" She said, "We wouldn't bring him on no date. Bring him home?" She said, "Man." This was Rose Tio talking. She said, "Look," she said, "my mother was a very forgiving person." She said, "If he was hungry, she'd have fed him, but she wouldn't let his black ass in the house." Louis Armstrong! He's the equivalent of Elvis Presley in later years.

Gagliano : Well, there you go.

Martyn : They wouldn't let him in the house. But that tickled the hell out of me, you know, wouldn't let him in the house.

Gagliano : Well, that would certainly be how you would describe Elmer Talbert.

Martyn : Well, he died in that Flint Goodridge place, didn't he?

Gagliano : Evidently he did, but I'm not sure about that. As I do further research on this, I'll probably find out. I would imagine that Elmer didn't have long to go, and all of his systems were shutting down.

Martyn : What about Lawrence when he got sick? Where did he go, do you know?

Gagliano : No, I regret not knowing too much about the details of his death, but I don't. I know he had that stroke, and basically from that time on, you know, I didn't see him but by this time I had already left the management of the band. My activity with the band really ended in late '55.

Martyn : When does Percy come into the picture? Did George tell you? When does Elmer Talbert go out of the picture?

Gagliano : Oh, I loved Percy. In my opinion, the band was at its best when Percy was the trumpet player. When I listened to that session with Percy and Talbert together, it just blew me away. Elmer, he got sick, and when he got sick he couldn't play anymore, and then he died. I know that George had played with Kid Howard before, but evidently Kid Howard was not his first personal choice. I'm guessing at that. I think he had a real appreciation for Percy Humphrey's playing, and I think a lot of that stemmed from playing with Percy and the street boys. I mean, if you ask me, this is what I would think. I think this notion of two trumpets. You know, the Oliver thing, although I never heard him talk about King Oliver and all of that as being a major source of inspiration. But if you know, as you do, that George came up as much in the parade tradition as anything else, that when he's playing in a parade band, he's going to be playing the little E-flat clarinet, and he's fighting against three trumpets, one or two trombones, usually one, and maybe an alto horn or baritone horn, and then the tuba or whatever you call those other instruments.

Martyn : But getting back to Percy, so George never came to you and said, "I've got a new trumpet player coming in here, he's Percy Humphrey"?

Gagliano : No. Man, I'm telling you, I don't think George would tolerate me interfering, I might have suggested and said, "What about so-and-so?" "No, no, uh-uh." But that decision was purely his, and I didn't interfere with it. I mean, when he wanted to take on – although Kid Howard was never an overwhelming favorite of mine – when George wanted to use him, I had nothing to do with either encouraging him or discouraging him.

Martyn : Well, here's something that you probably don't know. Well, you might know. Alton wasn't a fan of Percy Humphrey at all. Alton said, "He was the worst trumpet player we ever had in the band," because—and I knew Alton very well, I mean, much better than I know you. But we were on the road together for nine years, you know, although I never roomed with him because he snored. He was a terrible snorer, like a steamboat. Oh, man, could he snore. Nobody wanted to room with him.

Gagliano : And he said Percy was the worst ....

Martyn : He was the worst trumpet player George ever had, for him. He didn't say for the band, now. He said he's fitting in the band all right, but he said, "I didn't like Percy." I said, "What didn't you like about him?" "Well, he wasn't a jazzer." He said, "He's like Alvin Alcorn. He wasn't a jazzer."

I suppose I should have had a tape recorder there and said, "Well, what do you mean by a jazzer?" But I didn't. But that's what he told me.

Gagliano : I guess I wonder if he could have been thinking about trumpet players who stick strictly to the lead.

Martyn : I don't know. I should have – you know, the world is made up of 'should haves'.

Gagliano : Because in my listening to Percy on these records, he is not playing strictly the lead. Albert Walters was playing with Percy, and they each had a solo somewhere in there, and I got the impression that Walters was down the line, you know, pure lead, and Percy was embellishing it, you know, working around it, not unlike George Lewis plays around. But Percy, he commanded attention. I mean, you knew him. I don't know, did you know him better than I, or I knew him better than you? I never had much of a relationship with Percy. He wasn't very much of a conversationalist. I looked up to him, you know, and I didn't feel like I could – no, I just didn't talk to him that much, but I listened.

Martyn : He absolutely – he was the funniest man. He demanded respect without opening his mouth.

Gagliano : In later years when I would go to the Jazz Festival and I'd see Percy and I'd go up to talk to him, I think he remembered me. But he wasn't – let's put it this way: He wasn't very effusive about meeting and talking about things, you know. He'd say, "Oh, yeah. How ya been?"

Martyn : Yeah, and then he'd take the glasses off, like it helped him talk, and then he put them back on. I never understood what to do that for, but I knew him very well. I never had a conversation about you with him, I must say, but I did talk to him briefly about Alton, but his attitude was, "Well, them young boys, you know, like ...." I guess Alton was a young boy. But, no, the more I think about it, I know Alton was born in 1911, Percy was a little older, but he wasn't old enough to be his father or anything. But I don't know, Alton was kind of a – I don't know what you'd call it – Peck's bad boy in that band. He was always doing stuff.

Gagliano : Yeah, he was.

Martyn : Maybe – I just thought of something else. Alton was an official in the union. He was what they called a walking delegate, which meant he carried a little badge so he could come into your club and say, "Union," and want to know where was all the papers and how were they taking the intermissions and why was there no water up on there for the band and all that kind of stuff. And I think Alton being Alton, he took his position a little bit too seriously. I wouldn't say he ever abused it, but where Percy was – I think Percy was treasurer at one time when I joined the union. I know Sidney Cates was in there. So maybe Alton had a little backwash from Percy being above him in the union.

Gagliano : Yeah, that could have been.

Martyn : But he made the distinction that Percy wasn't a jazzer – jazz man was his word – and neither was Alvin Alcorn. But he enjoyed playing with them, so your guess is as good as mine. Did Percy keep up with George's band before he officially joined it? Did he know there was a *Look* article? Did he know they were at the El Morocco?

Gagliano : I don't recall ever talking about that with him. I would think he had to be aware of George's relationship with Bunk from his playing up in New York those four to six months. He had to know all of that. You know, the only significant conversation that I remember having with Percy was why he didn't want to go on the road with the band. He told me flat out. He said, "Man, I can't leave my insurance debit." "I got to keep my insurance going, and I can't afford to go out of town any extended period of time, because I don't want to lose my debit." That's what I remember.

Martyn : What is debit?

Gagliano : That's the term they use to characterize that kind of a route. They'd go and knock on doors and collect the premium.

Martyn : Not to sell insurance?

Gagliano : No. Well, maybe they did. But the debit was collecting the premiums that became due either once a week or once a month or whatever. But you're talking about nickels and dimes, you know, twenty-five cents. And I don't understand the economics of this, where people could spend their whole day going out and maybe collecting seven or eight dollars of premiums.

Martyn : It's not like he knocked on your door and said, "Mr. Gagliano, where's your $700 for last year's insurance".

Gagliano : No. They were like the little books that the grocers had. They would write down in the book twenty-five cents or fifty cents or a dime or whatever. Now, I'm no expert on this. Okay? But that's what my general recollection of a debit was. They would go from house to house wherever these people had these policies. Generally, these were burial policies. They were like life insurance, but they were probably geared to paying for a funeral.

Martyn : Like the benevolent societies .

Gagliano : Yeah. But I got the impression that Percy must have had a fairly good debit route, and at that particular time in his life this was probably his major source of income. It was certainly a dependable source of income, if it wasn't a great source. I have no idea what his economic involvement was. I would presume he got a commission on whatever he collected. I presume that, but I never discussed that at any depth with Percy. The only thing I remember us talking about was, "I can't go on the road for any extended periods of time." Now, he could go on the road, for instance, and did go on the road, when we went to Oxford to play two or three concerts and maybe were gone two or three or four or five days and maybe a week. He could do that.

Martyn : Like using up his vacation or something?

Gagliano : Yeah. In fact, he came on a number of those with us.

Martyn : So he was self-employed.

Gagliano : Well, I don't know whether you would call him self-employed or not. If he was an independent agent for an insurance company, yeah, I guess he would be self-employed. He'd be working on a commission, not a salary.

Martyn : Would he be picking up for like the major insurance people like Allstate and State Farm and all that?

Gagliano : No, they didn't write that kind of insurance, no. No, these were small companies that more often than not had an alliance with some funeral home. I'm guessing at this now. I'm guessing. I'm not being authoritative about it. He could have been writing straight life insurance. I don't know of any health insurance that was – maybe there was something going on back then, but I don't know of it. I had to believe that – well, my own mother would buy a bunch of these policies herself. Before she died, she put in my hands two or three of these policies written by local companies where the death benefit was like two or three hundred dollars, and the premium on it, I could go back to the books and I could see entries for like twenty-five cents. In today's economy you can't even envision what that was like back in the thirties and the forties and the fifties.

Martyn : But it was strictly blacks? I mean, what Percy was doing.

Gagliano : I'm assuming it was black, but I had absolutely no knowledge about what his route consisted of. My guess would be that it would be primarily a black neighborhood. That doesn't mean he couldn't be writing insurance for poor whites.

Martyn : The only one I know that picked up insurance besides Percy was Peter Bocage. And I asked Peter about it one time. I said, "What do you have to do, Pete, exactly?" He said, "Well, most of the ones I deal with," he said, "are dignified people." I guess he meant Creole people. I'm sure that's what Peter meant now. But he said, "Most of the

Jim Robinson

Joe Watkins and Alcide "Slow Drag" Pavageau

people I deal with are dignified people. Once in a blue moon," or whatever expression he said, "one of them can't pay, and I tell her, 'That's all right, Mrs. Daniels, don't you worry. I'll get you next week or next month,'" or whatever it was. So it seemed to be about give and take, and I guess Pete would put a quarter in or seventy-five cents out of his own pocket. She'd pay him a dollar fifty or fifty cents next time.

I never talked to him about insurance at all. But he did tell me that—why did he not go? Oh, because of that.

There was somewhere that they went out and they took Albert Walters on the trumpet. But we're getting into the story again. I'm trying to keep it with Percy with the band. Where was the first time you saw Percy with the band, at one of the Jazz Club concerts? Can you remember?

Gagliano: I think that probably would have been .... I might have caught him on a funeral or some parade thing. I don't have any specific recollection of the first time I met him, but I would think it would be very reasonable to think that one of my earliest encounters with him would have been – well, you know, he was on the WTPS radio show. It could have been there. I don't know that he ever did, because I know that that started with Talbert, and I know Talbert was still playing with the band through '50. Subsequent research at the Tulane Hogan Jazz Archives indicates that Elmer Talbert was seriously ill in Flint-Goodridge Hospital with kidney failure in November, 1950, and that he probably died of uremia in Charity Hospital in December, 1950. Obviously, I would have been aware and had met Percy at the concert that the band played for the Jazz Club in 1949. No, it couldn't have been. Elmer Talbert was our trumpet player then. In fact, one of the things I was listening to last night, Percy was playing second trumpet too.

Martyn: But, look, with Percy – well, let me just ask you this: What did the other guys in the band call you or what did George call you and the guys – did they call you Nick?

Gagliano: They just called me Nick.

Martyn: Not Mr. Nick?

Gagliano: No.

Martyn: Not Nick Gagliano , Mr. Gagliano ?

Gagliano: They might have started that. I don't know that they did. But if they did, I would have told them, "Cut it out, man. Call me Nick. That's my name."

Martyn: And they all called you that?

Gagliano: As far as I know. Might have cussed me behind my back once in a while, I don't know.

Martyn: But when Percy came into the band, did you get any feedback from the musicians? Did any of them say anything to you?

Gagliano: Not that I remember. I thought Percy coming in with us was a very positive thing. That's why I was disappointed that he elected not to go on any extended trips with the band that we were doing. But we weren't really doing many, you want to call it, extended tours. I don't think that the tours that I handled was ever any more than two or three weeks.

Martyn: Let me ask you something else. Did any of them talk about Bunk anymore, or was that all dead and forgotten?

Gagliano: Yeah, that's all dead and forgotten. Not after the initial conversations I would have with them from time to time in the late forties and before I would have became their, quote, "manager," unquote. No. I'm not suggesting they didn't continue to think about it, but there wasn't a lot of discussion about that.

Martyn: Well, even before I thought about co-writing that book on Bunk, the musicians around here, other than George, Jim, and Alton, the ones that were in that band, there wasn't that many – unless they were real old. Real old ones knew something about Bunk. But the younger ones, I remember talking to – Bunk was all I knew, because that was the records I came up listening to at first, and I had thought when I came to New Orleans, everybody would be talking about Bunk. But if you talk to say: DeDe Pierce, you know, they wouldn't even know who you were talking about. "Huh? Who? Bunk. Bunk who?"

Gagliano: That wouldn't surprise me.

Martyn: What was the politics of George and the band?

Gagliano: Never came up. If you asked me, I would think that they were apolitical.

Martyn: Well, I know later years Alton was staunchly Democrat, because, well, for the obvious. You'd think he would be anyway, you know. But I know he was because we talked about it.

Gagliano: Well, I would imagine that all of them would have been registered Democrats.

Martyn: If they were registered at all. I mean, they had that process here where they gave them examinations to see if they could vote. I mean, can you imagine Jim Robinson and Slow Drag passing that examination?

Gagliano: No, I couldn't imagine that.

Martyn: I mean, I can honestly say I never had a conversation with Slow Drag. I recorded with him. Never had a conversation with him. I don't know what he thought about anything.

Gagliano: I mean, you can understand then why I'm considered to a degree a manager, and I'm dealing with these guys, and the relationship was physically not as close as you might think it would be, because I'm trying to make my own way in life. I was able to get through Tulane, and I'm embarking on a new career. But I was very much touched by their telling me about all of the stuff that they had done in New York and how they had lost their major, you know, their big opportunity, and telling me that they're looking forward to having another chance and that they wanted me to be part of it. That was very touching to me. You know, at the time when we started our relationship, I'm in college. My claim to maturity was that I just spent two years in the navy in World War II.

Martyn: Do you think that George surpassed where he was with Bunk in the end?

Gagliano: Oh, absolutely.

Martyn: You're sure of that?

Gagliano: I mean, to me. Because he was out of the shadow of Bunk by then – you know. I mean, the true strength of Bunk's band was revealed in George. I'm not trying to knock Bunk in any way. I'm sure that he was the catalyst for all of this getting started, but in terms of musical ability at that particular time, I don't think he stood up to George's challenge.

Martyn: Well, Alton Purnell, who, as I've told you through these interviews, was the one I knew best, we had our band together, you know, him and me and Joe Darensbourg, Louis Nelson, and whatnot, "The Legends of Jazz". But Alton said, "Man, that never was Bunk's band. Bunk never had no band. That was George Lewis' Band. Yeah, it was George's band, I'm telling you." That was his take on it.

Gagliano: Well, he's right in terms of playing around New Orleans, because in all of the period when these guys were playing together, Bunk was frittering away his time in New Iberia.

George Lewis, Lawrence Marrero and Alcide "Slow Drag" Pavageau recording at Joe Mares' Studio April 6 '54

Martyn : Well, that's just like they take Nick Gagliano 's band. You've got a band. They're the same people. I come along, and they put me in charge of it and call it Barry Martyn's band. But you've had this band together for twenty years. That was the point Alton was trying to make.

Gagliano : That's okay, but he was the vehicle to get them business.

Martyn : George did get to some – well, not George, Bunk. Let's just say Bunk Johnson's band. They got to some dizzy heights. I mean, to be in Vogue magazine and ....

Gagliano : I'm trying to tell you. He was the media participant in all of this. I mean, it was his historical context, that made him the frontman to create this resurgence in the old music.

Martyn : Well, it was a publicist's dream. I mean, here's this old guy playing out in the boon docks, driving rice trucks and trashing rice out in New Iberia, you know.

Gagliano : Not only that, and you've got Louis Armstrong saying, "Hey, if you want to know about the old days, go see Bunk Johnson." I think it was a great thing for George and the guys to get with Bunk. But nobody outside of the Ninth Ward of New Orleans knew anything about George Lewis. If it wouldn't have been for the historians' search to resurrect Bunk, then George Lewis would not – well, I'm not saying that he would not have – but I think it would have been a very different thing in George's life. He just would not have had that boost that Bunk gave him. Now, granted, they were down on Bunk as having blown the opportunity, but to be fair about it, it was Bunk that gave them the opportunity. I mean, that's just show business. That's the way it is. Bunk giveth and Bunk taketh away. In essence, Bunk blew it. That didn't make the regret any less intense. Well, when you got down to George Lewis, if you're a publicist and trying to write about him, number one, he didn't have anything to say. You know, man, he wasn't the world's best talker.

Martyn : Where did the rest of 'The Men in the Band' live? I mean roughly.

Gagliano : Slow Drag lived down in the Quarter in the vicinity of the Dew Drop, his hangout place. Annie, his wife, she was a mainstay in the church somewhere around there. It is also interesting to note that in each of these various listings, the spelling of the last name was always different. The reference to the "Dew Drop" as Slow Drag's Hangout was incorrect; it really was Cy's Tumble Inn Bar and Lounge, located at 738 Burgundy Street at its intersection with St. Ann Street. [See New Orleans Directory]

Martyn : Well, they used to live on St. Ann Street.

Gagliano : You know, I don't ever remember visiting Drag at his house. I don't remember any visit there. I would visit George and I would visit Lawrence Marrero.

Martyn : Why did you pick them?

Gagliano : I don't know. I don't know. Well, George was , you know, that was a given. As far as Lawrence, Lawrence was able to talk to me and we could converse. I had an interest in his banjo. In fact, he got me a banjo, which I still have. He didn't give it to me; he said "Do you want to buy a banjo, I have a friend that wants to sell his?" I said, "Well, okay. " I got it for ten dollars. I never did ever sit down with Lawrence and ask him to teach me.

George called him "brother-in-law" that was really reserved for Lawrence.

Martyn : Yeah, but they weren't any kin at all, were they?

Gagliano : Oh, no. No, culturally they were brothers, brother-in-laws. They treated themselves like a sort of a family, and Drag knew that whenever George had a job, Drag and Lawrence had a job. Now, Jim felt the same way, but he realized that being trombone, he was expendable. I mean, Lawrence and Drag and Joe Watkins, I mean they were the staples, you know.

Martyn : So Joe Watkins, he was actually the first interview I ever did. I did that January 20, 1961, and he told me when he joined George's band, which he was in there when you came along – so all right, well, when he joined George, he came from Herb Morand's band. That was who he was playing with, and George asked him would he come play with him and he said, "Yes," because I don't know why. Perhaps he didn't get along with Herb Morand. I don't know. But whatever. He joined George and he said, "What style do you want me to play on the drums?" And George said, "Autentic style. Autentic." And it struck me as what a funny way of putting it, "autentic." What would George mean by that, do you think? Of course he was mispronouncing, "authentic."

Gagliano : Well, I guess the best thing I could tell you was that he felt the drummer had to be felt, not necessarily heard. I used to get a kick out of when the band would play "Mama Don't Allow," which is a staple, you know, and it came time for the drum solo and I'm watching these college kids. Joe played ensemble drums, his obligatory part, and I'm looking at these guys. They're waiting for some kind of a drum solo. Some kind of showboat, but that would never happen. So I guess the best way that I could tell you is that George probably meant you ought to be felt and not overheard, and that's a simplistic way of putting it.

Martyn : Well, George was very hard on drummers. He was hard on me, and I was the one who employed him. I was going to fix the tour, and he was hard on me, you know.

Gagliano : Well, let me ask you a question. What type of thing would he get on you about?

Martyn : He hated woodblocks. He didn't like those clack-clack, clack-clack, clack-clack.

Gagliano : Oh, that's why he didn't like Baby Dodds.

Martyn : Well – oh, he told you that?

Gagliano : Well, that's partly – I seem to remember that.

Martyn : I think he respected Baby enormously.

Gagliano : Oh, yeah. Well, he had to because Baby had gone on to fame in New Orleans way before George ever got going.

Martyn : Before George came on the scene, you know. But he hated that. He didn't want anything but—he wanted the cymbal. He said, "Look," he said, "I don't mind you playing the first chorus on the snare drum," he said, "but then get on that cymbal and stay on that cymbal all the time," which I did. I loved him. I mean it was fantastic. I mean, Christ, in 1965 I was twenty-four. Well, Jesus, when you're twenty-four. Joe told me. He said, "He'll worry you half to death, man." He said, "Don't pay him no mind." He said, "He's got a good heart," or something like that. But he said, "You be ready if you ever have to play with him," because Joe had died by then, you know, when I played with George. Well, I wasn't the sponsor, but I was the one who suggested to the sponsor they brought George Lewis over to Europe. And then they wanted my band to do it, the whole tour, and we did. So that's why I say George was always hard on drummers, you know. Cié told me the same thing. Cié Frazier told me, "Man, I can't mess with him. He don't know what the hell he wants." But I suppose any bandleader has got the right to tell you what does he expect of you in the band, you know. It depends how much respect you have for that bandleader, and I had the ultimate respect for George. He wasn't giving orders to people or anything like that.

Gagliano : No, not very often. No. But he'll look at you with those eyes, even while in the middle of a solo when he's doing his thing, and he's looking at whoever he's looking at. That's the way he would tell them that, hey, man, something's not right here."

Martyn : Yeah, yeah. It's probably because Slow Drag never was any technical player, what can we say? I mean he was a pretty basic bass player, but George kept him in there all that time, you know.

Gagliano : Yeah, I never did understand musically – I always felt that Drag and Lawrence and Joe made a very, very decent rhythm section. I remember occasionally I would see Drag pull out his bow. What is he going to do with that? Yeah, I mean he didn't know the fingerboard that well.

Very seldom he would bring out the bow I'd say, "Man, this is a new dimension for Drag." But here again, I think the bass is something that George feels that you've got to feel. The rhythm section—I guess you'd have to put it—I guess to some extent this explained the little tension that existed between him and George Guesnon. I think that George Guesnon was from the reading school. And he was probably a good musician and he knew what the hell he was talking about, and I think he looked down on George to some extent, and on Lawrence as being primitive ....

Martyn : I know he looked down on Lawrence, yeah.

Gagliano : .... unschooled, untutored, unlettered. In other words, aboriginal.

Martyn : I didn't know Lawrence. Lawrence was the only one of the band I didn't know. Well, Elmer Talbert, but they died before I came here. In fact, Lawrence had just died before I came here. I mean just, you know. But George Guesnon I knew very well. George was a good friend of mine.

Gagliano : He always said Lawrence played out of tune, and a lot of times he did.

Martyn : George told me that Lawrence came to him out of the blue sky and said, "I want you to teach me some of the stuff that you are doing so I can use it more with George." Now, I don't know whether that's true, but I never knew George to – I've know him to exaggerate a bit, make things a little bigger than they were, but I've never known him to come with an outright lie. I knew him well enough to say that.

Gagliano : I've only been exposed to George Guesnon maybe two or three times in my life.
And I liked him, thought he was a sort of a different kind of guy.

Martyn : Well, he was certainly that.

Gagliano : I thought he was an excellent banjo player. That much I could understand. But as I read now, I could now understand the friction that would have existed.

Martyn : For instance, he and I were once – don't know what we were doing. We were at his house. He used to live at 1012 North Roman, a nice little house he had there. It was a shotgun house, one storey, and I used to go there twice a week, sometimes more. You know, in the daytime there was no music to hear, no bands playing. I'd go by George, and we'd talk about music and all kind of things. He had a little – wasn't a windup – it was one of them little funny boxes about as big as that box there, and he plugged it in and we played the record of George playing the verse. I think it was, "Baby Won't You Please Come Home" with Shots. And he said, "Look, ..." he said – I think he must have had the record there – ".... what I'm trying to tell you about Lawrence. You can hear he's got a great beat, but listen to those terrible chords he's playing there." He said, "I can't understand how he can't hear that they're the wrong chords." He said, "They're just so wrong."

I mean, I'm a drummer and I taught myself music in later years, but when I first came here, I wasn't that good – I'm not that good a musician now – but I'm a musician, you know. I can write music slowly and all that. I said, "Jesus Christ." I mean I'd heard the record before, but how could Lawrence be out there playing that string of verse changes. It doesn't fit with anything. It's just, you know, it's just the wrong chords. I thought what the hell? I wonder how he could ever hear that?

Gagliano : Maybe that's what I interpreted as being out of tune, playing the wrong chords.

Martyn : Could have been that. I mean, I don't know. I wasn't there. It's hard to talk about somebody you never met.

Gagliano : The problem, though, is that Lawrence was such a likable guy. He was the favorite of all of these college – man, they loved Lawrence. He had a personality and an aura about him that was just unusual.

Martyn : Did he smile on the stage a lot?

Gagliano : Oh, yeah. Yeah, he would have a sly smile, you know, like, "Man, I got you now."

Martyn : He never took many solos, did he, by comparison?

Gagliano : Well, the band never did, except in some of these signature kinds of tunes like "Mama Don't Allow," but that was geared to spotlight every person. Let's put it this way. That song was the reason for having a solo. That's part of the song. All right? All the other stuff was basically, you know, you're part of an ensemble and you have to have your sound blend in with everybody else. Now, that wasn't exactly true with Lawrence because, as you pointed out, a lot of Lawrence's stuff did seem to stand out because he was playing a little bit out of tune, or he was, as George Guesnon suggested, playing the wrong chords. To the ordinary listener, Lawrence was just hip. Lawrence always brought down the house at the college concerts with his solo in, of all tunes, "The World is Waiting for the Sunrise".

Martyn : Lawrence didn't often play the wrong chords, but when he did, you just couldn't imagine how he couldn't hear it. It was so wrong, you know. It was like you're in a normal conversation and you start f-ing. You know what I mean? It stands out, you know. If I'm sitting here and I say, "Well, that f-ing band was so-and-so," you think, "Did he really say that?" And then it's going to stand out in that tape.

Gagliano : You know what? What was the problem with bebop? Bebop and all of that kind of stuff had a lot of discordant stuff in it, right? Maybe there are people out there who like discordant music.

Martyn : Huh. That's a point.

Gagliano : I don't know. I mean, how else do you describe some of this stuff that had been played in the fifties and sixties as jazz music?

Martyn : Yeah, yeah, yeah. What did George think of all that?

Gagliano : "Live and let live. It ain't my stuff. I don't know how to play it and I'm not gonna – I don't know. I just don't understand what they're trying to do." In my opinion, with me George was not a big conversationalist. He was really very laid back and he let people do the talking. But Lawrence, he was a little bit more garrulous than George was. Oh, yeah, he was more outgoing. Alton was fairly outgoing.

Jim was very outgoing, but you know Jim was always angling for some booze. I mean – and maybe I shouldn't say this. Maybe this is not the truth – but practically every time I would see Jim, he would sort of put the arm on and, "Give me a bottle. Bring me a fifth, man." Well, I never did that because I didn't want these guys to be drinking on the jobs you know. And I knew that George, early in his life, had a drinking problem.

Martyn : But never when you met him. Well, we know about Howard. Howard used to drink a lot, but Jim really, I would say from my knowledge of him, which was quite extensive, not as big as yours, but I played with him on recordings and tours and stuff. Jim, you never honestly knew whether he was drunk or sober. He was just the same way, you know.

Gagliano : I never could have a decent conversation with Jim. I never could and between him and Drag, it was just impossible.

Martyn : Oh, Slow Drag was – I never understood a word Slow Drag said.

Gagliano : But these were benevolent guys. I loved them and there was no tension between us. It's just that we couldn't communicate.

Martyn : Well, Slow Drag, what was that thing he used to say? "He turned around and I turned around. He turned around and I turned around and then this," you know. But he used to say that all the time. I'm thinking, well, who turned around? What is he talking about?

Gagliano : I can't really criticize the people who may be looking at our interaction, because I could never have any great conversation going with most of the guys, although I could certainly sit down and talk to George and with Lawrence. Alton Purnell, of course, was, as I mentioned, he was my roommate on the college tours. He was the only guy that felt comfortable, I guess, bunking with a white guy.

Martyn : I can't imagine in my wildest dreams why anybody would converse with Jim or Slow Drag. I mean, what would you talk to Jim about? I mean, I don't know where you'd start a conversation with him. Well, I had a conversation, if you could call it. I said to him, "Jim, didn't you learn trombone in the army?" And he said, "Huh?" I said, "In the army, when you were in the army, didn't you learn to play the trombone there?" He said, "Who?" I said, "You," and it went on like this. "The trombone, you know. Weren't you taught the trombone in the army?" He said, "I don't know what you mean." So I had to give up. Somebody must have interviewed him and made some sense out of him, you know, because I've seen it written in books that he learned trombone in the army.

Gagliano : Okay. So it's not me.

Martyn : No, no. It's definitely not you. And as I say, Slow Drag – you knew Miss Annie, huh, his wife?

Gagliano : Yeah. She was quite an intelligent woman. I mean she wasn't dumb. But, I didn't understand their relationship.

Martyn : I couldn't figure out what did she have in common with Drag? What did they ever talk about, you know?

Gagliano : I guess it was survival. Think about it.

Martyn : Was he married to her when you first met him?

Gagliano : I thought he was, but I never knew him to have any other lady besides Annie. So whether or not they were married, I have now really established that George was actually legally married the first time to Emily. I think that's her name. Because I've come across the certificate.

Martyn : Was Joe Watkins married to Edna in those times?

Gagliano : Yeah, yeah. That was his wife. They were up above a drugstore or something else. Where the buses stopped. I'd go there a couple of times, you know. I don't know what the business was, but I had occasion to go to visit Joe a couple times.

Martyn : Yeah, I went there to see him. No, Joe was quite eloquent, I felt. Didn't you?

Gagliano : Oh, yeah, because Joe was basically – you've got to understand his work – he was as a janitor, okay. So a janitor's work could take you into white toilet rooms where you would be maybe giving out – working for tips. On the other hand, he could be a janitor in an office building cleaning up after hours. I don't remember exactly. He never did tell me exactly where and how he worked. [See New Orleans Directory]

Martyn : Well, when I knew him, he was a bank guard at Whitney on Carondelet, is it, or one of those little streets there.

Gagliano : A bank guard?

Martyn : Yeah, for the outside, or inside, wherever it was.

Gagliano : Well, that wasn't janitor work then. He had stepped up a little.

Martyn : I was going to say he'd moved up then, because he told me, he said, "Yeah, I used to be a janitor, but now," he said, "I've got this. This is great."

Gagliano : Well, all during the times that he was a janitor, all were just barely squeaking by.

Martyn : Well, let's go through them. Joe was a janitor. Slow Drag, God knows, what could he do?

Gagliano : He was primarily working in construction, either like a tile carrier or some maybe less skilled kind of a job working as a helper. I understood that Lawrence was a carpenter or did carpentry. *[See New Orleans Directory]*

Martyn : Well, Alton – I know in '52, probably before that, Alton had a job. He was a walking delegate for the musicians union, for 496. I know he was that because I talked to him about it and I've got a picture of him with George's band. They were making a recording, and Alton was there and Lester Santiago was there and – wait a minute – this is the recording session with Red Allen. Then it dawned on me. I knew Alton used to work for the union, walking delegate. Alton probably came as a representative of the union. So Alton was working for the union, but that was '52. I don't know about '49.

Gagliano : That was in the time when we were in our traveling mode.

Martyn : Well, when did you first see Alton play with the band?

Gagliano : My recollection would be when we played that first concert at the Congo Square in 1949.

Martyn : So when you saw George at Manny's, he didn't say, "Well, I've got a seven-piece band really with a trombone and a piano"?

Gagliano : No. I knew that Alton Purnell had been with Bunk and George, and I knew the guys from that. I remember when the Jazz Club told me, "Yeah, we want George to put a band together." I said, "Okay. How many pieces?" Well, at the first concert we used, on trumpet, Percy Humphrey.

Martyn : Where was the first concert that George played?

Gagliano : It was outside in the Congo Square. This was the for Jazz Club, 1949. And it was that concert when the Jazz Club agreed to bring in George's band. That's when they talked to me. "Can George put together a band?" I said, "Sure he can."

Martyn : Alton said, "Oh, that Bunk Johnson situation." He said, "Man, that wasn't Bunk's band. George had that band," he said, "and they got Bunk to come in and play trumpet with George Lewis' Band. That's how that was." He was adamant about that. I didn't know Lawrence, but I've got ears and I'm a musician. I would say the best one in the band for music was Alton, not because he's a friend, but I would have thought Alton – Alton wasn't a genius of music, believe me – but I think he knew more than the other ones.

Gagliano : He was a great piano player, and he fit in well with George. The only difference was in his outlook on life. He was a little bit more aggressive.

Martyn : And younger too.

Gagliano : Yeah, and younger. And I think all of that went together, and so that's why I indicated to you that sort of

Alton and I were assigned to share rooms on the college tours.

Martyn : Well, I guess they seemed to me set in their ways, the ways of Dixie, the ways of segregation and all that, whereas Alton didn't seem to give a hoot for any of that, you know. He'd go where he wanted to go.

Gagliano : Well, that's not totally true, not down here.

Martyn : Not down here, no. Well, I knew him in Los Angeles.

Gagliano : When he was out of this area. Yeah, I would imagine, yeah. I would believe he would do that. But the other guys, they were older. They were more influenced by their living pattern in New Orleans .... a little bit of the rebel in Alton. People that have all of their lives been involved in a particular cultural setting, they're not going to be able to change overnight. And in some cases, maybe the guys just didn't feel comfortable in change. But I think they ultimately worked it out as time went by. I can tell you there was a great awakening to these guys when they went up on these concert tours of the colleges.

The only time that we really did have what I would call a rehearsal was when we'd go to one of the concerts at the colleges and we'd try to learn the college song. Inevitably, we would get Alton, who could read, and he had a piano, you know. And if you want to pick out a tune, you can use the piano for it. And then we'd get a couple of students to whistle the damn thing. And we'd try to pick it. We picked it up on a couple of occasions because it was successful.

Martyn : When I co-wrote my book on Bunk, came to light many, many things. Bunk was always scrounging money from Bill and the other people. It seemed like it was his duty as a black man to bum money off the white men.

Gagliano : That wouldn't surprise me. But I don't think that would be George's attitude. I think George did it, if he did it, he did it out of tremendous need, almost desperation. You can almost read his words, you know, the way he would put it to Bill, "Mr. Bill, I really need this. Could you send me twenty-five dollars?" And he said, "I'll sure pay you back when you come back down here." Bill Russell was back up wherever he was living.

Martyn : Canton, Missouri, I think.

Gagliano : And they would carry on this correspondence was like it was almost weekly.

Martyn : Well, I must say, in my knowledge of all the musicians in New Orleans I've worked with, hundreds, hundreds, the black ones, I'd say twenty white ones, about four hundred black ones – I don't know why. It wasn't planned – well, I guess it was planned. But anyway, doesn't matter about that. But only one ever tried to hit on me for money, and I don't mind telling you, because he paid me back. It was Joe Watkins, and Joe I knew probably second or third best of any of the musicians. He was the first New Orleans drummer I ever saw play live in my life. When the band came in '59, he was the first one. I was too scared to go and tell him. I must have said, "Hello, Mr. Joe Watkins. How are you?" I guess. I can't remember.

But anyway, when I came here, he was the first interview I did, January 20, 1961. And we got to be such good friends. I hate to say it because it's in my book, but it's interesting to bring up here, he asked me, "Would you mind if I wrote to your mother?" And I thought, well, no, because he had been to England, so he had met people. And he was married to Edna. Edna was still living at that time.

I said, "No, she'd be tickled pink to get a letter from America." You only got that in the war, you know, people writing to from the U.S. and so they kept up a correspondence. They never met, but they kept an unbelievable correspondence going till he died.

But he was so badly off, it was just ridiculous. I mean, his leg was rotting. I mean, he couldn't do anything. But anyway, Joe almost was adamant not to go to Charity Hospital, but he couldn't do anything, and one day he asked me, he said, "Man," he said, "you know, we've been friends a long while." He said, "I never asked for anybody for anything." He said, "Could you loan me fifty dollars?" I was a poor kid. I said, "I think so. Yeah, I'm pretty sure." I could have borrowed twenty dollars off Bill Russell if I'd had to, because I could see what this poor man was – he couldn't go out of his house and nobody there would look after him. In the summer, no air conditioning, just sitting up there in a dirty old vest and sweat pouring off him. I lent it to him, and he paid me back a dollar a week, just sent me a dollar bill in an envelope, to England yet, but he paid me. He paid me all the fifty dollars back. But all the rest of them, I don't remember them ever asking. Did they ever ask you for money?

Gagliano : Oh, yeah. Well, it would be sort of like in a joking way. What I remember about that was I remember Slow Drag's wife, Annie. Every time I would run into Annie, she would be behind me for something for her church, for her church, always for her church. And then, of course, Jim made some occasional remarks like, "Man, I could use a fifth of liquor," something like that. But other than that, no. They didn't try to pester me for that. And maybe George told them,

"Leave him alone," but I don't know that.

Martyn : I don't think that he would have had to. I think they would have realized, "Well, this is a good guy. He's trying to help us," you know. But it didn't seem in the George Lewis band, of all those men, even Slow Drag, crazy as he was, he never said, "Can you lend me a couple of bucks so I can go out to buy tobacco?" What did he smoke? Black Draught, I think it was called. God, it was the most .... were you ever be around him when he smoked his pipe?

Gagliano : I don't recall.

Martyn : God, you'd have recalled if you'd have known. It was the stinkiest damn tobacco. It was called Black Draught. I don't know why Draught. God, did it smell.

Gagliano : No, I don't remember Drag's stinky tobacco, but I had the same problem at my home when my father smoked those skinny, crooked and very dense Italian cigars, that I called charoots, which I think could hold its own for stinkiness fight against the Black Draught.

Martyn : Well, I don't think I ever smelled anything as bad as that stuff Slow Drag smoked.

And he smoked it in the apartment, and all the time, you know, smell that damn stuff.

But it's funny, that that whole band, I don't know, they just got along so well, you know. Was there any ever arguments in them that you can remember between this one and that one?

Gagliano : No, I can't recall anything. I seem to remember maybe there was some problem with Kid Howard once in a while, but maybe even that's not fair to say.

Martyn : Well, I guess it was four of them. Let me see. Is it four? Alton, George, Jim Crow, and what's his name? Slow Drag. They had been in that band with Bunk, so I guess that would kind of gird you against, you know ....

Gagliano : You know, they had this brotherhood thing where actually Bunk sort of isolated himself and he drank. I guess Bunk had a sort of a attitude toward some of the guys that they didn't know how to read music, you know, and he was supposed to be a good reading musician.

Martyn : Which I'm certain he was, from the research I did.

New Orleans City Directory

Resident Listings for members of the George Lewis Ragtime Jazz Band

Note: Spellings of name are as listed in the directories.

1930:
George Lewis, musician, 1319 Governor Nicholls Street; no wife listed
Alice Zeno, no listing
Lawrence Marrero, musician, 126 Pauger Street, no wife listed
Alcide Pavageou, painter, 1225 St. Philip Street, no wife listed
Avery Howard, laborer, 1324 Lamanche
Percy L. Humphrey, Jr., Chauffer, 3927 Hamilton
Nathan Robinson, laborer, 541 3rd Street
Nathan Robinson, Jr., laborer, 548 3rd Street

1935:
George Lewis, longshoreman, 416 N. Villere Street, no wife listed
Alice Zeno, 1125 Tonti Street
Mildred B. Zeno, maid 1603 St. Philip
Lawreence Marrero, no listing
Alcide Pavageau, no listing

Avery Howard, cement finisher, 1515 St. Philip
Percy G. Humphrey, musician, 4519 S. Robertson
Elmer Talbert, presser, 905 N. Claiborne Avenue
Nathan Robinson, laborer, 522 4th Street

1940:
George and Geneva Lewis, musician, 827 St. Philip
Alice Zeno, no listing
Lawrence Marrero, no listing
Alcide Pavageau, no listing
Avery Howard (Mary), laborer, 1515 St. Philip
Percy G. and Mary I. Humphrey, agent, Liberty Industrial Life Ins. Co., 4519 S. Robertson
Elmer Talbert (Lillian), presser, 19231 St. Peter
Jos. Watkins (Edna), janitor, 1315 Iberville

1945-6:
George and Jeannett Lewis, 827 St. Philip
Alice Zeno (widow of Henry L), 910 St. Philip
Lawrence Marrero, helper, Hotzman's Furn. Store, 907 Burgundy Street
Alcide Pavageau, no listing, except the following possibility:
Morning Star Baptist Church 626-28 Burgundy Street
Avery Howard (Norma), empl. U.S. Cold Storage, 1112 St. Philip
Percy G. (Ethel) Humphrey, musn NOPE, 4519 S. Robertson
Elmer J. Talbert (Lillian), Supreme Cleaners, 625 S. Rampart Street
Joseph M. Watkins (Edna), helper, U.S. Government, 825 N. Galvez

1947:
George and Jeannette Lewis, no listing
Alice Zeno, no listing
Lawrence Marrero, helper, Holtzman's Furn. Store, 907 Burgundy Street
Alcide Pavageau, no listing, except the following possibility:
    Morning Star Baptist Church, 626-28 Burgundy Street
Avery Howard (Norma), empl. U.S. Cold Storage, 1112 St. Philip
Percy G. (Ethel) Humphrey, musn NOPE, 4519 S. Robertson
Elmer J. Talbert (Lillian), Supreme Cleaners, 625 S. Rampart Street
Joseph M. Watkins (Edna), helper, U.S. Government, 825 Galvez

1949:
George and Jeannette Lewis, Musician, 1819 Dauphine Street
Alice Zeno, no listing
Lawrence Marrero, helper, Holtman's Furn. Store, 907 Burgundy
Louis Pavageau, carpenter, 910 Burgundy

1952-53:
George (Geneva) Lewis, musician, 3327 DeArmas Street, Algiers
Alice Zeno, no listing
Lawrence Marrero, no listing
Alcide Pavageau, no listing
Avery Howard, (Norma L.), porter, Tulane Univ., 1112 St. Philip
Percy G. Humphrey, (Ethel G.), agent Good Citizens Life Ins., 4519 S. Robertson

Elmer J. Talbert, Jr., 625 N. Rampart
Joseph M. Watkins, (Edna), porter, Sears, 825 N. Galvez
Also:
200-202 Bourbon, El Morocco Lounge, night club
333 Bourbon Mardi Gras Lounge, Sidney Davilla
424-26 Bourbon, club slipper, night club
423-27 Bourbon, Silver Frolics, liquor, Pete Conforto

1954-55:
George (Geneva s.) Lewis, 3327 DeArmas
Alice Zeno (widow of Henry), rear 910 St Philip
Lawrence Marrero, musician, 1846 Industry Street
Pavagau, Alcide L. and Annie R, musician, Geo. Lewis Dixieland Band, 910 Burgundy Street
910 Burgundy Street also listed as morning Star Baptist Church, and
738 Burgundy (corner at St. Ann), listed as Cy's Tumble Inn Bar and Lounge
Avery Howard, jr. (Norma M.), musician, Geo. Lewis Band, 1517 St. Philip
Percy G. Humphrey, (Ethel G.), agent, Good Citizens Life Ins., 4519 S. Robertson
Elmer J. Talbert, Jr., driver Stephens Buick, 625 N. Rampart
Jos. Watkins, (Edna), musician, Club Slipper, 832 N. Galvez
Alton (Esther) Purnell, ass't business agent for Musicians Local 496, 1875 N. Rocheblave
Esther also listed as machine operator Escalante Cigars

1956:
George Lewis (Veletta), musician, 3327 DeArmas
Alice Zeno (Widow of Henry L.), rear 910 St. Philip
Lawrence Marrero, No listing Alcide Pavageau, no listing
Avery Howard, Jr., musician, Paddock Lounge, 1517 St. Philip
Percy G. Humphrey, (Ethel G.), agent, Good Citizens Life Ins., 4519 S. Robertson
Alton (Esther) Purnell, musician, 1875 N. Rocheblave

1957:
George Lewis (Veletta G.), musician, 3327 DeArmas
Alice Zeno (widow Henry) 3327 DeArmas
Lawrence Marrero, 1846 Industry
Alcide Pavageau, no listing
Avery Howard, Jr. Musician, 1517 1/2 St. Philip
Percy G. Humphrey, (Ethel G.), agent, Good Citizens Life Ins., 4519 Robertson
Jos. Watkins, (Edna), 832 N. Galvez
Alton (Esther) Purnell, 1875 N. Rocheblave

1960:
George Lewis, musician, 3327 DeArmas
Alice Zeno, (widow Henry) 3327 DeArmas
Lawrence Marrero, no listing
Alcide (Annie B) Pavajeau, musician, self, 932 St. Ann Street
Avery Howard, Jr., musician, 1517 St. Philip
Percy G. Humphrey, (Ethel G.), agent Good Citizens Life Ins., 4519 S. Robertson
Jos. Watkins, (Edna), 832 N. Galvez

Chapter 4
"Look magazine and El Morocco"

Martyn : Let's go back to 1949. Did you see that this music was in danger of dying?

Gagliano : In my limited scholarship on the issue, I've got to believe that the efforts of Bill Russell and his group when they came down here in the forties, the early forties, and started recording these guys and then getting out those records, even on a very limited basis, I have to believe that that was the seed that started the renaissance of traditional jazz that sort of took real root by 1950, when it had gotten back to such a point that *Look* magazine would devote an article, as it did, to write about George Lewis and his band.

Martyn : Was any of the *Look* article to do with you?

Gagliano : No, although, let's see, I would have been in the role of his manager at the time. I would know what was going on. There was an interesting situation here. At the very bottom of the first *Second Line* dated May, 1950 was a statement, "Be on the lookout for the *Look* magazine article coming out in June." So somebody in the Jazz Club was already aware that that was coming out. Curiously, in the subsequent issues of the *Second Line* after the Look article was released, no mention was made of the *Look* article.

Martyn : Well, how big was that when that came out. How big was that article to the band, to you?

Gagliano : Oh, it was tremendous. At least I thought it was. I mean, to my way of thinking, it gave the ultimate credibility to George Lewis, and from that time on, I mean, it broadened – George Lewis was basically an underground musician, okay? *Look* magazine brought him out of the underground, made it headline. Didn't make him any better to the people who knew who he was and how he played. Didn't make him any better, but it gave him the mass appeal.

Martyn : I wonder what was the circulation of that magazine in those times?

Gagliano : Well, we knew it was national.

Martyn : Well, national, but how big was it?

Gagliano : *Look* magazine? Yeah, was behind *Life* or was it running close to *Life*. *Look* magazine, in my view, it was the poor man's *Life*. It was a modern, more popular version of *Life*, but with heavier reliance on pictures. It had a lighter feel and a more popular feel. If it was national, it had to have a circulation of a couple hundred thousand.

Martyn : Oh, I would think. But it drew George to national attention, if not international attention. I mean, I know that magazine got over to England quite early, because people were collecting it. Did George ever meet up with Stanley Kubrick later, to your knowledge? I know there's a photo of Kubrick playing drums with the band from the *Look* photos. He was a drummer of fair quality according to Dick Allen.

Gagliano : Not to my knowledge, George never met with him again after the *Look* article.

Martyn : Did George know who he was later? Did he say, "Oh, that's the guy making these famous films. He's the one took our picture"?

Gagliano : At that time I didn't even know who Kubrick was.

Martyn : No, at that time I don't think anybody would have known.

Gagliano : No, but as it turned out, according to the thing, that Kubrick was certainly a fan of George. How he got that way, I don't know and I wouldn't – no, George had never discussed that with me.

Martyn : Well, there's all sorts of stories about that magazine article. Stanley Kubrick came and people wanted him to write articles about Sharkey, and he wanted to know where George Lewis was. Do you see that as true?

Gagliano : Well, let's put it this way. I read the account about Bob Greenwood and his people sort of, the way they put it, they kidnapped Kubrick. But I don't think that was totally true because it appears, from what I've read since, that Kubrick knew about George Lewis before. So probably it didn't take any kidnapping for Greenwood to divert Kubrick over to Manny's, rather than to go hear Sharkey at the Famous Door. I think that that's partially how it happened.

Martyn : Who would have been the people that wanted Kubrick to do the article about Sharkey?

Gagliano : I have no idea.

Martyn : Was there any faction then?

Gagliano : I didn't know about it. Greenwood seems to think, you know – I was not a part of that active jazz fan that was dealing with it every day. I am a working engineer. Music, jazz in particular, would be, at best, a hobby for me. So I abhorred going to the Quarter. I think I mentioned this to you, that whenever George was playing in the Quarter, I had absolutely nothing to do with it. George made his own deal, and that was fine with me. And I'll tell you, the 1945 comeback of Bunk Johnson and George Lewis and the guys was really a thing that put the guys back on their feet. Prior to that, George was forced to work on the riverfront as a stevedore. He's constantly getting hurt, and when he gets hurt, he doesn't get paid. In those days, the idea of any stevedore being compensated legally for an injury was, there was no thought of it. It was like, to them, this is a fact of life. You got hurt; you can't work; you can't get money. The idea of suing anybody for something that you experienced, even though it might be somebody else's fault, didn't occur to them at that time.

Martyn : Well, especially being black, on top of everything else.

Gagliano : Yeah, especially being black. But you see, that's the thing. The so-called greedy lawyers came in in later years and started to pursue these rights for these people. Yeah, they were somewhat greedy, I suppose, but initially it was a recognition that these people should have been paid for the injury that they suffered. Of course, all of our workmen's compensation laws that came in after that recognizes that. But all of this was before that.

Martyn : Well, I remember interviewing McNeil Breaux, the bass player, out in Oakland. He's a New Orleans boy, you know, and he told me this horror story. He said, "My daddy died when I was sixteen," or something. I said, "What did he die of?" He said, "Man," he said, "he went into the hospital with a perforated lung," or something, "and they took out the wrong lung and he died." I said, "Well, couldn't you sue them?" He said, "Are you kidding? A black man in Louisiana suing a white doctor?" And you can't equate with that, you know.

Gagliano : That was a fact of life. That was a fact of life. You've got to realize George had been through the mill. He had seen so much adversity in his life to get to the point where he now was, you're either going to get a lot of wisdom from that or you're going to get a lot of bitterness, okay? So basically I would suggest that George did not have the bitterness thing about his role in life, however hard it was. So basically he learned from life what he could. I would have to say that at that point, George was at the beginning of his period of recognition, some money coming in. But that was tempered always with a recollection as to where he had come from. And what he was doing now was so much better than what he had been through earlier. Now, at this time in his life, he doesn't have to go out and work on the waterfront. He could make enough to sustain his standard of living just from his music. He never once, to me, ever expressed anything like the plight of the black man – No, just that life was hard. Life was hard for him. Life was hard for his mother, and he definitely wanted me to go see his mother, visit her and understand how she was doing. As I told you before, she was an eighty-some-odd-year-old woman living in a one-room walkup with no toilet facilities, no running water. I'm at that age now. I'm at the age that Alice was, probably, when I met her. And realizing my own physical condition, even though I'm reputed to be in pretty good shape for my age, I can imagine how difficult it would have been to live under the conditions that she had to live under. There's no way we, as white people, could imagine trying to live under the conditions that they were forced to live under. And let's face it. They were forced to live under them, and that's the unfortunate thing. And of course, regardless of what you think about me or what all the other people think about me and my role, I was there to try to repair and try to somehow recover for them what they lost through Bunk Johnson's personality and feelings.

Martyn : But you weren't a crusader either, were you?

Gagliano : No, I'm not a crusader. I'm trying to help these guys make a little bit of a living. I didn't ruffle any feathers at that time. Nobody was ruffling any feathers in the forties. Everybody was geared to trying to survive. You almost have to be a student of the Depression to understand what it was like in the thirties. When we had this Depression, there was no Social Security. There was no Medicare. None of the programs that we have today were in existence. If you fell on hard times, you either starved or you would find some family member that would take you in. It was the family that was the social agency at that time.

Martyn : When was George Lewis' band named? I know you told me you came up with the name. Tell me a bit about the name, Ragtime Band.

Gagliano : It was just born out of an idea of trying to suggest that this band was part of the original formation of the music, and I didn't realize at the time that ragtime was really not considered as – you know – ragtime was a precursor. It was a heavily structured music, very intricate, beautiful stuff when it's played right. I love ragtime, but it had a connotation of being old. So I suggested this to George and he said, "Okay." And I just said, "I think this might be a good name to use for the band and it might give you some further –" I was trying to get the personality of the band. For instance, there was some reference on one of the old records, they called it the George Lewis Band and it really wasn't a band; it was a trio.

Martyn : Did George, when you suggested Ragtime Band, give any arguments?

Gagliano : No, because, maybe George would have known more about what ragtime was than I did. I don't remember any great debate around it. I just made that suggestion and he went along with it.

Martyn : Well, it worked, I mean, for sure.

Gagliano : I think it worked, but I mean, as I told you, later, in the later years, I was embarrassed having learned that this really didn't fit the band, but it may have fit the time.

Martyn : Well, yeah, that's a good way of putting it, and I think it did a lot for George with that. The *Look* article was out after they went into the El Morocco, right?

Gagliano : Yeah, the Look article came out within maybe a month after we opened at the El Morocco.

Martyn : Oh, so the El Morocco was first and then the Look article.

Gagliano : Oh, yeah, that's my recollection.

Martyn : Did that swell the people, the crowds at the El Morocco?

Gagliano : Yeah, I'm sure it did, and I would think that the club management did its best to capitalize on it. Now, look, I'm relying on my recollection as to the timing. I'm going to go back into my notes and I'm going to tell you specifically. I can tell you right here. It says here that the *Look* article came out on June 6, 1950, and we opened at the El Morocco on May 9, 1950. So we were there four weeks when the *Look* magazine article came out.

Gagliano : I had nothing to do with setting that French Quarter stuff. I knew nothing about the process, and I never did interfere, for instance, with George's methods or his personnel or any of that. I had nothing to do with that.

Martyn : Well, how would you decide between you and George if you were going to handle something, or would he say, "Look, Nick, I've got this covered. Don't worry about it"? Or would you say, "I'd rather you did this"? Who decided that?

Gagliano : It just happened. It happened. Just like the thing with the El Morocco. The only part that I played in it, as I remember, was that when I was at this frat party with the band, that I had booked them into this frat party, and then this guy from the El Morocco came over and wanted to talk to somebody about maybe the band coming over to play at his place after the gig, and I talked to him. I said, "Okay." I said, "Hold on a minute. Let me go talk to George." I said, "George, do you think you and the guys would feel up to going over to the El Morocco to play a session over there?" He said, "Sure." So I said, "Okay." This frat party was being held at the Parisian Room in the 100 block of Royal Street. The El Morocco Night club was at 200 Bourbon Street, about a block and a half from the Parisian Room. Sometime between 9 and 10pm, while the frat party was in full swing, I was standing alongside the band stand, when a man introduced himself to me as Frank Spinato, the owner of the El Morocco, and asked whether the band would like to come over to the El Morocco to play after the frat party; I called George over and he readily agreed and said the band could come to the El Morocco a little after midnight. As it turned out, about an hour or so later, the frat party turned into a brawl, and was shut down by the police, and the band went right over to the El Morocco. I stayed at the El Morocco for no more than an hour, and left George to work out the details of how long would they play, and what they should be paid. At no time was I involved in discussing money for this appearance, but I assumed that George would insist on union scale. And I had no direct involvement in the long term engagement at the El Morocco that followed.

Martyn : Was that a big deal for them if they'd have gotten the job at the El Morocco?

Gagliano : Absolutely it was a big deal. Now, they didn't know what was going to come of it, but you've got to understand at that point George Lewis and the band had never played, as far as I know, Bourbon Street or at any of the clubs. So what this meant to the band was that they could work every day at their music, and the only thing they had to do, they had to somehow accommodate whatever their day jobs were with this, and I've got to believe this was an economic boon to them. This was the first time that they were working full-time at music. Well, I think that playing for an audience on Bourbon Street would probably be much more stressful and less enjoyable than playing for a fraternity or a debutante dance or some company picnic or whatever. Certainly it didn't match up to any kind of a presentation that the Jazz Club did where you had people who knew and understand, to a certain extent, what jazz was all about, and they were very, very much impressed by what was happening. But, you know, the people on Bourbon Street, there's a mixture. It was tourists, and I'm sure there were a bunch of knowledgeable people coming through that knew that George Lewis was playing there. Nobody danced at the El Morocco I remember that it was sort of a wide place and it had a bar, and the band was tucked behind the bar on somewhat of an elevated platform that had some velvet curtains

(Above) The El Morocco
(Below) The Band and Alton Purnell at the El Morocco

all around it, you know, to gussy it up. Then the people would be out here in front, and so there was no dancing or anything. It's just people would just come in there and drink, and the management wanted to encourage drinks, so they didn't mind, I suppose, the band taking ten or fifteen minutes off every set just to clear the place, you know. And I don't know that I went down there two, three times while the band was there for over a period of a couple years.

Now, when we broke up that night at the frat party and I walked the band down to the El Morocco, I probably stayed there a while to listen just to get them started. Then I left. What happened after that was done totally by George in conversation with the management of the place, and I would imagine what he did was probably sign up for scale, with him getting the typical leader's fee. I think the Paddock had started with Celestin, and I think this is what gave the El Morocco the thought that George Lewis would be a draw. In the Bob Greenwood file in the Tulane Hogan Jazz Archive, there is a letter from Bob, dated may 11, 1950 to Joe Roddy, who was the author of the *Look* magazine article that was released in its June issue, and reporting to Joe that the George Lewis Ragtime Jazz Band opened at the El Morocco Club on Bourbon Street several nights before, for a two week engagement with an option for a month. There is another letter from Bob, this time to Bill Russell in Ohio dated may 17, 1950 about how well the El Morocco gig was working out for the band, and that the club management exercised it's one month option after the second night. He further stated that the band was playing six nights a week, and that they played until 4am that past Sunday. The management wanted the band to play until 5am but the band begged off. He also stated that Emile Barnes, a noted clarinet contemporary of George's was playing at Manny's with Billie and DeDe Pierce.

Martyn : Right. So the El Morocco was before the *Look* article.

Gagliano : Yeah, the El Morocco opening was not instigated in any way by the *Look* magazine article, but evidently, Bourbon Street started with the Paddock, and may have got Sharkey at the 500 Club. This is basically Sharkey's band, with a mid-performance appearance of Pork Chops and Kidney Stew, you know.

Martyn : Did they ever dance with George's band?

Gagliano : I never remember them ever dancing with George's band unless it had something to do with some of the concerts where Sharkey was. We never had any relationship with them. So to cap this thing about the El Morocco, I would suggest that the management was looking for a group that would compete with Papa Celestin, and would compete with Sharkey. I don't remember what they did before they had George. I know they had some kind of music. Well, yeah, they were there pretty much over a year, year and a half.

Martyn : When the Look article came out, George was obviously playing at the El Morocco.

Gagliano : But the photographs were all at Manny's.

Martyn : Right, and one of them is in George's backyard with that big old microphone they had. Did they capitalize in any way on the Look article by giving the magazines to the customers?

Gagliano : I have no idea. They had a big poster outside, a big plaque or whatever, tells you "Come here. Look magazine's greatest jazz band in the world,"

Martyn : I've got some photographs of the day they opened, and I'll come out and bring them to you, show you, because they had something outside, and I think it went back to your ragtime thing. It said something like "Jazz as it was in the ragtime era," or something, "George Lewis." But there was a big, big thing outside about it, you know.

Gagliano : Yeah. You know, I can't tell you how long from that so-called audition to when George started. I thought it was almost instantaneous, but I was not involved in negotiations.

Martyn : Was George happy? Well, obviously he was fiscally happy, but was he, as a bandleader, happy he got his band into that place? Did he say that he was?

Gagliano : I'm sure that he had some misgivings about the type of audiences that he was playing for and what kind of reaction he would get, but apparently he must have got a great reaction because they wouldn't have kept him there if he wasn't bringing in people. Yeah. The guy that ran the El Morocco, I remember his name, and his name was Frank Spinata. Eventually he graduated into respectable business, and he became an automobile dealer with Spinata's whatever it was, Chevrolet or Ford or whatever, Dodge, Chrysler, on Canal Street in the vicinity of Galvez right in front of the Deutches Haus, the community center for the New Orleans German Community.

Martyn : Okay, I think I know what you're talking about. It's on the uptown side.

Gagliano : On the uptown side.

Martyn : It was on a corner.

Gagliano : Actually, now, I don't know whether Frank Spinata was fronting for somebody else, but he was the guy that I understood was the owner of the El Morocco. Yeah, he was a nice young fellow at the time.

Martyn : Oh, he was young?

Gagliano : Relatively. Maybe at the time no more than thirty-five.

Martyn : Well, then, he was old compared to you.

Gagliano : Well, he was old. I would say he would have been ten or fifteen years older than me. But he did not project to me like the gruff – like the guys who operated the Silver Slipper. I found out, I know who those guys are now. The big culprit was a guy named Ciro Callico and I found out that later, you know, he was reputedly one of the Mafiosi in the city, and his thing was to operate clubs and restaurants down in the French Quarter. That was his gig.

Martyn : So you don't think that the El Morocco was mob?

Gagliano : I don't think it was. No.

Martyn : George never said anything much about that. He said, when you quizzed him, "Oh, yeah, yeah, we had a nice time there," or something like that.

Gagliano : Well, no, when you stop and think about George's economic condition, to my way of thinking, I seem to remember at the time that the solution to all of our problems was to get a day gig on Bourbon Street. See, they saw that

George Lewis – c.1949

Papa Celestin was playing every night at the Paddock. They were aware that Sharkey was playing every night at the 500 Club. I mean, for them to get a six-night-a-week or five-night-a-week – somehow I've read where while he was at the El Morocco, he was also playing at Manny's. Now, I don't know quite how that was accomplished, but if it happened – I'm not going to say it didn't happen – but when George went into the El Morocco, my involvement as his manager basically stopped, regarding jobs around the city because the band was tied up regularly.

Martyn : On that gig.

Gagliano : With that gig. As long as he had that gig, I had nothing much to do. As to us getting that job. The account in Tom Bethel's book is fiction. I have no idea where he got that from. When I read his account, I think I remember is that some woman at the El Morocco called to them when they were walking by. But that's not the way it happened, because I know what happened. The guy came and talked to me.

Martyn : Now, at the El Morocco, you say you didn't go there that much because you were not enamored with the French Quarter.

Gagliano : Well, to be quite honest with you, I probably did, but I have no specific recollection of it, and as I told you before, I didn't handle George's negotiations with the New Orleans club operators. I did a lot of the independent booking with fraternity parties, debutante parties, and various things like that, but when Bourbon Street beckoned, George basically did the negotiation, probably on the basis of union scale, and I was not involved. It was just an understanding that my efforts were not necessary. The band was not in any negotiating position to get any kind of big money at these clubs, and consequently, I think the perception was that "We're going to get union scale," and that was going to be it. And there was apparently no need for me to get involved in it. It was just an understanding that just cropped up. It wasn't anything premeditated, although I didn't want to get too deeply into the French Quarter culture because I didn't think that this was the venue for presenting the band in its best sense.

The club owners want you to cater to the requests. And it didn't have the type of crowd reaction that you have at a dance, and I think the musicians will tell you that. And so playing at the El Morocco, up on the stage maybe with a bunch of tourists, drunken tourists listening here, it's just not conducive to them playing real good music, in my opinion.

Martyn : There's a billboard outside the El Morocco. And it says something about "Bringing back the old-time music, George Lewis and his Ragtime Band." Was that just their perception of how they should advertise it, or did you ....?

Gagliano : Yeah, I had nothing to do with that.

Martyn : So you didn't suggest to them they should say "Bringing back the old-time music."

Gagliano : I have no recollection of suggesting anything to those people.

Martyn : And I don't think George would have done, would he?

Gagliano : Well, probably not. And I'm not saying I didn't interface with them. I just don't remember. The one thing that I remember specifically about the El Morocco engagement was who I thought the club owner was. As I mentioned before, the club owner that I understood was a fellow name Frank Spinata. I came across some later writings about the El Morocco, I'm looking at it and these articles define a fellow named Sero Calico and Eddie Kid Wolf as the managers. Well, I can understand that the managers could be different from the ownership.

You know, these could be guys that are outside trying to drag people in, and so that doesn't, to me, interfere with my recollection of Frank Spinata as the owner. And I know I talked to Frank on a number of occasions. And as I found out later after he somehow, I guess, got finished with his French Quarter experience, he became an automobile dealer. With his dealership on Canal Street. And that's what I remember about the El Morocco. And it was a long time. They stayed there well over almost two years.

Martyn: Well, what did they do about Manny's? Just leave it?

Gagliano : You know, I'm not sure about that, because as I'm reading certain things, I get the impression that he was playing at Manny's occasionally at the same time he was playing at the El Morocco. But I don't understand that, because when he played at Manny's, he played primarily on Saturday night. I had an impression it may have been Friday and Saturday, but what I've been finding out in the little ads that I run across, say in the Second Line, with Manny's, it says "Dancing, Saturday night, 9:30 to 1:30," and that's refreshed my memory. So their playing at Manny's was on the weekend only.

Martyn: Did George ever make any comments to you about the El Morocco? I mean, did he ever say, "Oh, I don't like it there. It's too hot," or anything?

Gagliano : Yeah, the thing was, okay, we were trying and George was trying to solidify some regular flow of money for the family. And as far as I was concerned, this was the ultimate for us here in New Orleans, regardless of whether I felt that the audience was a proper audience or the setting was – it didn't make that much difference because I was zeroed in on trying to give George an income that he could call regular. And I think that I'm satisfied in my own mind that the long engagement that we had at the El Morocco was what set George on the road to some financial security, not that he ever had real security, but as I had indicated earlier, it was during this period that he began to save money in order to buy the lot in Algiers, which, ultimately, in 1952 allowed him, for the first time in his life, to own his own home. That was a milestone for us.

Martyn: Why did he select Algiers?

Gagliano : Because it was cheap. Yeah, and not only that, but when you think about it, the Algiers neighborhood is very close to the French Quarter, although it's divided from the French Quarter by the Mississippi River. But you could catch the ferry in Algiers and you're dumped right at the entrance to the French Quarter on Canal Street.

Martyn: When was the bridge built?

Gagliano : Oh, man, the bridge. I seem to remember – I would think that that bridge – what's now called the Crescent City Connection, was not built until sometime in the fifties.

Martyn: So it would have been built when George was working at the El Morocco.

Gagliano : It may have been built during that period. I would suspect that when he was building his house – now, remember, I have a deed that tells me the exact date when he bought the lot. I have information that indicates that he moved into the house – Okay, July 21, 1950, George and Jeannette buy a lot on D'Armas Street, okay? That's when they bought the lot. Now, you notice that was in 1950. We started playing at the El Morocco in 1950, and when he started to get this regular income as the leader of the band he would be getting double scale. So I don't know what the musicians' scale was at that time, but whatever it was, he got two shares.

Martyn: And it was less in the colored union than it was in the white one anyway.

Gagliano : It wouldn't surprise me. But what I'm getting at is that that engagement at the El Morocco allowed him to save some money to ultimately buy the lot. I understood that he bought a lot of used building materials from the destruction of some project or something. I don't know – all I do know is that in 1952 they moved in and he had a house.

Martyn: Would they have taken a mortgage on the lot or would they have bought it cash out?

Gagliano : I do have an indication where George was paying off a mortgage.

Martyn: The situation that it was here in those times, could he borrow money from a white bank or did he have to go to a black bank.

Gagliano : There were no black banks. The first modern black bank that I know of is Liberty Bank. It was formed by a fellow named Allen McDonald who has become a very well-to-do member of the Creole establishment. I know that Norman Francis, who is the vaunted president of Xavier University, a real fine man, was also involved in the formation of that bank. I would think that a number of the black establishment that was important in the civil rights struggle in the sixties, you know, to integrate the schools, I think that group got together and eventually formed the Liberty Bank. My understanding was that it – well, let's put it this way – I would say that the initial ownership group was totally black.

Martyn : That means to say that all the black people that wanted loans and everything would come to this one bank?

Gagliano : All I can say to you is that the black community finally had a bank and that these people stated that their primary purpose in forming the bank was to serve the black community, which was being underserved, probably, by the white banking establishment. I don't know that to be a fact. But let me put it this way. To answer your specific question, I do not know that George ever went to any bank at that time to borrow money. I do have indications that he did borrow money from individuals, because I remember there was a period of time when they fell behind and I had to, you know, get them out.

Martyn : Let me ask you this. I don't want to make this a racial issue in this book, but it just interests me, I suppose, and it's worth putting there. In your profession, were there black lawyers that black people went to totally, and were there white lawyers that didn't accept colored clients, or how did that all work?

Gagliano : Well, at the risk of being a little verbose about it, let me start out by saying that all of the black lawyers up until around let's say the mid-fifties, they all went to Southern University, which was the black university that was the prototype of Louisiana State University. LSU is the big state university in Baton Rouge, and Southern University was its counterpart for the black community. And as I recall, their domicile was right outside of Baton Rouge in Scotlandville. In the mid-fifties, after the Brown versus Board of Education case came in, which ruled separate but equal unconstitutional, then the white law schools were then required to take in blacks. And when I started Loyola University law school in New Orleans in 1954, Norman Francis, for instance, who became ....

Martyn : The bank guy, yeah.

Gagliano : Very high up in the community now. Norman Francis was a member of a class back at Loyola, and I remember that in my entrance freshman class at Loyola in 1954, I think we had two black students, and then in subsequent years, they started to come in greater numbers. So now you had black lawyers who are graduates of predominantly white schools, and then you had black lawyers who were the graduates of Southern.

Martyn : What did George think of all this racial situation? Did he ever talk to you about it at all?

Gagliano : Not at all. No, about it because at the time that I was with him, keep in mind that Brown versus Board of Education didn't come out till around 1954, whatever, and that would be just about the last active year I had with George. 1955 was where I made I guess you would call my clean break from him and turned over everything to Dorothy Tait. At that time, you know, the idea of integration in New Orleans didn't get hot until 1960.

So basically, I don't remember having any great discussions with George or the band about all of this. There was just nothing there to talk about. We're living here in this community. We've got to live with it. Now, in a sense, I'm risking things by having myself as a young white guy out there managing a black band.

Martyn : Did it manifest itself in any way?

Gagliano : No, it never did because I was never the boisterous type about it. I'm doing what I'm doing for George in what I would think whatever would be the most effective manner, and we had no political agenda to deal with. One of the things that, as I told you, allowed me to get bookings for the band was the tremendous help given to me by Myra Menville, who had all the social connections and were willing to share those with me and help me get inroads to get these deb parties and that sort of thing.

Martyn : Well, did people like Myra, who I met but don't remember very well – Helen Arlt, I know very well. I mean, what were their attitudes towards all of this that was going on racially? I mean, did they think you're a little strange managing a black band?

Gagliano : No, certainly not Myra. Myra was very taken up with the fact that I was rather what I'd say liberal in regard to the relationship between the white and the black community. Certainly Helen, I think, felt the same way. Dr. Souchon was a sort of a funny guy. I never could figure out where he stood, but he was always very helpful to the band. We were not crusaders at that time.

We were in a live-and-let-live situation, and you tried to do the very best you can to earn money and to survive the ravages of the Depression. As I told you, the series of letters that I've read between George, and also Jeannette, to Bill Russell in '42 and '43 and '44 really tells a story of how poor they were. George was down to no money and said, "Mr. Russell, could you lend me twenty-five dollars?" Twenty-five dollars, like as if that kind of money makes a difference between whether you eat or not.

Martyn : Well, I guess it's not very easy for us to tell how black musicians lived because we never had to do it.

Gagliano : You may never have seen the conditions under which the true black musicians – now, I'm going to tell you – as I said earlier, that in the black community there is a bit of integration, the segregation issue between the light-skinned blacks and the dark-skinned blacks.

And consequently, the people that were the light-skins, they were probably able to better earn a living and to have a little bit better standard of life than the black blacks.

Martyn : Well, they must also have had a better education, which is the key to everything.

Gagliano : That all stands in, you know. The Creole light-colored black community really stemmed from the free blacks. While the other people were enslaved, they were out there doing their thing in the community, not that they didn't have prejudice against them by the white community because, you know, the white community was always up in arms about some of these people passing as white, you know.

Martyn : What kind of education did George have, do you know?

Gagliano : If I was to gauge from talking to George, analyzing his handwriting and stuff, I would say George probably maybe had gone through the fifth or the sixth grade. And even then, George, had a habit of playing hooky. He was always absorbed in trying to learn how to play music. But that's not to say that he spent a lot of time on it, because he had to spend a lot of his time scraping up nickels and dimes and pennies helping his mother try to see that they could survive.

Freddy Kohlman's Band at the Mardi Gras Lounge – 1952. Wendel Eugene (tbn), Willie Humphrey (clt), Thomas Jefferson (tpt), Freddy Kohlman (dms), Clement Tervalon (sbs) and Dave Williams (pno)

Martyn : Well, I mean, he wasn't much of a talker, as we both know anyway, but I mean, when he did talk, he said some peculiar things. Once we were in Trafalgar Square in London – we were right in the band bus and he said, "Look." I thought he was going to say, "Lord Nelson." Horatio Nelson, he's up on the top there, but he wasn't pointing. "Look at them birds, man." And I said, "What about them?" He said, "They're seagirls." Girls. Not gulls. Girls. I said, "Seagirls? How you know that?" I mean, how did he know they're all feminine birds? He said, "I see them 'round New Orleans." I said, "What? They're a different color?"

I'm thinking he's got some profound way of knowing that these are all female birds because they got gray heads. And he was getting a bit angry. Not angry, but he said, "Man, that's what they're called, the whole race of them." Race of them. "They're called seagirls, man."

I said, "Oh, okay." And I thought seagirls, Jesus Christ, you know. Where did he get that from, you know? And a lot of the things he said weren't grammatical. I mean, black people seem to me to have problem with tenses and plurals, you know. Would you say George was an ignorant man?

Gagliano : No, not at all. Not ignorant. No. Let's say that he was unschooled for the most part, that education for him was very not too much important to him as it was to his mother, Alice, who constantly was behind him to go to school. No, George was an intelligent person. In my opinion, he was intelligent. He didn't write fluently. He didn't speak fluently. He was very reticent about speaking, and many times when he was announcing the band, you know, he would just say, "We're going to play this and this." And he had a hard time dealing with microphones, projecting his voice.

Martyn : Well, where would he learn microphone technique?

Gagliano : I guess he picked it up after a while, you know. But George has never been, to me, a very great

Sid Davilla, owner of the Mardi Gras Lounge, guests with the band. Jim Robinson, Percy Humphrey, Sid Davilla (clt) Joe Watkins – Mardi Gras Lounge 1952

conversationalist. You know, I guess the concept of George, to a New Orleans native, has got to be fundamentally different from the people who were looking at George as a tremendous musical icon, and it was a surprise to them when they were introduced to the adulation that they would ultimately get. And that's where the college tours began to seep into their consciousness about their own personal individual worth.

The El Morocco engagement ended, in March of 1952. That same month, George and Jeanette moved into their new home, the first home that they ever owned in Algiers. And I recall, from my records, that they had bought the lot in 1950 and apparently George, together with Lawrence Marrero, Slow Drag, probably during the day, while they worked the nights at the El Morocco. During the day, they were helping George build his house.

In November, the band started playing at the Mardi Gras Lounge. In December of '52, we had the record session with Decca at Artisan Hall. And that one was with Percy.

Martyn : That's right.

Gagliano : Percy is now with the band. Percy is playing with the band at the Mardi Gras Lounge. Right. And I think that's where it was. But, I think when he was playing at the Mardi Gras Lounge, he was also playing at Manny's. And I think what happened is that, as I was looking through all the previous Second Lines, I noticed that the Mardi Gras Lounge carried an ad that was featuring Freddy Kohlman's Band. And then, as – as we get to November, now it's still the Freddy Kohlman Band but also featuring George Lewis. So, apparently, the Mardi Gras Lounge had two bands playing and George was playing maybe two nights or three nights a week and he was also playing at Manny's.

Martyn : Well, Freddy Kohlman's Band was also recorded at the Artesian Hall by Decca. In other words, they did two sessions one with George, one with Freddy, but there's quite a lot of stuff that was recorded by Freddy Kohlman's Band.

Let's see – oh, Wendel Eugene was on trombone. And then, in the rhythm section, they had Clement Tervalon, who's generally a trombone player, playing the bass, and "Cousin Joe." And they had Cousin Joe sitting there. So, they – when it came to the Artesian hall recordings, they recorded both bands. And they recorded a lot more of Freddy's Band than apparently they did of George's because there's only three numbers by George's Band. Magnificent. "Georgia Camp Meeting" "Chime Blues" and I think the other one was "Burgundy Street Blues".

Well, I had occasion. We owned the Paramount record label – GHB did – and Decca wanted to buy Paramount's for Decca. I think it's MCI now. But, anyway, and I said, "Well, we'll swap, but we need to find out and if there's more stuff in the George Lewis recording session of such and such a date. I guarantee you there's more." They went back and checked all in their vaults, files and they said, "No, there's no more than that."

So, all I can presume is that they never did record more than those three numbers and yet Freddy Kohlman's Band, there's about 20 numbers. So, all I can say is, that one appealed to the guy in charge more than the other band, you know.

Gagliano : At the Mardi Gras Lounge. George's band, presumably, could be the fill-in band. And it tells me that, if George is playing at Manny's, then that had to be on a weekend and that he was playing weekdays, you know, at the Mardi Gras Lounge, and probably Freddy Kohlman was playing the weekends at the Mardi Gras Lounge. I mean, Freddy's Band was a much more commercially-oriented band than George's.

Martyn : Okay. Let me ask you about Sid Davilla about who ran the Mardi Gras Lounge.

Gagliano : Well, he was a clarinet player with fairly decent talent. And he knew what was happening around the time and I think, from the concerts that the Jazz Club put on and all of that, he had to know that, among the black bands that were – that were playing that, you know, the George Lewis Band was, you know, right up at the top. And so, when he had the opportunity, I guess, he put him in at his lounge. And there were times when he would sit in with them.

Martyn : And he owned the place?

Gagliano : Well, he owned it or he fronted the place, let's put it that way. Yeah, the ownership of all of those places in the French Quarter were very much suspect. But the word was that Sid Davilla's mother was a – as I remember, she apparently was considered to have some means and that it was her who put him in – you know, bought him a lounge so he'd have a place to play and operate. It was called "Sid Davilla's Mardi Gras Lounge." When I got into trouble, if you want to call it trouble, was because I got a little bit too close to the band when they were playing at the Mardi Gras Lounge. And, of course, I knew Sid Davilla. He was okay. This would have been like around '52, after we had started to go on these tours to Ohio and stuff. Apparently, I was mistaken, in that the band was then playing at the Silver Slipper, on Bourbon Street, about a block away from the Mardi Gras Lounge, and it was for the management of the Silver Slipper, fronted by Sero Callico, that I arranged for the Gene Mayl's Dixieland Rhythm Kings for a two-week replacement gig while the George Lewis Ragtime Jazz Band went on its annual mid-west college tour in 1954. My recollection was that the Mayl group did not go over big at the Silver slipper, and after the first week, there was an altercation between one of the management

Gene Mayl's Dixieland Rhythm Kings of Ohio playing in New Orleans Robin Wetterau (pno), Jack Vastine (bjo), Gene Mayl (tuba), Ted Bielefield (clt), Bob Hodes (cnt), Charlie Sonnanstine (tbn)

people and one of Gene's side men, and this was the trigger for terminating the engagement, which was a major embarrassment for me in my efforts on behalf of the Gene Mayl band. There is an interesting account of this whole episode in the November/December, 1954 of the New Orleans Jazz Club's Second Line Magazine, in connection with the Jazz Club's annual Jazz Festival at the Municipal Auditorium in which three local bands were presented along with a special out of town band, Gene Mayl's Dixieland Rhythm Kings of Dayton, Ohio. The Jazz Club article praised the Mayl band's performance, suggesting they were showing the local bands how the old Dixieland style of music should be played. The Jazz Club rendered a special apology for the rough treatment accorded the band at a local Bourbon Street night club, unnamed, which was the incident that was described above, just about two weeks before the Jazz Festival. And I remember this one occasion when the band was playing at Mardi Gras Lounge and we were going to take two or three or four weeks off to go on the tour, and the club manager asked me if I knew who he could get to replace them. Well, I should have told him, "Call Paul Barbarin," but I didn't for some reason. I told the guy, I said, I told him, "I met a group of young white guys up in Ohio." This was Gene Mayl's group. I said, "They've got a record album out," and I said, "and they play real old-time, maybe more of what would be considered old-time than what George is doing," because they were trying to mimic an earlier—you know, Gene playing the tuba and all that. And okay, I got them a gig.

I called Gene and asked him if he wanted to come to New Orleans. "Oh, man, gee," you know. Well, within a week the management of the club was dissatisfied—they just weren't drawing anything, and I think it was a mistake on my part to even feel that they could work out on Bourbon Street.

And I'm also certain, at this time, that a couple of the guys that were managing this club were really Mafia, and so after that first week they came in. He said, "Yeah, we've got to cut this. We've got to kill this." And I said, "Look, these guys came down here. One more week?" He said, "It was a two-week gig." And I said, "Well, got to figure out a way." Well, they figured out a way. They got into a fight and they beat the hell out of one of the guys, and I felt so bad about all this.

Martyn : Who beat the hell out of who? You mean one of the band guys got beaten?

Gagliano : My guess is that this henchman-type manager of the club provoked some kind of an incident with the band. I wasn't there. All I know is I heard that there was a fight and they sort of beat up on one of the sidemen, and that ended everything. And so I just washed my hands of the Quarter after that for good.

Chapter 5
"THE COLLEGE TOURS"

Gagliano : Let me tell you what I remember best from the El Morocco thing, because this led to the Ohio concerts. Evidently, somewhere in 1950 or 1951, John Ball came to New Orleans and heard the band at the El Morocco. George called me up and told me, "Hey, Nick", He said. "This man from Ohio called, wants us to come up to his college in Ohio." And he says, "He's trying to make arrangements to do that." He said, "But he's been having trouble raising enough money." I remember that. And then somehow or other, I got in contact with Ball, and then that led to the ultimate first set of concerts, which was in 1952. The El Morocco engagement ended, I think, in February of 1952. And then I've noticed that we have here that the first concerts in Ohio were in May of 1952. That means that there was a period of time, say about three months, between when the engagement at the El Morocco ended. And if you ask me what was it that caused that to end, I can't give you an answer. All I know is that it ended.

Martyn : When John Ball came here from Ohio, did he come with George Lewis's Band in mind, or did he just – I mean, if he'd come with George's Band in mind – he'd have had to or talk to somebody who had seen the band at Manny's or the El Morocco or someone and said, "Oh, there's this great band down there called George Lewis and his Ragtime Band," you know.

Gagliano : I think it would be logical to believe that John came particularly seeking to hear the band and to explore the possibility of bringing them up to his college.

Martyn : So, do you think that he had it in mind to bring them up to his college, before he saw them even?

Gagliano : That's – that's conjecture on my part, but I think it's a reasonable conjecture. John Ball didn't give me the impression that he would be coming down to Bourbon Street just to sample the livelier lifestyle. That – that doesn't fit my perception of John Ball at the time.

Martyn : He was very bright, very aware of what was going on when I knew him but, of course, I knew the time I got to know you, which is what 20 years ago.

Gagliano : Oh, when we met, John ultimately came to know that I was a graduate of Tulane University. Which I think gave me some personal credibility with him, I believe. And, of course, he, being a Professor of English Literature at Miami University, although I didn't know too much about the university at the time, but he had to have stature and he's also the Director of the Archives at Ohio Folklore. He said he wanted to try to raise enough money to bring the band up there, "But it's going to take me some time."

And that's what happened. It took him a year, at least a year, in order to – for us to put the deal together and part and parcel of putting it together was him getting together with George Rosenthal and getting Rosenthal's money ....

Martyn : Yeah, to put in the pot.

Gagliano : .... to kick in with whatever the University and the Archive was willing to pay. And maybe, with all of that, they – they were able to generate enough money where we felt that it was feasible for us to go up there for three, four or five days, or whatever it was.

Martyn : How did you get Percy to go? He hadn't been regular with the band for long.

Gagliano : I mean, I don't recall. I'm sure George took care of that.

THE MIAMI FOLK ARTS SOCIETY

The Miami Folk Arts Society is a small, informal group of students who have in common an interest in the traditional songs, tales, dances, arts, crafts, and customs of man. There are no membership requirements, and members come from many different departments in the university.

Meetings are held about once a month, and generally include a program given by a member, a faculty member, or a guest. During the year a range of programs is given, with emphasis on different aspects of folk life and culture. When possible, programs include the playing of recordings or the exhibition of pictures or films.

At least twice during each school year the Miami Folk Arts Society cooperates with the Artists and Lectures Series to secure campus-wide programs, open to the public, on the folk arts.

Martyn: And talked him into it.

Gagliano : And remember, that was only for no more than a four or five day trip. As I recall later – Percy was willing to travel, but only for very short periods of time. Now, if you go play a gig at, like when we went to play at the Beverly Cavern, he would not go. And that's when Avery Howard came back in the picture.

Martyn : So, getting back to the premise of these things then, the five-day tour that you went up for John Ball, you said the band went on the train and you'd go up there.

Gagliano : That's my recollection. That's my recollection, because I could only go there for the weekend. And I flew up there. I spent Saturday, Friday – maybe it was Friday night – don't remember. Yeah. I mean, I was going to tell you then the next set of concerts we had then built around George Rosenthal. John Ball's thing was now in February or March 1953. This time, I was able to expand the scope and I know that I'm pretty much probably traveling with the band or probably took my vacation. Because there, my notes indicated that we played at the University of Indiana in Bloomington. We played at the DeKalb University in Green Castle, Indiana. We played at the University of Cincinnati again. We played at Miami. I remember then going to Chicago. We played an afternoon that I remember as a Sunday Clam Bake by the Hunt Club.

The Hunt Club is not the name of the vendor. It was the name of whoever was sponsoring this thing. And then I have a notation that we played the Rosenthal gig in Cincinnati again. And I also made a note here that, on March the 5th during the tour, while the band was in Chicago, there was a record session for Jazzology. And this was the trio, with George, Lawrence and Art Hodes. And that took place while we were on that tour but, frankly, I have no recollection of it and I had a feeling that – that, as I told you, most of the recording things, George seemed to handle that by himself.

Martyn : Let me go back to the first tour first. So, the band went up on the train.

Gagliano : Oh yeah.

Martyn : How long did it take the train to get up on the train to Ohio and those places?

Gagliano : Overnight. Basically, I would compare it to the "City of New Orleans" going to Chicago. I think you left in the afternoon, the early afternoon, and you got there maybe late morning the next day. I don't know which train we took. Maybe it was the "City of New Orleans." Maybe it went through Cincinnati on the way to Chicago. So, I would think it took, you know, less than 24 hours.

Martyn : Did the band know they were going to be staying with the people, or did they think they were going to a hotel?

Gagliano : No, I'm sure that their lodging was going to be all part of the deal. And that we were trusting them to take care of this in an honorable way and it – it was more than that. No, the first concert, the Ohio concerts of 1952 are our first trip out. And these men, in my opinion, were overwhelmed at the kind of reception that they got personally and from the fact that all of these people are in John Ball's entourage, I guess the most prominent of which was Reverend Kershaw, Alvin was his first name. They all vied for who was going to stay with whom.

Martyn : So, there was no color prejudice up there in the Ohio?

Gagliano : No. And this is what I'm trying to tell you is odd even though they'd been in New York. They – you know, they went through all of that thing in New York. New York was very hospitable and their very first – when I say "their very first," I'm thinking of Joe Watkins. I'm – well, I'm thinking of George too. George, Jim Robinson, Joe Watkins, and Drag. Alton had a little bit more sophistication than they did. But the other guys, man, this was – this was a revelation for them on how they could be treated by white folks.

Now, of course George had an understanding and his family with his mother George Lewis' mother worked with a relatively prominent family, white families, in New Orleans. She never worked for anybody else but white families. And, of course, George got a certain – you read stuff about that Alice would take George with her to work but one of the first families that she worked for, when they found out about it, that George Lewis, a little kid, was playing with the white kids, that family told her that they shouldn't be there. Later, when she got into working for the Renshaw family that changed. They apparently were very, you know, solicitous about her and her children and they didn't have any prejudice about whether he should come there or not.

So, George has been through this in New Orleans, but what he experienced in New Orleans was under the, shall I say, the sponsorship of his mother who had always told him "Remember your place." Because, with Alice, it was a matter of survival and she was not an activist. It doesn't mean she didn't have her personal integrity. She did and didn't like to have, you know, all of the restrictions put upon her. But she was living in this society, and this was what she felt she had to do to make a living.

Martyn : Well, anyways, so when they get off the train in wherever they went . I assume that John Ball was there to meet them. What was the first town?

Gagliano : Well, the first concert was at Cincinnati. But, remember, Cincinnati, as I recall, was only about 25 or 30 miles away from Oxford where Miami University is. I would assume that John Ball picked them up, delivered them, or introduced them, to their respective hosts .And then, after that, got back together again and probably and then I think I remember driving with the group to Cincinnati. And after I flew up and met John Ball and his wife, they came to pick me up and that's how I got there.

John and Helen Ball

Martyn : Okay, he had his wife with him when he came down here. What was her name, do you remember?

Gagliano : Helen.

Martyn : She came down here with him.

Gagliano : What year was that?

Martyn : Oh, it was when I first met you 20 years ago, probably.

Gagliano : I was talking to Marilyn, my wife and she distinctly remembered visiting John and Helen and spent an evening at their home when we were returning home from my one-year stint teaching at Rutgers Law School. When we came home, we decided, by this time, my wife is three months pregnant, you know, and I'm coming home from the end of this one-year or nine-month contract at Rutgers University. I'm now coming home to figure out what I'm going to do with the rest of my life. I had no job lined up, but I had whatever confidence I had still. I was still not worried about it. We decided that we were going to take a tour coming back home. We went – we came back home through Canada. Then we came down to Ohio and down to Kentucky.

Martyn : But anyway, so you are out there and the band is kind of surprised that the people are treating them so nice.

Gagliano : I think the people there held them in great esteem and they – you know, from what I understood, there was a competition for who got who. And I know that Kershaw took a liking to two guys. He had two at his house. I know that George and I stayed at John Ball's house and I'm not sure where the other people were, but there was an entourage of folks who offered to take them in and they – they were placed. And that's where they stayed. And so it was not a very – I wouldn't call it an imposition, so to speak, for them to be called upon to play privately. Because this was part of John Ball's overall aim with respect to recording the band. All of this was being done to provide artifacts for the archive of the University. The idea that, eventually, Reverend Kershaw was to have the church service was held on the second trip. And I know this tour that I actually traveled with the band. In fact, the only one that I really did was in 1953 because, in '54 – well, I know – I started law school in August of '54. In 1954, I noticed we did the tour again, I was with the band on that tour in '54, because I remember a second concert at some of the places.

Martyn : Were this places co-ed?

Gagliano : Yeah, I'm not sure of De Pauw University. I'm not totally sure of Miami, but I think it would be co-ed because it was a state school. I can't visualize a state university being other than co-ed, so I'm guessing. But I can tell you that Western College for Women was considered to be, in some respects, a sister university to Miami. And, as I recall in later years, it was actually taken over. It was actually pulled into the Miami system. But, I would have to guess that they were co-ed. Now, De Pauw University was a small university. It may have been – it may have been a – a religiously-affiliated university. It was considerably smaller than the others we played for. But they were every bit as enthusiastic.

Martyn : Well, I mean, the people responded to the band from the word "Go"?

Gagliano : Absolutely. It didn't take a lot of warming up. And this is my recollection. I think by the – by the second or third number, I mean, they were hanging. And then, you know, you couldn't get off stage when we were finished.

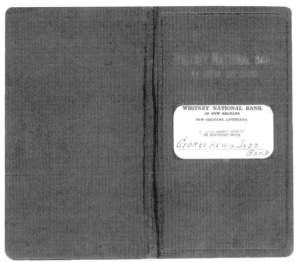

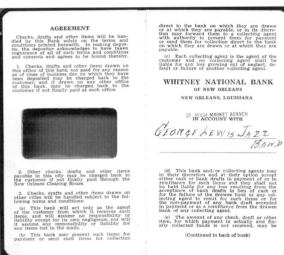

Bank Account opened by Nick for the Band

Martyn : I mean, I suppose John Ball took a lot of credit, then, for bringing them there?

Gagliano : Oh, I'm sure. If I looked at the time line, the first concerts over there were in the month of May of '52. The second concerts were in February. So, May to February, less than – around six or seven months. And then, this time the college tours were in February and March, and that's what happened in 1954 and I don't remember . We're in the middle of the second semester of the year. I don't know why the initial concerts were in May. I guess that was because that's when John Ball was able to scroll up enough money to bring us up there. If you're thinking about it from a university point of view, it may have been probably a bad time. But I don't think, to a true jazz fan that would have made any difference having a chance to hear George and his band.

Martyn : Do you think they'd a made the same as they made here, like a local scale or went and made more or what do you think? I mean, did you know?

Gagliano : I think we probably made a little bit more. But I – the only physical problem that I remember in handling the finances for the band was, when they were playing, I think, at a place called the Royal Room in Hollywood, when I had – I don't know, I think I mentioned to you in an earlier recording that we had set the band up on basically a cooperative basis. George would get two shares, the side men would get one share and another one share was reserved for expenses and me. I was involved to the extent that I received the money, managed it and paid the taxes on it. Probably the band members didn't even file any of their tax returns. But, the one bad thing that happened was that one of the checks, or one of the payments from the Royal Room never did occur.

Martyn : You mean it bounced?

Gagliano : Yeah. Either it wasn't made or when I paid in the check, it didn't clear. So we were in sort of a panic. I had to tap everything that we had around here reserved. The boys maybe didn't even know about it because they got paid. And – and, later on, I told – when George was on one of these tours, I remember we did – we did a record session for some memoir in Yellow Springs, Ohio. Do you remember who that might be?

Martyn : No.

Gagliano : Anyway, we did a session and I had him send me the money and I told George, "George, this money that I'm getting from this record session is to partially make up for what you lost on the Royal Room." George said, "Okay." In later years, I find out that the guys in the band were bitching about not getting their money for that session, you know. So George probably didn't tell them, you know. I said maybe that they – they weren't – I've heard that they were sort of grumbling about me or something about why they didn't get their money from that record session? I said, "Guys, I talked to George about that." I said, "We had lost a check, a bank check, at the Royal Room, you know. You all got your money. So that was to partially get the band, you know, the administrative fund, back up to."

Martyn : Were there any particular gripers in the band?

Gagliano : I had heard that it might have been Alton and maybe Kid Howard and possibly Joe Watkins. But, as far as I know, that was it. But, to me, George didn't – he was not a very voluble, forthcoming person about troubles, you know, and so it doesn't surprise me that the guys – although I find it hard that they wouldn't have known about it. Because, what would happen is, I would get the money by check from the club and I had a – I had a bank account, as I remember, in the name of the band and I would deposit the money and then, maybe in advance of that, I would send George checks pre-cut. Distributing the money, so that there'd be no foul ups. But what had happened in that particular case is that, when – probably what happened is I got the check and the damned thing bounced. And so I told George and here I am, I'm drawing checks on the George Lewis bank account, thinking that I'm going to have that money in the bank and it didn't have it, so I had to scramble, you know. I was proud to say that the guys didn't lose any money on it and maybe, as far as I know, maybe George didn't even tell them. But, what I really don't understand is whether we terminated the engagement on the or maybe it was the last week of the thing, or whatever it was, you know, so I don't really know whether they knew about this.

Martyn : Is that the only time it happened?

Gagliano : Only time it happened, one time that I can recall.

Martyn : Well, you know, that's good.

Gagliano : Well, we were playing for good people.

Martyn : Was anybody else that came to the college concerts that'd say, "Look, I love this band. I'd like to book it for such and such"?

Gagliano : Yeah, I'm sure that happened.

Martyn : What did the guys do in the day time with their time?

Gagliano : I guess they were being entertained by the family but, for the most part, I think John Ball would have had arranged informal sessions. The band would be playing at his – in his basement. I don't know what they did. I guess they were fed and rested.

Martyn : Well, you were staying with George, you said.

Gagliano : It was George and I staying with John Ball.

Martyn : Okay. What did George do in the days and then, sleep a lot?

Gagliano : What did he do? I don't remember that, you know. I was a guest of John Ball. Whatever John Ball arranged for us, we did. And I just remember that, you know, we had the usual get up, have breakfast, we'd chat and then, first thing you know, later on in the day or late morning, then John would say, "Listen, I've got the Gene Mayl band coming over at such and such a time, we're going to set up in my basement." And that's what happened.

Martyn : What did George think of Gene Mayl's band? Did he ever comment to you?

Gagliano : Oh, I thought he was very happy playing with them.

It's very different from his band. Yeah, it was very different. But, it's powerful and he doesn't play with as much conviction, but it's good. And George fits in extremely well with them, you know.

Martyn : Well, let me ask you this. How did Paul Barbarin get into the sequence?

Gagliano : I don't know how he got the job to go out there, but he went and did the same job for the same people, for John Ball and whatnot, you know. But that was long after George and them. In their concept of New Orleans black jazz as a cultural attraction, Paul Barbarin fit in very well. They all had big backgrounds. Well, Paul himself, had a bigger jazz background. I mean, he made recordings with Louis Armstrong in the 20's and stuff. And so Paul was a big name. But none of the others particularly.

VICTORY WALK
AINT She Sweet
Yes Yes In Your Eyes
Angry) GIGOLD
X Cant Give You Any Thing Love
Oh Alice IM CRAZY
X Panama BOUT MY BABY
X ICE Cream ROSE OF RIO GRANDE
Welking With King
X What Sorry Now
X Every Body Love My Baby
X Alex Rag Time Ball
Putting Egg In One Besk T
X THATS A PLENTY
Yearning WOLVERINE
Louisiana BLUES +
X JADA LIZA JANE
MELONCHOLY
X ALL OF ME
Aunt Hagar Blues
X Miss New Orleans
X INDIANA BLACK & BLUE
X WALK Thro The City
X Just A Little While
After You Gone
X MILNEBURG

(MANY WHAT YOU PLEASE) HOME X MACK THE KNIFE
X Bourbon St Parade
DIPPER MOUTH
X Savoy Blues
Tin Mingo
Doc Jazz
Washbash Blues
X Fidgety Feet
X Mary Land
X High Society
X Must keat Ramble
X Tin Rooff Blues
RUNNING WILD
Hebie Gebies
EVERY Body Love My Baby
Sawnie River
X Jazz Me Blues
CARELESS LOVE
Second Line
Shine) Confessing
Canel St.
Dont Give Up Ship
X Just A Close To Walk
X Rampart St Parade
X Dark Town Struters O
Jelly Roll
Climax
X Bill Bailey
X Clairnet Mambee   X SAINTS

Ohio (MA) SAN SISTER KATE
MOVE The Body Over
OVER The Waves
Hawains Skyes
NoBody knows
Lillie Of The Valley
Yaka Hula
X MARGIE South
X AVALON
X Birth Of Blues
Bye Bye Blues
DINAH
X FAREWELL Blues
Aint Got Nobody
Alliways Be In Love With You
X Dont Talk About Me PLEASE
Grey Bonnet
Sleepy Time Gal
X Some Body Stole My Gal
STumbling
Changes Made
12th St. Rag
Yonder In N.O.
To Old To Dream
Tulips That's My Baby Now
SUNRISE

Chania Town
X Shiek
X DALLAS BLUES
X BYE ALL BYE
OLD MAN MOSE
SENSATION RAG
X Thats A Plenty
X HINDUSTAN
X I Found A New Baby
Lazy River
Lime House Blues
Linger A While
X MY GAL SAL
NAGASAKI
LADY Be Good
X Suger Blues
GEORGIA BROWN
Three Little Word
Tiger RAG
Someday Sweetheart
Sleepy Time Down South
St James Infirmary
GETTYSBURGS MARCH
BALLIN JACK
X BEAL ST BLUES

Alton Purnell's song list for the college tours

I think it was '55. I think. But I'd have to go and look at the contract. I was just beginning to get out of it. But, you know what, that's also the year when – that may have been also the year that I talked to Paul and booked him in Childs Paramount in New York .

Martyn : Well, probably because I remember George somewhere on one of the records – I forget where it is – and they're talking and they said, "Oh, a friend of mine's got his band out on the road right now. They're in Boston," I think he said. "And his name is Paul Barbarin and he's got a very fine band." I don't know what he was describing Paul's band for. Maybe because you had done the deal with Paul to go to there.

Gagliano : I don't know.

Martyn : But, on that first tour when Percy went there. Who picked the numbers?

Gagliano : George always picked the numbers.

Martyn : Always?

Gagliano : As far as I know. Right. Now, we might have gotten around a table with Alton and George, and me because, you know, I would ultimately write up the program, whatever it was.

And I think, certainly when we made this first one, I was the announcer for the – for the band, which I didn't think – that didn't sit too well with John Ball.

Martyn : It's that the first one with Percy where you were talking about the New Orleans funeral traditions?

Gagliano : Yeah. I couldn't remember. I ought to get that whole load of records and play them all over to myself again, you know. Well, I told you that there was some confusion about that because I know that the initial announcer was not me. And then I came on in about the middle of the band and picked it up. If you go and listen to the first '52 concert of the Oxford Series. Listen to the first voice, it ain't me. And it's not John Ball. John Ball's got a fantastically distinct voice. But, you know what John Ball wanted to do? John Ball wanted George to introduce and I understand that. And he did that the second time. You know, I got the hint.

Martyn : Whose idea was it to play the funeral sequence?

Gagliano : As far as I know, it was ours, a part of our deal. It must have been at the McAlister in '49 concert that we first did the funeral concert.

Martyn : Was it your idea or George's?

Gagliano : I don't remember. It probably was my idea. It was my idea to play it in the context of tying the three different modes of music together and explaining why these particular things were used at that particular time.

Martyn : Well, it's very instructive to people who don't know anything about New Orleans and its culture to see what they do as – what they're calling Jazz Funerals now. I know they weren't calling it a Jazz Funeral.

Gagliano : No, not at that time. They were just funerals, you know, funerals with music they were called. And I have to confess to you something that – as I hear back my presentations, I think I played it too – put too much humor and with not enough dignity for the occasion and I suspect that maybe this is what – one of the reasons that John wanted to let me know that maybe I should be in the background. You know, this is archival music, so let George – let George do it. Well, George's fine, you know, at – at announcing. He would say, "Now we'll play blah, blah, blah."

But I felt that, in order to introduce this college crowd to this thing, it would be better for me to do it, to explain it. The only thing I find wrong with it is I should have treated it a little bit more less humorous. The one thing that I cringe every time I hear it, is I referred to the body as the "stiff." Well, look, this is all spur-of-the-moment, man. This stuff, I didn't write it down. I was just extemporating.

Martyn : And it took place at the start of the second half, correct?

Gagliano : Always after the first set-up and where we could then especially get lined up for what we had to do is, we had to change Lawrence's role from banjoist to a bass drummer.

Martyn : And he brought his own drum down?

Gagliano : He brought his drum. We made sure he brought his drum. It's the only reason he would have brought his drum because we had to premeditate that this was what we were going to do. And he brought his drum. And then we had to figure out what to do with Drag because he was the Marshall and he would carry a parasol and then what to do with Alton Purnell. Well, Alton came in at the very end. I mean, by the time that we got into the third number, hey, you know, everybody played. Probably, Lawrence put the bass drum down and started playing the banjo and so forth.

Martyn : Well, I'm going to tell you something that maybe you don't know. When I had my band with Alton, we used to do that sequence too. And Alton would be the Grand Marshall and he was a great Grand Marshall. He'd get off his piano and go back on the piano and put on his sash and a little derby hat, you know, come front of stage with his parasol.

Gagliano : Well, he had the props but Drag didn't have any props.

Martyn : Well, Alton had all the right moves for the Grand Marshall. He was a great Grand Marshall and he did that for the last three years. I'm surprised he didn't do it with you because the intervention would have been there but maybe nobody told him, "Alton, why don't you be the Grand Marshall?"

Gagliano : No, because that was reserved for Drag. The Grand Marshall was leading the guys through the audience.

Martyn : I was with a broadway show for eight and a half years and we were just doing the show with that, it never fails, when you go into the audience with a band, it never fails, it always spreads it out and it's so elementary, the thing to do. I mean, it just – you don't even think about it.

Gagliano : I have a feeling that I'm going to claim credit for it. I had to believe that we were probably the first jazz band to play concerts at university venues.

Martyn : I wouldn't be at all surprised. What was John Ball when the concert finished, like the first one, was he overjoyed?

Gagliano : Oh, very, very happy. He said, "Now, we've got to do this again." And that's why I said, within seven months, we're going back, on an expanded basis. And now we're playing two or three – we played – as I said, we played the University of Indiana, we brought in DePauw University and then we did the Hunt Club in Chicago and we did – we had George Rosenthal's party at the – at the Newport Yacht Club. What do you know about the Newport Yacht Club? Did you know the background?

Martyn : No.

Gagliano : It was a brothel.

Martyn: Was it really? I didn't know that.

Gagliano : It was – it was the Red Light District for Cincinnati. It's still within Kentucky.

Martyn: Oh yeah, I know it was across the state line.

Gagliano : It was across the state line. "Man" – I said, when I'm talking to John Ball, John Ball would never tell me about it. The Yacht Club. So, I'm thinking it's a yacht club. And, when we get there, we go it's basically an old riverboat steamer. That's moored to the bank. And I said, "Hey, is this the Newport Yacht Club?" and he said, "Yeah, that's what they're calling .It was a brothel." I don't know how many years.

Martyn : I might have told you this, but George Rosenthal's wife at the time, who was called Jean and, later in Los Angeles, she married the owner of Bullocks Wilshire a big trendy department store. They say it's like it's a Macy, you know, like our Downtown Macy. She married the – this guy. His name was Bloch. So, her name is now Jean Bloch. And I had a phone call – I used to book my band, Legends of Jazz, which had Alton and Louis Nelson and all you know. And I – she says, "Yeah, is this the band that's got Alton Purnell," and I said, "Yeah." So, she said, "Well, we'd like to book you for such and such a date to play at my house," and I said, "Okay" and I told her what the price was. I don't know – it was a couple – a couple of grand in those days, you know. I mean, we didn't go out cheaply. And then we get to the house and she's all kissing Alton and Alton's hugging her and I'm thinking, who the hell is this woman? And it turns out, and I said to Alton, because she's got guests arriving, I said, "Who's that dame, Alton? Is that the lady that owns the place?" and he said, "Oh, she used to be married to George Rosenthal." And he said, "Well, I knew her from playing at the Newport Yacht Club, which is no longer, all those years ago." I said, "Good grief." And out comes a little guy taking pictures. He said, "Do you mind if I take some pictures?" I said, "No, knock yourself out." So he took some pictures and I said, "Look, if they ever come out any good, I'd like to get a copy. Have you got a card?" and he gave me this card and it said he took all the pictures for *Jazz Ways*. Do you remember that book *Jazz Ways*? His name was Skippy Adelman. He was part of Jean Rosenthal Bloch's circle of friends in Los Angeles. And so no one knew each other and it was – it was fabulous. I don't – I keep meaning to call Jean Bloch to see if she's still alive. I believe she must be 80, you know. But she was in good health. I keep meaning to call her because I'd like to try and get to interview her about her recollections through George Rosenthal.

Gagliano : Well, I had the impression that Rosenthal is sort of a rich guy.

Martyn : I think he must have been, yeah.

Gagliano : And he thought nothing about spending a couple of thousand dollars but I don't think he ever thought about paying the whole tab or bringing the band up from New Orleans. He would make the deal when he knew we were in the neighborhood, you see.

Martyn : But you can't blame him for that.

Gagliano : But he – he was considered to be very friendly to the band. He was very supportive of whatever they did. Any time they were in the neighborhood, man, he would try to get them to play – he'd sponsor a party.

Martyn : Well, in fact the person who gave me the acetates of George's band. It's called "The George Lewis Band in Kentucky." And, like we said, it's just because the place is in Kentucky across the state line. And one of the guys that were there and helped set the job up was named Preston McClanahan and he's a bass player. He's a guy from Cincinnati, or wherever he come from. I don't know is he any good as a bass player. But he was a big fan of Chester Zardis. He's like one of them old time bass players.

And I had dealings with him with these acetates. He got in touch with me and said he had these acetates with the George Lewis Band, was I interested? And I thought, well, they're probably going to be the same old songs, you know. And the band, when Percy was there, it was a whole different lot of songs on there when Howard was there. So, but when he sent me the acetates and I played them, they were a lot of different numbers I've never heard George play before: "Just a Gigolo," "I'll Always Be in Love With You," "Lonesome and Sorry." I've never heard the band play them, never, and I've been around George and these men for years. They weren't high-fi recordings, but were fabulous.

Gagliano : I wouldn't doubt that this recording's this session in 1953 at the Rosenthal party was probably recorded. Was this the tape you're talking about or the record you're talking about had Kid Howard on it?

Martyn : Howard, yeah.

Gagliano : Well, that could have been '53. I'm sure there's a date on it. But it's probably out of that network of people along the State of Ohio. You know the men. They're just sort of like –

Martyn : It's strange how they all seemed to be in touch with one another and, you know. And there seemed to be no animosity. I mean, John Ball never, ever said, "Oh, them damned people with George Rosenthal". Rosenthal is, what I seem to recall, one of the lynchpins putting up enough money to bring the band up. And what would it have cost you then? I mean, what would the train fares have been in those days? A hundred dollars a man maybe? Two hundred dollars a man for the train fare?

Gagliano : I would have to say, for a period of time, I don't know, $2,000-$3,000, I think. Keeping in mind that they had no expenses at all. They were fed, they were housed, they were transported and, of course, in a sense, they paid for it with these informal sessions. For friends that greatly admired the band and this was such a rare instance for them, that this was a rare opportunity for both the band for them to really meet this group.

Martyn : I mean, we would never have got those Oxford Series tapes given to us if we hadn't been a 501(c), a tax exempt foundation you know.

Gagliano : That's true.

Martyn : And nobody – nobody would have given them to us.

Gagliano : You said this lady, Mama. What are you calling her?

Martyn: Mama Jazz.

Gagliano : Mama must have known something about the George Buck compilation.

Martyn : I mean, George you know, he's a good guy, but I would imagine she bought some CDs first from him and then, perhaps, she thought, well, since I've got these tapes – well, John Ball must have been in on it, because he was still alive because he came here to see me and we worked together on it – and I imagine they must have said, "Well, look, we haven't done anything with them all these years," you know. The people are all dead. The intent was to publicize their art, or whatever you want to call it. "Why don't we approach the GHB Company to see would they be willing to –put them out, to issue them." So I said, great.

It didn't come through John Ball, because I didn't even know anything about John Ball until he got in touch with me and said something, "I'm glad you are working on the project George Buck tells me you're the one in charge of putting out the Oxford tapes and I'm glad because I sort of instigated it." And he wasn't bragging or anything about bringing the band out there. So, I called him, I said, "Yeah, I'm very pleased." I said, "They're fabulous." I mean because George Buck had told me, he said, "Oh, it's old classroom stuff, all talking."

I don't know where he got that idea, you know, but – well, I guess they sent him the tapes and he might have sat on them for a year. If I see a box of tapes and they're labeled "The George Lewis Band in Ohio," or whatever they were labeled, "What in the hell are these," you know? So, I would have said, "What is that box of tapes doing out there?" So, George would have – "Oh, yeah, Mama Jazz sent those down and it's mostly all classroom materials" and I said, "Those are the priceless. It's got the George Lewis Band teaching jazz classes Percy and Purnell outgoing people like that." So I put them on and the very first tape is Percy Humphrey, which had never been issued, never seen the light of days. I said, "Jesus Christ!" and I kept playing tape after tape and it was music and I said, "George, it's not classroom material." I said, "Whoever told you that?" "Oh, I thought it was all talking." I said, "Jesus, this is all music!". So, I said, "We could have made arrangements to put these out. Now, do we have to settle with anybody," and he said, "No, they were given to us because they wanted them out and we're a 501(3) (c)." So, I said, "Well, hallelujah," let's get on them.

So I started to learn, then I got in touch with you and got in touch with John Ball, or John Ball called me or something. I don't know who called who. And then we finally put the whole lot out. We came to the end of the George Lewis ones and there are two full Paul Barbarin. So – so, why don't we put them out too, you know? I mean, because the agreement we had with the people like Mama Jazz and I guess John Ball was that they would take responsibility if anybody came out the woodwork that we weren't – we were just doing them, well, a favor, is another way of putting it.

But, no, I'll have to be honest, the one with Percy, the first one, sold immensely though. I mean, we never sold – we never had to repress it but it maybe got up to about, probably by now, 800 or 900 sold, which is incredible. The second ones were the ones it was three with Percy. The first one did extremely well. The second ones did reasonably well. Then they started dropping off because there were so many of them, you know. I mean, the ultra orchestra series is that long on CDs. I think there's about 15 or so. So, the more we got – we got to the end part of it, the sales were, you know, 300 or 400, you know, it dropped off a good bit, you know. But there were some people who wanted the entire series, you know. And but it broke even for us. But we were all tickled pink, George Buck included. But, I don't know if George and the guys had been alive and they had sent us those tapes in – because we were in business since '49, George Buck had started the company. If they'd have sent us those tapes in '56, '57, '58 and said would we do it, I wondered what would have been the attitude of George and the fellows? Would they have wanted money, or do you think they would have just said, well, it's for artistic reasons?

Gagliano : I think they would have been concerned about what the union would say, but glad to see them issued to fulfill what they had agreed to in '52, '53 and '54.

Martyn : Okay, so we have gotten, last time, Nick, to where the band went up to, the first college tour, okay, and we

Kid Ory with Jim Robinson

covered that reasonably well, I would think. It was in October of that same year that the band went out to play for the Dixieland Jubilee in Los Angeles.

Gagliano : That's right.

Martyn : How did they come to get that job or who did what, talked to who?

Gagliano : I really don't know how we got the Beverly Cavern thing, which is tied in with it. Evidently, when George's engagement at the El Morocco ended around March, I must have gotten more active in trying to do things. I don't remember any particular contact with the Gene Norman and Frank Bull concert. I just don't remember.

Martyn : Well, there was an occasion when – let me see. Who went out there? It might have been before George. It might have been the same time as George. I'm not sure, but it would have been the early fifties, no question. Was George Girard there? Johnny St. Cyr I think was out there already and they did a concert with Raymond Burke. Raymond Burke went out there, and George Girard.

Gagliano : You mean to play the Bull thing? Dixieland Jubilee. I have no recollection about how any of the stuff in Los Angeles and Hollywood occurred, other than the fact that I was involved in it. I can recall initiating the San Francisco thing because I had already targeted Doc Dougherty's place. And I just cold-called Doc one day and told him who I was, and he said, "Oh, yeah, yeah," and eventually we made a deal. I think our first engagement was either four or six weeks.

Martyn : That's quite a long time for a little band, isn't it?

Gagliano : Yeah, that's my recollection. Well, of course, you know, here again, we have to sort of amortize the transportation cost. I can also tell you that I did never go to San Francisco in person when the band was playing there, and the only time I saw the band active in a club in Los Angeles was this first concert in Beverly Cavern. Everything else I'm doing by letter or by phone. I'm sure it was some intermediary that came in and talked to those guys, and that's the way it's done. I know I did not have any particular contact with that group or with the Beverly Cavern, so there had to be some third party that maybe introduced us or talked about us, and then mentioned a contact with me, ad then we made whatever deal had to be made. Because I remember Papa Celestin went out there, but he went out there as a solo and he appeared with Ory's band, and George went out there and Ory was a frequent visitor there, but then old Ory's band lived in Los Angeles just around the little suburbs, you know.

Martyn : Yeah, every one of them, Joe Darensbourg, Andy Blakeney, and of course, Bud Scott had died by then. Bud died, I think it was 1949 or '48, it might have been. I can't remember.

Gagliano : I have the impression, a very faint memory that probably Kid Ory's band played at the Beverly Cavern before or maybe they were stepping down to let the George Lewis band come in for two weeks? I don't know.

Martyn : Was it a two-week engagement?

Gagliano : That's my recollection of it. I know I've read something about it being four weeks, but I have no recollection of it being four weeks.

Martyn : Well, I mean, were you aware of the Beverly Cavern?

Gagliano : No, not before ....

Martyn : You didn't know what it was?

Gagliano : No – I knew very well Doc Dougherty's club through my reading, but I don't remember ever reading about the Beverly Cavern. I have a feeling that the Beverly Cavern thing resulted from maybe the impetus to get the band up there for the Norman/Bull concert. In order to make it feasible to amortize the trip, we had to get a little bit of an extended engagement at some other place. Now, remember, we had to do the same thing on the college concerts. What initially held John Ball back from bringing us up there earlier was the fact that he had to figure out a way to put up enough money to cover the transportation costs, as well as pay the men and then keep them up there for about four, five, or six days, whatever he wanted, so he could do these impromptu recordings for the archives. So you had the same economic problem when you're talking about bringing a New Orleans band to San Francisco or to Los Angeles. You can't hardly do it.

Martyn : It's the same thing today, you know.

Gagliano : And then the Norman/Bull concerts, I don't think they were probably not paying the bands very much. I think bands were clamoring to get the recognition of playing on the damn thing, I believe.

Martyn : Well, there's a good possibility, that they were the ones that talked to the Beverly Cavern, you know.

Gagliano : It's possible.

Martyn : I mean, if they wanted George to bring the band out to play there, first of all, evidently you, he, between the two of you, or somebody had said, "Well, you know," as you aptly put it, "to amortize the transportation costs, we'll have to get more than just go there and play for a couple of days." And perhaps they said, "Well, let's try the Beverly Cavern." I mean, it's all supposition. I don't know. I wasn't there. But it's a good supposition, isn't it, when you think about it, if they would have contacted the Beverly Cavern?

And of course it was always a dream of mine that maybe we could go to Europe. But unfortunately, there was no way I could do it, especially when I had started at law school. But evidently, Dorothy Tait was able to pull it off.

Well, let me just ask a few more questions. We were talking about the Hangover Club, as opposed to the Beverly Cavern. We never did delve into the Hangover Club. Who got the band the Hangover Club?

Gagliano : Well, I did. I told you. I made a cold call to Doc Dougherty.

Martyn : Okay, well, how did you know of Doc Dougherty?

Gagliano : Well, basically through the *Down Beat*. Remember now, I'm still the Down Beat correspondent in New Orleans, so I'm an avid reader of *Down Beat*, and I'm aware of all the big clubs around in New York. But New York had several places where they're known for jazz like Jimmy Ryan's. These were all just names to me. The Blue Note in Chicago and probably a lot of other places. I don't remember any significant place in L.A., so the idea that the Beverly Cavern, I don't know where it cropped up, but it cropped up in connection with that first concert that we did.

Martyn : Well, when you called Doc Dougherty, did you get through to him?

Gagliano : Well, I think I did.

Martyn : What was his name? Charles wasn't it?

Gagliano : Yes, Charles "Doc" Dougherty. But I read about him, so somehow or other, I get a phone number for the Hangover Club in San Francisco and I called the number. And eventually I got to talk to him and I told him who I was. He said, "Oh yeah, I know about your band." I said, "Great," because we had already been to the Bull/Norman concert, so that gave us an up with those people. And he said, "Yeah, I would like to have your band up here and we'll try to work it out." And of course he was bringing in – I know he had Ory for a while, and, of course, I think he had the Yerba Buena Band, I think. This was later, I think, but they had Earl Hines's band with Earl Hines, Pop Foster, Jimmy Archey, the man who played trombone with them. I know they had that band, so that was an all-black band, I think. I'm not sure that he had an all-black policy, but I knew he was, in my opinion, from what I read, he was the premier jazz spot in San Francisco, and if we wanted to go and explore club dates while we're in California, that was the logical place to go. My recollection is I called, talked to him. He said, "Yeah, we'd like to have you. We'll try to figure something out. How much would it take?" I gave him a price. He said, "Well, you know let's try it." Somewhere along the line, we got back together and worked it out.

Martyn : What would they expect to make on a job like that?

Gagliano : I still think that the band was expecting scale.

Martyn : New Orleans scale?

Gagliano : No, not necessarily.

Martyn : Scale from San Francisco?

Gagliano : Whatever scale would be. I never did – I found out later – well, I'm reading about it now. It's something like – there was apparently, you know, like the Exchange Band – where the band exchanges between musicians. They had the same thing between cities, between the unions. I know they had a thing whereby you had to register as a traveling band and they would charge more money for a traveling band. Maybe that was an incentive to hire local people.

Martyn : Yeah, it probably was, but what are you going to do with local people? I mean, it's like putting the band down in New Orleans or bringing a band from New York City. More people would go, ostensibly, go and see the New York band because they can't see them every week, you know.

Gagliano : Right, sure. My recollection in San Francisco sometime in June.

Martyn : Would that have been the Hangover?

Gagliano : Yeah, that would have been at the Hangover. I don't know of any other place we played in San Francisco. I know in Los Angeles we played Beverly Cavern. We played a place called the Royal Room, and those are the two that I remember. In San Francisco it was always the Hangover and when we played in New York, it was at Childs' Paramount.

Martyn : Lizzie Miles and all them were out there at the Hangover when the band went up there. They were playing intermission act, I remember, because there's a recording with Lizzie singing with George's band at the Hangover. Smokey Stover was playing drums. Joe Robichaux from here was playing piano, who later joined George's band. Lizzie was singing, and there was a bass player, I think, and that was all.

Gagliano : So there was a relief band?

Martyn : No, they were like the intermission band. Well, it was obviously a little long because Lizzie – you know, to me she was always raving about George and his band and how successful they were. I didn't know that they were – well, I guess they were friends. They had run across each other at different jazz club concerts and stuff, probably, but she was always saying about how George was doing so good with his band, you know. But when they went up there, they recorded. They used to broadcast, remember?

Gagliano : Yeah, there was a broadcast from the West Coast. No doubt. It seemed to me that it would definitely tie in.

Martyn : Was George happy to do these things?

Gagliano : Oh, absolutely. You know, the band was still – well, the band always was struggling economically, you know. Eventually, if you think it's important enough in George's lifestyle, I could show you, you know, records that indicate that he's always been financially insecure, even after 1950. That gave us certainly a lot of recognition. It didn't give us a hell of a lot of money, but, you know, the recognition eventually led to somewhere. Now, at this point, you know, keep in mind that when I started with George, I was working full-time – well, not when I met George, but when we started working together in '49, and I had decided not to go out of town, to pursue my engineering profession and stayed home with a local construction company. And it was while I was with that construction company that I was devoting my free time to the George Lewis Band. I can't begin to tell you how the Norman/Bull concert was booked, or the Beverly Caverns, other than I believe it was a tied-in arrangement and it was tied in order to be able to cover the transportation cost.

Martyn : Do you think George wanted to go on those traveling trips because he was broadening his base, making his band more famous, or do you think it was just the money, or a combination or what?

Gagliano : Well, I think it was both. Keep in mind, now, at this time he's not working regularly in New Orleans, except maybe he's back on weekends at Manny's. We were also playing some periodic social events and stuff, because he didn't pick up replaying Bourbon Street until he opened up at the Mardi Gras Lounge later on toward the end of '52. And even then, I don't think he played at the Mardi Gras Lounge full-time, because I sort of indicated to you that he was sharing the load over there with the Freddy Kohlman Band. So I got the impression that maybe George might have been playing two or three days out of the week, probably in the middle of the week, and then playing the weekends back at Manny's, and then Freddy Kohlman and his group, which had previously been the house band, I guess, if you want to call it that, at the Mardi Gras Lounge, they took back the weekends.

Martyn : But by this time, Howard had come into the band, hadn't he?

Gagliano : Yeah, well, because when we were starting to do these projected trips, Percy had already said he couldn't do it, so Howard became the guy and he became the guy for local stuff as well. You had to integrate him into the band, you had to keep him active, and so really and truly, the only time after that that Percy would have played with us would have been in a two-trumpet situation. George is very loyal to his people, very, very loyal, and it was evident from all of his past experiences in being picked up as a young kid to play with other guys, he really appreciated the notion that they would keep using him, and I think this started to be ingrained in him that this is the way he should also treat his people. Hence, you had that very strong relationship between him and Drag and Lawrence Marrero, and then Jim, and then eventually Joe Watkins. Purnell was in and out. Of course, he was the expendable guy because some of the gigs didn't have a piano, so he didn't play. But whenever we did club stuff or we did concerts, Alton was always along.

Martyn : How did he feel about being expendable?

Gagliano : I don't know. I think it was a reality that he had to face that – it's not George's fault, that if people don't have a piano and they don't want to put in a piano temporarily, so, you know, well, they can't use the piano. And he can't sacrifice the other guys' opportunities. So I think it was simply a realistic thing that Alton certainly lived with, and, you know, he was noted as a solo player anyway.

Martyn : Well, he did do a lot of solo work. He was playing with Smiling Joe, you know, Pleasant Joseph. He was playing with a little trio with him around that time too. I remember him telling me all that, you know, and he said, "I preferred working with George," he said, "but couldn't always." He, just like you, was saying the same thing. He said, "But anyway, I was with Smiling Joe, so," he said, "I didn't care. Smiling Joe was a friend of mine. We grew up together, and if I wasn't working with George, then Smiling Joe would hire me because he played piano too.

Gagliano : Well, Smiling Joe was primarily known as a singer, as I remember.

Martyn : He played a little guitar, piano, but Alton was far and above. I mean, I worked with the two of them. There's no comparison, you know. In fact, Pleasant Joseph, he wrote a book and he mentions me in that book working with him. So by then Howard would come in. Did Percy just say, "I can't do any more"? Do you remember how that happened?

Gagliano : I wasn't part of the deal. I remember George telling me, "Percy don't want to go on any extended trips." That's what he told me. So basically I said, "Well, who you gonna use?" He said, "I'm gonna use Howard." And I assumed that Howard certainly was with us when we did the first Norman/Bull concert for the tour, because we had to do the two weeks at the Beverly Caverns.

Martyn : What were those guys' names? Gene Norman and Frank Bull, wasn't it?

Gagliano : Gene Norman and Frank Bull.

Martyn : What did you know of them when ....

Gagliano : Nothing other than I had read about them in *Down Beat*. Most of what I knew about the jazz scene was what I got out of reading *Down Beat*. Remember, I was still the New Orleans correspondent to Down Beat, not very prolific, because if I had done my job right, I would have been covering the rhythm and blues scene and the rock and roll scene which was beginning to emerge at that time.

Martyn : I was going to say was there much of a rhythm and blues scene in the city?

Gagliano : Yeah. Yeah, it was underground, though. It was in the black community primarily, until the records started to come out. But basically the big man in that was a fellow named Frank Painia, who owned the Dewdrop Inn and Hotel, and I understand that that was the central place for all these musicians to get together.

Martyn : Well, they had all kind of acts playing there. I knew his daughter, Frank's daughter, Lilly and I interviewed her too. But anyway, she said the same thing, that it was one heck of a place for people to congregate. They would book different acts and then they would play the Dewdrop, which was on LaSalle, apparently. You ever go there to the club.

Gagliano : No. I seem to remember that my then friend a black disc jockey. He died about a year ago. You know who I'm talking – Tex Stephens. I ran into Tex at some function and he found out that I was the local correspondent for Down Beat, and that immediately gave me some credibility. And he said, "Man," he said, "why don't you come with me?" And I said, "Well ...." I sort of was hesitant at the time. You know, we were still in the Jim Crow years, and I had to be concerned about that. But he could have probably gotten me into the place and I could have probably covered the scene if I was that eager to do it, but I was really not that eager to do it. And if I was looking at this from the viewpoint of my activity with *Down Beat*, then it was a vast mistake, because, for one thing, *Down Beat* was not necessarily all that interested in traditional jazz.

Martyn : It never seemed to me to be.

Gagliano : They reported on it.

Martyn : Yeah, when they had to.

Gagliano : But I think they became more involved in the bebop era and Stan Kenton and big bands, big swing bands, because that was what was commercially selling, and *Down Beat* wanted to sell magazines.

Martyn : Well, I think, for instance, Frank Painia's place, the Dewdrop, when artists would come, they'd play like a week, two weeks there, even people like Ray Charles and all those kind of people. They played at the Dewdrop, but then they'd send them out – there was another guy, Hosey Hill. I don't know whether you ever heard of him. He was a black booking agent, Hosey Hill.

Gagliano: No, I never did.

Martyn: And he used to book the acts that came to the Dewdrop, he'd book them in all the country towns, you know, they'd play Raceland and – oh, you know.

Gagliano: They were amortizing the cost of moving around the country.

Martyn: Exactly. Exactly what George meant. Did George ever talk to you about the rhythm and blues scene? What did he make of it?

Gagliano: Yeah, you know, he didn't say too much about rhythm and blues because basically that was another aspect of black music. I guess he got a little excited about bebop. "I don't understand that stuff." Certainly he could understand rhythm and blues, okay, but when you start getting all the discord involved in bebop and there was really, I guess, very little melodic line in a lot of it, but then again, once in a while they would play a tune that had – I don't know whether it was true or not – that had bebop origins.

Martyn: I think what happened was both of the camps adopted like – what am I thinking about? Well, I remember Howard used to play "Jumpin' with Symphony Sid," which was a George Shearing – not really bebop, but it was a blues, but Howard would play that, I remember. The thing was, Howard came into the band and Percy kind of bowed out.

Gagliano: Yeah, because Percy could not make the extended trips. And because he couldn't do that, George felt the need to keep a cohesive group together and adopted Kid Howard as his trumpet player. And Kid was good – a lot of times he was good. A lot of times he was bad. Well, let's say less good. Let's call it less good. And apparently it appeared to be the result of two things, as I saw it. One was he did have some problem with his lip and the other thing was drinking. When he drank, he became very mediocre, I mean to me.

Martyn: I remember seeing him on parades, and if he had those dark glasses on, you knew he'd been drinking.

Gagliano: You knew he had tipped.

Martyn: Yeah, always with those dark glasses. It was a funny thing. I mean, even if the sun wasn't shining, he'd have them dark glasses if he'd have been drinking, you know. But he was a strange man. I mean, my dealings with him were a bid odd, to say the least. He was the only one of the New Orleans musicians that I thought was a bit of a – tried to be a bit of a slickster. I can't really explain what I'm getting at, you know.

Gagliano: Yeah, I think he dressed a cut above the other guys. I think he thought of himself as, I guess, a ladies' man. I don't know if he was or wasn't.

Martyn: Well, if you look at the pictures that Bill Russell took after the Climax recordings in the Gypsy Tea Room, George had all them in just shirts and, you know, scrappy, but I mean, there was Howard in a two-piece suit and tie.

Gagliano: It's an interesting point. All the years that I was with the band – of course, I was very close to George's wife, Jeannette. I met Jim Robinson's wife. I never had any significant relationship, but I met her. I knew who she was. Slow Drag, I knew his wife.

Martyn: Annie.

Gagliano: Annie. Lawrence Marrero, I knew his wife. I met Alton Purnell's wife. I never met Howard's wife. If, in fact, he had a wife.

Martyn: Yeah. Well, I remember he lived with his mother for a long, long time. Then he married a woman who had two girls so that would be his stepdaughters. No, I don't remember. I went to Howard's house when he was living on Charbonnet Street down by Martin Luther King High School there. I went to his house. I went with a friend of mine to discuss making a record with him and he seemed like he was the only one home. There wasn't any women there or men or children or anything. He cooked this beautiful fried chicken dinner and all the trimmings, but he seemed like he was – gave me the impression he was the only one in the house, the only one at home.

Gagliano: Well, that would tie in with my experience, because as I say, I never met a wife. Nobody was ever identified by me as his wife. I've never been to his home. I didn't know where he lived. Of all the men in the band, I had the least, contact with him.

Martyn: Percy lived right there near Napoleon Avenue where the big hospital is there. What the hell's the street where Percy – South Robertson. He lived on South Robertson for years and years and years. I mean, when I first met him, he was living there. An amazing thing, I went to his house nearly forty years later and he still lived in the same little house. The front door needed painting from the time I went there till forty years later, and he had the same furniture, this beat-up old couch.

Gagliano: But you don't want those people to change. I mean, you know, that's the criticism for a lot of these artists.

Once they get some money in their hands, they totally change character and they change all sorts of things, but –

Martyn : Well, a lot of the younger musicians, I feel, that I knew through the years changed. If you gave them a recording session, they would take the money and go down and put the payment on a new – well, not new, second-hand Cadillac, you know. It meant something to them. The older musicians, I guess, saved their money. I don't know what they saved it for because, you know – but they did. I mean, Alton Purnell, when I knew him out in Los Angeles, he lived in a funny little house. I mean, it just was a little wood-frame house. It was nothing. And Alton wasn't making a lot of money, but he was probably doing better there than his counterparts, Slow Drag and Jim where doing here. Oh, it just came to me. Esther was Alton's wife.

Gagliano : Esther.

Martyn : Yeah, Esther, and you know she remarried him – well, not remarried. They didn't get divorced, but he left and went to California. She went back and lived out there.

Gagliano : Yeah, you told me that, and I was glad to hear because she was a nice lady.

Martyn : Oh, she was fabulous, yeah. But anyway, so Howard came in. Percy went out. All right. There wasn't any more changes, was there? There was one. I don't know what you remember of this and I might be jumping ahead a year or two. I probably am, but I remember when I interviewed Cié, he told me one time he went out to California with the George Lewis Band.

Gagliano : Cié played the Persian Room.

Martyn : Joe didn't want to make the trip, I don't know why, and Cié went out there. But when he came back, he told George, "I want you to take Joe back because I can't get along with these fellows." But that's what he told me, you know. So then Joe came back. But who was the most loyal of the band to George, do you think?

Gagliano : Well, clearly it would be Lawrence and Drag. If I was to say who would be joined at the hip with George, it would be Lawrence and it would be Drag. Trumpet players were sort of a different breed, you know. I guess they played the lead and maybe they felt more often than not they ought to be the leader of the band. Nobody could. The only guy that could approach George, I think, in musical ability is Percy. But okay, the personnel in the band, I would have to say that the closest two to George would have been Lawrence and Drag. Then I would say maybe it became a tossup between Joe Watkins and Jim Robinson. So who does that leave?

Martyn : Alton.

Gagliano : That leaves Alton, and Alton had the problem of having to give up his appearance with the band when there

Frank Bull introduces Joe Mares at the Dixieland Jubilee festival at the Shrine Auditorium – 1954.
George Girard on trumpet.

Frank Bull *& COMPANY* *Advertising*

Frank Bull
Mel Roach
Hank Konysky

August 12, 1954

Mr. Joe Mares,
520 St. Louis St.,
New Orleans, Louisiana.

Dear Joe:

I just spoke with Al Van Court who tells me he has received a letter from you in which you stated that you thought Johnny St. Cyr should come to Los Angeles a couple of days before our Jubilee and work out with George Lewis' band. This is agreeable to us and will you please advise how Johnny will want to travel.

I am in hopes that you can confirm Jack Delaney, Raymond Burke, George Girard, Armand Hug and Sam deKemel for appearances here on October 15th. I'm anxious to get a firm commitment so I can prepare our advertising. We also want you to come along and be introduced and present this group at the performance. We will provide a top drummer, possibly Nick Fatool, a prominent bass and there are several in Los Angeles who are familiar to you (Phil Stevens, Artie Shapiro, Marty Korb) and a banjo or guitar man, possibly Nappy LaMare or George Van Eps. This will round out a very wonderful combination.

As I explained to you during my visit, because of the large number of men and the expensive overhead, this is not a big money maker for anybody. I'm sure you and the men will be thrilled performing before a packed house at the Shrine of nearly 7,000 jazz fans.

Publicity is tremendous and of national scope, and our Jubilee has been the show case for many bands. To mention a few, The Castle Jazz Band; The Firehouse Five; Rozy McHargue's Ragtimers; George Lewis, etc., all got their start.

Mr. Joe Mares   -2-   August 12, 1954

We will entertain the men royally while they are here and to augment their income as soon as you let me know that they are available we will attempt to get other engagements for the Saturday and Sunday following our show. I would like to hold the expenses to around $1500.00 for your group. This can be done if you can get the boys to travel by automobile. Al Van Court told me that Delaney was willing to drive. Please don't think that I'm chiseling, but we do have to watch the overhead.

I'm looking forward to meeting you again here and I'm positive you will have a wonderful time. At your earliest convenience will you please let me know whether or not the group can make the trip.

Kindest personal regards.

Cordially yours,

Frank Bull

FB:jtd

Frank Bull's letter to Joe Mares suggesting that Johnny St. Cyr should appear with the George Lewis Band at the Dixieland Jubilee Festival.

Letter dated August 12 1954

were no pianos available. So by necessity, he couldn't have been as close to George as the other three guys. Now, when Elmer Talbert was living, I would put Elmer in the same category as Lawrence and Drag, because there was a very close relationship there.

Martyn : I think you said you did not go to the Hangover, but you went to the Beverly Cavern?

Gagliano : Just to rehash what I just said, the only West Coast trip I ever took in my life was this weekend trip when the band played the concert, the Bull/Norman Concert, and I also went that same weekend to the opening of the Beverly Cavern. And I also told you that I did not travel with the band to California because they had to leave earlier to get there and I was on a limited schedule, so I had to fly up out the weekend.

Martyn : What made you go that time?

Gagliano : Well, because, to my way of thinking, it was a very important breakthrough because this was really – as far as the George

AUdubon 1824 MAgnolia 7429

JOE MARES JR.

SOUTHLAND RECORDS
New Orleans Jazz . . Made In New Orleans
520 ST. LOUIS STREET
NEW ORLEANS 16, LOUISIANA

Aug.17,1954

Mr.Frank Bull
1239 N.Highland Ave.
Los Angeles 38,Cal.

Dear Frank:

Thank you,on behalf of the boys,for your kind offer. I'd be delighted to supply you with a firm commitment at this time,but can't,because of these reasons.

First,George Girard is away on maneuvers with the National Guard,and can't be reached until Monday,Aug.23.However,I'm sure he'll want to make the trip.Jack Delaney,Raymond Burke,Armand Hug and Sam Dekemel are prepared to come. One of the difficulties is,however,that they can't afford the time involved in driving,so would have to come by air.Round trip fare for the group would be $1086. The boys need to draw at least $125 per man in order to handle their replacements. That would amount to $625,or a total of $1711.25. If you're able to cover these expenses,I don't think anything will stand in our way. Naturally,I wouldn't miss it for the world,myself,but of course,will pay my own expenses.

I had the opportunity to speak with Nick Gagliano last night about Johnny St Cyr sitting in with the George Lewis band. As their manager,he objects to having St.Cyr added,because the band is so completely set that he feels it wouldn't work out well.As a result,you'll have to make your own arrangements with Johnny,which may work out even better than the original suggestion. Johnny,too,will want to travel by air.

In the event that your budget will stretch sufficiently to cover these expenses,please advise us in regard to available accomodations in Los Angeles for the week-end.

Thanks again for your interest and best personal regards,

Cordially yours,

Joe Mares

Joe Mares' reply to Frank Bull – August 17, 1954.

Lewis Band is concerned – set aside individual accolades or whatever, talk about the band, I had the feeling that appearing at the Bull/Norman concert was a great step forward, and no doubt it led to our being able to go back to the West Coast several times. So to me it was a breakthrough. Now, you say to me, "Okay, Nick, you're telling me that's a breakthrough and you can't even remember how it happened." I realize there's a contradiction there, but that's just the way it is. I just don't remember it, and I am very, very chagrined that I don't have my damn records of correspondence, checkbooks, and all that from that era, which got lost sometime in the period when I left my mother and father's house and went out and got married. I know I never did throw the stuff away, but somehow or other – and I may find it. I may find it somewhere in this house under a pile of stuff. I can't even get to it right now because I got so much stuff, and I have my brother over here with his crap while he's temporarily building an addition to his house out in the country. So I have his stuff, I have my stuff, got all of my kids' stuff here. You know, I could start a storage business in my attic. And I have this room back here, and it could very well be somewhere buried at the bottom of all that debris. One of these days, I'll find it.

Martyn : Well, call me when you do.

Gagliano : The Dixieland Jubilee was promoted by Frank Norman and Gene Bull in *Down Beat*. And so that's what I knew about them. That's all. And I'm going to say this to you. In later years, the band went back there, and they might have played. They played the first one in '52. I think they went back in '53 and maybe went back in '54. I don't know. I just don't remember. So I can't tell you anything about who they were other than that they were promoters, but they must have had some kind of standing in the jazz community, because they had to have that standing in order to have a lot of these big names to go play for them. But then again, if we played – my recollection is, reading all the stuff I've been reading – that we played in the fifth Jubilee concert. Now, if that was the fifth one and this was in 1952, then evidently they might have started in 1947.

90

(interview with Floyd Levin by Barry Martyn June 24th, 2001)

Frank Bull and Gene Norman were the two most popular disc jockeys in Los Angeles. They each had daily radio programs and they got together to put on this "Dixieland Jubilee", they used their radio programs for six months ballyhooing the event and they were able to pack the Shrine Auditorium every single year for about eleven years. George and his band were brought out; I would think 1950 or 1951. He came out several times, that was a good band. Next to Kid Ory, I think that was the best New Orleans band I ever heard. I think they did two "Dixieland Jubilees" and they were hired to go into the Beverly Cavern, our jazz club got together and decided to meet them at the train and we arranged housing for them. Monette Moore, a blues singer from the old days that lived here; she and a couple of her lady friends provided housing. The band split up and they stayed with these different people. We met them at the station. They climbed down the steps and here we were yelling and waving and they ran back in the train, they were frightened. When we explained who we were we really became very friendly with them and we went "en mass" to the Beverly Cavern and they had a packed house. There was a great difference between them and Ory, a different sound. It was more primitive. By comparison to George Lewis, Ory's band was more sophisticated. It would be pretty hard to compare those two bands because there was no basis of comparison, the rhythm sections had a different feel. Alton was certainly a different kind of piano player than Buster Wilson. Buster was delicate and frilly where Alton was powerful, swinging and hard. I know they had a lot of fans here. They packed that place every single night. They were booked in there for, I think, a month and we noticed when they got off the stand they would disappear into the kitchen where they would sit around a little table and drink coffee and such. Once I went back and said, "Why don't you come sit with us and have a drink with us? They were very nervous about that because in New Orleans, they weren't allowed to mingle with the audience. Little Alton was the one that broke that. He broke it down first. He was drinking in those days and he went back and told them "C'mon they're not going to bite your head off".

Monette agreed to put the band up for economic reasons. I think she was charging them probably something very moderate. We had parties over at her house. She had recorded very early, around Bessie Smith's time. Anyway, she wrote lyrics to Burgundy St. Blues. She talked to all the guys in the band about locations round New Orleans where people would meet and the man that owned the company that did the recordings asked her to do that. I can't remember his name. It was done in what used to be called the KSJ Studio on Melrose right next to R.K.O., Joe Darensbourg was involved in that recording, he was sort of, I wouldn't say the producer but he had more experience than the guy who was paying for the productions. He asked Joe to be there and Joe sort of ran that whole session.

At the Beverly Cavern Alton was featured with the rhythm section only in George's band once in a while. He had his little bits like "Caldonia". When the band left to go home that first time, Alton didn't want to go home, he didn't like New Orleans. He grabbed onto my wife Lucille and I had to pull him away and put him on the train. (end of interview)

Martyn : Everybody who reads this book when it comes out is going to know who Gene Norman and Frank Bull are, you know. I mean, their names are automatically linked with the Dixieland Jubilee concerts, you know, in Los Angeles. Weren't they at the Shrine Auditorium?

Gagliano : The Shrine Auditorium.

Martyn : See, I played the Shrine later years. 1970, it's a massive thing. I think it holds six thousand people. When the band went up to Ohio on that first trip in May of '52, what was the biggest theater they played in?

Gagliano : The only thing I have and what I remember was a figure like 1500 people.

Martyn : So the Shrine Auditorium would have probably been the biggest they had done to date.

Gagliano : Oh, yeah, yeah. I seem to have a vague recollection of flying in to Los Angeles, arriving there somewhere around midday. Somehow somebody picked me up. It was still broad daylight, and they're driving me to the Shrine Auditorium and I see this great big old place. I go in, and then I remember being backstage with the band, and then after that going to the Beverly Cavern. All I know is that they got a great reaction to the band, so I wouldn't even begin to suggest whether it was better or worse than anybody else. I just don't remember. And I don't even remember who else was on the ticket, but I do seem to recall meeting a bunch of sort of famous musicians backstage, which is like nothing I had ever been exposed to.

Martyn : I mean, I suppose George must have realized the importance of doing something like that.

Gagliano : Oh, absolutely, and I think when he started to – George knew who some of the big names were in the business – he had to, you know. He had that exposure with Bunk Johnson in New York, and I'm sure he met a lot of these guys, and I'm sure he understood that that was a very important breakthrough for us. And again, it would have been a follow-up. I say it's a follow-up, but let me be sure. I can tell you that the appearance at the Bull/Norman Jubilee was in October, and we had previously played the first concerts in Cincinnati and Miami in May. So you had about five or six months between the two. I don't know that there was any connection between the two because I don't know how much national publicity, if any, the concerts in Ohio got.

Martyn : Do you think George would have paid the band the same money, double the money, a little bit more when they went out of town for the weekend?

Gagliano : Yeah, I would think he did. He would get double and everybody else would get one. It was split on that basis.

Martyn : But I mean, if they went to Los Angeles, do you think he would pay the band double than if they worked in New Orleans?

Gagliano : I think it would be dependent upon how much money they got for the engagement. As I told you, my discussion with George – and I can't tell you that this was done in everybody's presence. It was probably me and George – I just said, "George ...." I guess what I'm telling him is, ".... I'm not in the position to be an employer – have to pay these guys, have to hold off Social Security, income taxes and all that. You don't want to do that either, I guess. So I don't know how they do it in real life, but that's the way you should be doing it." But I said, "Maybe the best way to get around that is to consider the band to be a cooperative band." "What's that?" Says George. I said, "Well, you own it together. Whatever money you make, you share, and you share it according to an understanding as to what and how you're going to distribute the money." And he said, "Well, how would you do it?" I said, "Well, you tell me what's scale." And he said, "Okay." So I said, "Well, let's take whatever we get, cut it up into a total of nine segments, thinking about a seven-member band." The seven members would get a share each, George would get an extra share as the leader, and one share was going to the expense pot or to me. I told him I would treat that as if it's my income. "Whatever I can write off, I'll write it off, and whatever I can't write off, well, if there's any surplus, I'll just go ahead and pay the tax on it." But it had to stay in some semblance of availability for things that might crop up, and of course, they sure as hell did crop up when we went and played at the Royal Room in Hollywood. If you ask me how we got the Royal Room gig, I don't know. I don't remember that, but I do remember setting up the thing where the Royal Room people would send me the check and then I would cut checks. In fact, basically every week I would send George the checks in advance. When I'd get the check from them, I'd put it in the bank.

Martyn : Where did the band stay when it went out to California, for instance.

Gagliano : I have a feeling that there was sort of a network of friends that they had where they could temporarily lodge when they'd go on some of these trips. Now, I would think that Los Angeles would be a good place for a number of reasons. We had a number of musicians that left New Orleans to go live over there.

Martyn : That's absolutely true. I know that.

Gagliano : And you had a couple of distinctive black neighborhoods in Los Angeles, so I would think all of that gave them the opportunity to find reasonable places to stay. Keep in mind that they would never be there more than a month. I do remember the Beverly Cavern thing being a two-week engagement. I have also read something in the Jazz Club Second Line that says it was for four weeks, but I remember two weeks. I don't remember any engagement that we ever did that went beyond four weeks.

Martyn : But you know, I just thought of something. I'm interrupting you, but I seem to recall somewhere along the line I read that some of the musicians in George's band stayed with Monette Moore.

Gagliano : Well, that sounds good, because Monette, you know, recorded with them. Right around in there when she did sort of a monologue on "Burgundy Street Blues."

Martyn : I'm sure that somebody told me that the band stayed with Monette Moore or most of the band stayed with Monette Moore. I think she had either a big house or she might have run some little rooming house, small rooming house. It would have seemed logical that that's how they got to know her if they did stay with her and then how she became on this recording session.

There's one recording session that I meant to ask you about. I think we mentioned it but didn't know much about it, either one of us. In March, early part of March '53, George Lewis and Lawrence made a recording in Chicago with Art Hodes.

Gagliano : Yeah, that was done when we were on an extended tour. That would have been in the second year that we went back up into the Indiana and Ohio area. That would be '53.

Martyn : March of '53, college concert tour at University of Indiana.

Gagliano : Yeah, cause I have a note here that it says, "On March 5, during the tour while the band was in Chicago, there was a record session for Jazzology with George, Lawrence, and Art Hodes on piano." And I'm saying my note is I have no recollection of that. A lot of these recording sessions, George made the arrangements himself. Or maybe it was through the union. The only recording session that I recall being involved with, I mean real directly, would have been the thing with Bob Clark to record the Ohio State thing, and that was because he wanted to record that concert and he tracked us down at the auditorium where we were, and, like, it was in the morning, a late morning, and he says, "Man, I'd like to make a deal to record the session tonight."

Anyway, we came to an agreement on it, and I seem to have a feeling like he paid us something like either 2,500 or 3,000 dollars for it. But you know, I thought that all of the recording rights were going to be really for George because these were in his name, and George paid them for the session and that was it. That's the way I look at it, you know. I don't know how it is in the musical world. Do sidemen get royalties?

Martyn : No, generally not. Look, in my musical world, I don't even get royalties. I never do recordings for royalties. I made this great deal. I said, "Look, Nick, you want to record my band? Right now I've got a little three-piece band. I want 500 apiece for them and I want to take 1,000. That's 2,000 dollars. You give me 2,000 dollars." If you want to go sell it, if you issue it and put it out and you want to go sell it to your next-door neighbor, knock yourself out. But then that's me. A lot of people prefer to go the other way, you know.

Gagliano : Well, I remember that Bob Clark, besides the 2,500 or 3,000 dollars he paid up front, that we were going to have a royalty arrangement.

Martyn : It was issued in a little box set, wasn't it?

Gagliano : Yeah, I have that. Two twelve-inch LPs in the box. It had an insert that I had done with Clark. He went and he had it printed all up, and then finally he issued the records. Then after he issued the records, he sent me a couple copies, and then I never heard from him again. I don't know what happened to him, but we never got any royalties or anything. I think he lost money on it, but who knows.

Martyn : Yeah, who makes money on jazz? None of the New Orleans variety. Did George and the band sell records on their tours ever?

Gagliano : I don't recall ever doing that. If I'm looking at the itinerary for 1953, I see a college concert tour and I've got a University of Indiana, DePaux University. For some reason or other, DePaux stands out to me and that was because we were sponsored by the fraternity and they put us up in their dormitory. And this was in February and March, and they sleep with the damn windows open. So here we are. It's like eleven o'clock at night, maybe later. The guys had played the concert and then they came back to the frat house and probably did a little middlin' around, and then it was time to go to bed. So they said, "Okay, we've got you all set up up in the dormitory. Got a lot of blankets and stuff." And said, "Want you to know that we have the windows open." And man, I'm horrified. I'm saying to myself, "My god, how are these guys gonna make it?" Well, I don't know whether I protested. I doubt that I did, but they said, "Well, whatever." They said, "We'll do all right." They said, "We got enough clothes on." I said, "Okay." That room was so cold, but we got through the night. We got up. That's one of the things imprinted in my memory, that I had one hell of a time thinking about how that would be. And I assume that this was probably the first time we went there. I know we didn't go there before, and I know we came back and played there again. We went back and played at the place again, so I know I was there twice. Again we played the Hunt Club.

Martyn : What was the Hunt Club exactly?

Gagliano : Well, what I'm trying to tell you – I have it as the Hunt Club, and I think that's not the name of the place where we played. I think that was the name of the group that sponsored us. Somewhere along the line, I've read the name of the place where we played, and it wasn't the Hunt Club. It was something else. And I do specifically remember the first time we did it they called it a clambake, the Hunt Club Clambake. And I said, "Gee, I wonder why they're calling it the clambake." He said, "Because we gonna have clams," and this is the first time in my life I ate clams.

Martyn : Well, places like that, men and women came?

Gagliano : Oh, sure, as far as I know. So I'm looking at this and I'm seeing that I have a listing in February for the concerts. Oh, oh, we also played at the Blue Note in St. Louis. That's a club. Then we went from there to a concert at the University of Indiana, of which I have no particular recollection.

Martyn : Where is that? In Bloomington?

Gagliano : Yeah, Bloomington. And then the concert at the and Greencastle event, and I guess we must have slept up in the dormitory again. Again, it's February. And then I have the Sunday engagements, same thing like before. Sunday engagement at the Hunt Club. And then on March the third I have the concert at Ohio State. Now, this must have been the time when – I must have taken a vacation period through all of this – because I remember being at Ohio State. I don't really have any great recollection of the University of Indiana. So I have a notation here. It says, "These engagements were set out in a notebook," that I still have.

Martyn : When George and them were touring and you were with them, if they had an off-night, did they ever go to see anybody else's band?

Gagliano : I remember playing – I remember in – I'm not sure. Probably after the Ohio State concert, I think we were invited to go to someplace, and there was a place where other musicians were and it was sort of like a session going on. That plus all the times when we were with Kershaw and the John Ball people in Miami. But other than that, I don't ever remember intermingling with other bands or other musicians. But then again, I was only with the band on limited situations. So I mean, my experience would not necessarily be typical of what they did.

Martyn : Did they rehearse while they were on the road?

Gagliano : No, I think I mentioned the only time we ever had what was like a rehearsal was with Alton and maybe Lawrence talking to students and trying to learn from them with the school song. And I think we pulled it off successfully one time and then another time, they just blew it off, so then we played "Beautiful Ohio" as a – that's a waltz, isn't it?

Martyn : Yeah.

Gagliano : Yeah, well, that's what we adopted and it went over all right.

Martyn : So George wasn't big on rehearsals all the time you were in the band, then.

Gagliano : No, not to my – no. I know I gave somebody a flip answer once who asked me, "Did the band ever rehearse?" And I said, "Rehearse? Man, you've got to be kidding me." No, they probably did on their own, but not in a formality. When we went on these sessions, when we went on these concerts, the only thing that would account for a rehearsal would be when we would work out some of the physical details of how to put on a funeral scene.

Martyn : Whose idea was that?

Gagliano : Well, I don't know. It could have been me.

Martyn : So they were doing it that early then?

Gagliano : I would have thought so, because George and them. I don't think it ever occurred to them to do this. So I have a belief that I probably formulated it and I probably announced it. I can tell you very definitely that I was on the record in Miami when I announced it at the first Miami University concert. I've got to believe, although maybe we did. Maybe we didn't. Must have done it at the University of Cincinnati, which we played first. You know, what could have happened, we could have played Miami first, then gone to Cincinnati on Saturday night and played Cincinnati, and then the next day went to the Newport Yacht Club.

Martyn : Well, no, but it's more the general feeling of what the band was doing on those concerts. I mean, what was the biggest difference to you in listening to them in the concert halls and listening to them at Manny's?

Gagliano : Oh, they were so – well, there's no real logical comparison, because at Manny's they were dealing with a five-piece group playing a limited bunch of tunes for dances, okay. And here we are on a concert stage with seven and sometimes eight players and an audience of over a thousand people that are going bananas within the second number. And I'm sure you must have edited a lot of that stuff out when you did the LPs. And there's no doubt in the world but that the audience reaction is going to spur these guys on. The audience is good and they give them everything.

Martyn : I mean, did they play stronger and harder?

Gagliano : Any musician does. I mean, even beboppers, I'm sure, do, you know. But for George and them, I mean, and especially that these are all white kids, you know. I mean, seeing all these white kids going bananas over a band, you know. But we had a taste of that with the frat clubs and the deb parties, but of course the venue was not nearly as conducive to – but, you know, now, remember the frat club bands led to the engagement at the El Morocco got to be a very boisterous affair.

94

Martyn : Yeah, yeah. Well, it's boisterous music really, isn't it?

Gagliano : Well, you know, you got two things here. You have music critics who will write that the concert setting is not nearly as exhilarating as the setting in a black dance hall. Now, of course, I don't know what their experiences were in a black dance hall. I'll be honest with you, I never had that experience, but I can begin to think about what it might be. But I can't begin to understand how, after having witnessed these concerts and the reaction that we got from these college students, I can't imagine a dance providing quite that level of excitement. But in addition to all that, very seldom did these kind of bands play for black audiences.

Martyn : I mean, I remember talking to Alton about that. He said, "Who in the hell would play for them? They never had any money." He said, "They would pay us off in chitlins." But when you're in Ohio, you're talking introducing the New Orleans funeral sequence, and very well, very expertly, because, I mean, I've played hundreds of funerals, and that's just about how you described it. How did you know enough about it to describe it? Did you ask, or did you go to funerals?

Gagliano : Oh, well, by this time, you know, there was a bunch of guys in the Jazz Club that were parade followers. "Man, where we going? There's going to be a parade next week." So we would go out and we would listen. It was real highlight for me to catch a marching band, and so I became enamored of parade music. I to this day love march music. And so getting to see and hear one of these bands with all of these great musicians was a highlight.

Martyn : And funerals, too, you'd go to?

Gagliano : Oh, yeah, been to a few. Not many, but a few.

Martyn : So you knew what the drill was.

Gagliano : Oh, yeah, I knew generally. I knew generally the technique. The drill, so to speak. I'm not an expert at it. Basically what I did was pretty much impromptu. I don't know how much thought I put into it, but I'm sure George and some of the guys – I sort of told them, "George, I think it would be a great thing for us to introduce the parade tradition to the students." I'm assuming that I did that. We all agreed that we would do it to start the second half of the concert.

Martyn : Why did you start the second half with that?

Gagliano : I think we would have time to get it set up and get Lawrence to strap on the bass drum. I remember specifically we told Lawrence Marrero to take his bass drum with him. So evidently we must have agreed before we went that we were going to try to do something. I'm guessing, but I think and there would be no reason for him to bring the bass drum if we were not going to do that sequence. I don't know whether we had any conversation with John Ball when we set up the first concerts. Maybe it was some kind of a consensus, "Hey, how about doing this?" I don't remember that. As I mentioned to you in the very beginning, the tragedy in all of this is that I can't find all of my original correspondence and other facts from the era, but I noticed this little book that I had made for some reason which I can't recount. But I'm making a listing of several letters. First of all, I'm writing a letter to a friend who was in Minnesota, I believe, and it's dated 8/6/53.

Martyn : Who is the person you're writing to?

Gagliano : It was a young lady that I had met, as I recall, at one of these Newman Club conventions, expressed some interest in the music, and so I was writing a letter to her telling her what we have just done and are proposing to do. So I wrote this letter in August of 1953 and I'm stating that we did a number of college and private concerts and dance, or whatever, parties. All of this took place between the end of February and the beginning of March. We played at the University of Indiana; we played at De Pauw University in Greencastle, Indiana; played at the University of Cincinnati; Miami University; and we played in Chicago at the Hunt Club; and we played in Cincinnati for George Rosenthal. As I had indicated to you earlier, every time we were up in that area, George Rosenthal throws a party and has the band there. The letter is to a young college student. Emily Bednor.

Martyn : And so where is the University of Indiana?

Gagliano : Indiana is in Bloomington. And De Pauw is in Greencastle, Indiana. So all of these, you know, within several hundred miles of each other. University of Cincinnati, Miami.

Martyn : Where is the University of Cincinnati?

Gagliano : In Cincinnati, which is maybe about thirty or forty miles from Oxford, Ohio, where Miami is. And as I told you earlier, when we had our very first concerts into Ohio that John Ball arranged, this was in 1952.

The first concert that we played was at the University of Cincinnati, and the next night, or whatever, we played at Miami. I'm sure that John Ball brought Cincinnati into the deal to help pay the costs of transportation. I guess we could say the same thing with George Rosenthal, with his party at the yacht club.

So, carrying on in my letter, I'm stating that in May and June we had club dates in Los Angeles. Now, that would probably be at the Beverly Cavern, and San Francisco would probably be Doc Dougherty's Hangover Club. I notice in October we're back in Los Angeles, and I think that is probably the time when Dorothy Tait first heard and saw the band. I think that happened in '53, and then in November and December of that year, the end of '53, we had played at San Francisco, and that was the basic content of that letter.

Then I have another letter which I received. This was from John Ball. This letter is dated August 4, 1952, and it was his letter back to me. Now, John is writing me in August – I'm paraphrasing, of course—essentially saying that our next concert in Ohio, in Oxford, is not whether there will be one, but when. And then he referred to the wonderful three days when the band was in Miami, at Miami University and also refers to being out of town during September when we planned to visit Oxford. Now, I'm not sure what he's talking about there, because if he's writing this letter in August of '52 and he's saying that he's going to be out of town during September when we planned to visit Oxford, and then I go back to my previous letter and it shows that we played at Miami University, so it's possible that John Ball might not have been there. But on the other hand, maybe he made some rearrangement.

So it shows that we did, if my letter is correct, we played at Miami University. So what this note is, for some reason I'm making a little bit of an inventory of some of the letters that I had. And this is the notation of that letter to Miss Bednor and then this is a notation of the letter from John Ball. Then finally I have a letter here that was dated February 8, 1954 to Toni Caccioppo. That's a cousin of mine who lived in Chicago, and I had invited her, as I recall, to be with me at the Hunt Club. That was in 1953. So, in essence, I'm telling her what's in store. "Get yourself ready because we're going to be back in Chicago." "We're going to St. Louis to begin the tour and we're going to be playing at the Blue Note." That must be for a weekend or maybe a week, because then the next item I have is February 24, University of Indiana in Bloomington. Then on February 26, '54, De Pauw University in Greencastle. And I also remember damn near freezing to death, and the men, sleeping up in that dorm with the windows open in February.

Then after the De Pauw University concert, which is on February 26, I have an entry, February 28 and I noted that it's a Sunday. I have a notation, 4:00 p.m. to 9:00 p.m. at the Hunt Club in Chicago.

Martyn : Well, you never know what you're going to find. Let me ask you a couple of questions of around this time here. What would the band do if they had a day off? What would they do?

Gagliano : You mean on the road? They'd knock around. I don't know. I don't even remember what the hell I did.

Martyn : At the concerts, the college concerts, were there any black people came to them

Gagliano : I'm sure there must have been, but it wasn't evident to me one way or the other. My recollection is that, it was basically a vast majority of white people. There could have been blacks, but either I was color-blind on the thing or didn't pay that much attention to it.

Martyn : Well, in those days, did they have segregation in the northern universities?

Gagliano : Oh, no. That's the thing about going north and that's what was interesting to the men in the band, because for the most part, was probably the first exposure to northern, shall we say, integration and the fact that they could go anywhere they wanted to go. They could go into a restaurant. It doesn't have to be like in New Orleans or in the South, where you had colored only and white only.

Martyn : Well, how did they react to the mixing.

Gagliano : I would think they were initially uneasy about it, but once they met their friends and their friends put them at ease. For instance, they had no problem with George Rosenthal. You know, his people knew the band from years back and they were very comfortable with them. When they came into Oxford, Ohio, which was a brand-new experience – well, for me as well as them – the people were so warmly presenting themselves to them and sort of fought over who was going to stay with whom. I mean, initially I'm sure this was a little bit of, shall we say, a pleasant shock.

Martyn : Were the people sincere?

Gagliano : I would be sure that they were, yeah. I didn't recall any superficiality about it.

Martyn : John Ball, was he like the crusader? Did he think he was doing something?

Gagliano : No, I don't think he was a crusader. Now, remember this. John Ball came to New Orleans and met the boys in the band. And at some point in time, and I can't even tell you whether he came to New Orleans for that express purpose or whether it was something else. Given John Ball's – what I recall of his personality, I don't think he would be wasting his time coming to New Orleans without a significant purpose. Now, that's my guess. He has to be what I would

George Lewis

Ragtime rhythm swayed the Res

Alcide "Slow Drag" Pavayeau
Bass

Jim Robinson
Trombone

George Lewis
Clarinet

Photos by
Don Gruelle

The "Res" was packed to capacity. People were standing on chairs or sitting on the tables and the walls could almost be seen going in and out as everyone yelled "Play that thing!" It was one of the greatest jam sessions of the year when the George Lewis Ragtime Jazz Band hit the Res.

The band was officially organized in 1949, when George Lewis began recording under his own name.

The ragtimers, who all have roots deep in the jazz tradition of New Orleans, gave the first of their college concerts at Miami in 1952. Because of the warm reception and cheering success that they had here, the band went on to play at other universities and colleges in the midwest. Since then, the band has had a warm spot in its heart for Miami.

Lawrence Marrero
Banjo

"Kid" Howard
Trumpet

George Lewis Ragtime Band publicity leaflet

call a very typical, shall we say, not timid in any way, but certainly not a flamboyant kind of a person. Very reserved, very traditional. I would call him rather conservative, perhaps, in his living arrangement and his social things. John was interested in history and folklore, folk art, and that's what John definitely expressed to me was his primary interest in the George Lewis Band. I don't know that he used the words, but I think the words that would fit is that the George Lewis Jazz Band was a living fossil of black music, black spirituality and music, in other words, the aspect of black culture that's represented by the old jazz band. He viewed them as authentic folk artists. Well, if you want my appraisal, which may be right and may be almost right, my appraisal is that when I accompanied the band for the first time to cover the Cincinnati and Miami University concerts in Ohio, 1952, I can tell you that this was my first encounter with them in an unsegregated situation. If you remember, the California concerts took place after that.

Martyn : That was the second time.

Gagliano : And then they were thrust into the California society with its liberality, I suppose. And I remember we had an afternoon before the concert, and I remember me and Joe Watkins and Slow Drag and maybe one other guy, I don't know, we were walking the campus, and I'm looking at Drag and, man, he's just wide-eyed. This is something like— obviously, man, he'd just never seen this. I mean, we have beautiful campuses here, okay, but they're really not of the scope of the campuses up in Ohio and Indiana. So they got a sort of an ability to spend a little time in a – it's not like you get on the stage, you play your thing, and you get out of there. No. We have a whole three days in the town, so they're getting a full dose of the smaller – I would put Miami University as in the mid range. Maybe it had a student body of eight to ten, maybe twelve thousand, most. But you go up to Purdue and you go to Indiana, you go to Ohio State, now you're into the twenties and thirty thousand group. And you go down to De Pauw University, which is a smaller maybe they had about four or five thousand students. But here we were in Miami, typical, I guess, middle United States college campus town, and we're walking around the campus looking at the buildings and I'm trying to explain to Drag what this is and what that is. Now, then after that, then the rest of the time we were off, they were with their respective family hosts.

Martyn : Well, who stayed with who?

Gagliano : I don't remember. I only remember that I stayed with John Ball, and I think George was with John Ball. I know Reverend Kershaw took on two of them. I think it was either Jim, Drag – two of the three, so Jim, Drag, and Joe Watkins. And then the other guys, I don't know where Alton – I don't know where they stayed. For instance, I can't remember any names from that situation other than John Ball and Dr. Kershaw.

Martyn : You were saying that John Ball regarded them as sort of folk artists.

Gagliano : That's the way he expressed it to me.

Martyn : But what did they regard themselves as, George and the band?

Gagliano : New Orleans musicians trying to scratch out a living. In terms of folklore, I would think they wouldn't really know what that was.

Martyn : Did they ever believe – well, this is a weird question. It's not a question. It's more of a statement, and then you give me what you think of it. I know in George's later years, when I toured with him the second time, not the first time, the second time, he came out with this speech about – on and on and on and on. It was about evergreens, and he was liking them to people's love of his music to evergreen trees and stuff like this. He told me. I said, "George, where'd you get that stuff?" "Oh, Miss Tait gave me that. I had to learn all that." I said, "Jesus. Is that what you feel?" He said, "I don't know what they're talking about, but I just recited it," and that he did, you know. And on one of the records from Bakersfield, the Blue Note record, George says, "Well, we certainly glad to be here," or something. He says, "We're the last of the New Orleans jazz bands." Well, that sounded like outside influence. Let's be kind, you know.

Gagliano : Yeah, that might fly in Bakersfield.

Martyn : Yeah. But did George ever think he was representing a folk art.

Gagliano : Well, certainly not in the beginning, okay. I'll give you what is my opinion of him. The first concerts that we played up in the mid USA, these were awakenings to the band, and I must admit it was an awakening to me. Now, I am born and bred, just like George Lewis, in New Orleans. I'm taking jazz music as a fact of life for us, nothing extraordinary, great to listen to, beautiful music, great to dance to, but part of our New Orleans culture, okay? So John Ball comes into the scene and he's a very cultured gentleman from Ohio, college professor, and apparently, as we came to find out, he was the director of the Archive of Ohio Folklore. So he was a folklorist. So during our exposure to John, it became clear that he considered the George Lewis Band to be a prime example of folklore, of the folk art, music arts of the southern Negro, and more specifically, the New Orleans black community. Then he expressed that to the guys. He

98

gave me the same belief. I accepted it. And as I look back on it, he's absolutely right.

So after we had been up there, we toured the campus, we saw the archive or whatever and we saw the reaction that we get, I said, "You know damn well we must be great folk art." Not in the sense of Pete Seeger or Joan Baez – who were mainly protesters. No, we were the purveyor of the daily music expression of the New Orleans black.

Martyn : We were going to talk a bit about Reverend Kershaw. What kind of a man was he?

Gagliano : Well, here again, John Ball, as I indicated, is very sort of straight-laced, college professor type, say in his mid-forties, well dressed, well spoken, married, living in the community. Dr. Kershaw was an Episcopal rector. He had been the rector of the Holy Trinity Church, or Cathedral, if you want to call it that, in Oxford. I guess in terms of the bigger Episcopal parishes, that would have been a relatively small one. But my recollection is that when he left Oxford, he went to Boston and became the rector of a major Episcopal cathedral in Boston.

Martyn : Did he think about the band the same way as John Ball did?

Gagliano : Oh yes. Probably thought of it the same way. Yeah, I would think so, and he also, of course, being a clergyman, he was particularly interested in their playing of the spirituals. And of course, almost immediately he says, "I want you fellows to come and play at my church."

Martyn : Were you at that first church session?

Gagliano : As I recollect, I was there, of course.

Martyn : What was that? Fifty-three, wasn't it?

Gagliano : That was the first time.

Martyn : What did the band think when they'd go to play.

Gagliano : That was all part of their awakening to a social system that they had never been deeply exposed to, although that's not to say that there were elements of society in New Orleans that was every bit as prestigious as what they had there. But in New Orleans, they never had any access to it. But to be revered for what you are doing in your music, your music being accepted was a great thing to them. And later on, I guess they began to understand about the idea of it being art. But art never would have occurred to them earlier on because their music is a part of their life and part of a way to escape the drudgery in the South.

Martyn : When they did the first church service, it was quite an unusual happening, I suppose.

Gagliano : Yes, it was an unusual happening.

Martyn : What was more unusual, that it was a colored band, or that it was a jazz band? What was the most unusual facet of it?

Gagliano : I don't know that that would have made a difference. Maybe. No, I guess it made a difference. Maybe I'm giving these folks a little bit too much credit for their liberality, but I guess when you think of it in a social sense, I guess the social divide between the blacks, aside from being a musician, and the high church Episcopalian are pretty broad, and so here you have this clergyman, very staid gentleman, tall, as I remember, very tall and had an imposing presence, and he's sort of basically fawning over these guys, not in an offensive way, but expressing to them his affection for what they are and what they are presenting and to incorporate into their music a spiritual dimension, because we were able to play for him at least eight to ten spirituals which we played regularly, and that just blew him off and – I mean blew him out.

Martyn : Well, how did the audience respond to it?

Gagliano : Well, there was no response. My recollection is the band played, and I don't remember anybody breaking up the aura of spirituality there by clapping and all of that. They just sat there and listened.

Martyn : Which would have been about the opposite in black churches in New Orleans.

Gagliano : And of course, Kershaw would get up and try to explain to his congregation who these men were and what their music really is. And he says, "You know, as a real dimension in their music is a spiritual strain that you'll be delighted to hear." And these guys are living with all of this. This is the funeral music they were playing. A lot of it was the funeral music, so it was second nature to them. And even in the forties, there was still this feeling that jazz was a sort of a sinful-type music, okay? And I think this was part of Kershaw's crusade to try to get that kind of a thought out of people's minds, at least in his congregation.

Martyn : Was he a crusader?

Gagliano : No, I don't think he was a crusader in the sense that we've had crusaders.

Martyn : Bill Russell told me that Gene Williams literally thought that jazz, if exploited and brought to the people, would stop wars. He literally thought that would stop wars. It would stop, you know – it would rectify all of the social injustices and all of the – you know. But that was Gene Williams. George and them did they like Reverend Kershaw?

Gagliano : Oh, absolutely, from what I gathered. Sure, as a reverend. And, you know, later on I noticed in some of the writings that I have seen that they referred to the Reverend Kershaw as the chaplain of the band. I suspect that that was a creation of Dorothy Tait.

Martyn : So were there any arguments in the band when they were on the road? Did they argue any about things?

Gagliano : I don't recall any. I'm sure there were later on. In the beginning, we were so intent on trying to recapture the opportunity lost with Bunk because of Bunk's attitude.

Martyn : It begs this next question. When did, and did he, in fact, when did George think, "I've now passed where I was with Bunk"?

Gagliano : Never did express any of that to me. You mean that he now surpassed Bunk in reputation?

Martyn : Do you think he thought, "Well, I'm doing better now than I was with Bunk"?

Gagliano : Oh, absolutely they were doing better, because there was more cohesion in the band, and they didn't have to deal with this divisiveness and the jealousy that apparently was sort of a hallmark of Bunk.

Martyn : In later years Alan Jaffe toured the colleges with the Preservation Hall Band. But he learned as he earned. He didn't know that much about jazz coming in, you know. And all the groundwork had been done by bands like you guys touring the college circuit.

Gagliano : The road was already there.

Martyn : Yeah, so he didn't have a hard road. I mean, I know Jaffe, when he came here, he used to ride a bicycle for

Bunk Johnson with Jim Robinson and George Lewis at the Stuyvesant Casino N.Y.C. – 1946

D.H. Holmes delivering bits and pieces to people, you know. But it wasn't long before he made it, and good luck to him. I mean, I knew the musicians. I didn't know him. I got to know him later on because he was right across from Bill Russell, you know. Bill was directly across the street on St. Peter, and he would come over there and ask us who we thought would work with who to put this one with that one. Sometimes "Don't put them together. Christ, you'll never get anything out of them two. They don't get along. They hate each other." I mean like Kid Thomas and Jim Robinson didn't like each other. Neither one of them liked the other one's playing. They didn't like each other as people. So don't fool with that, you know. In later years – I don't know whether you even know this, but none of the George Lewis Band – I'm talking, let's see, Howard, Jim Crow , Joe Watkins and ....

Gagliano : Purnell?

Martyn : No, Purnell wasn't here. Slow Drag. They wouldn't work for George. Neither one of them would work for George like before, and Jaffe wanted to put that band together. But George said, "Well, I'll be damned if you put out in my name and they don't want to work for me. The hell with them." And they said, "Well, the hell with him." So they winded up putting the – and I don't know the ins and outs, but I do know this is a fact. They put the band Emanuel Sayles' New Orleans All Stars, for the simple reason that those four wouldn't work for George. Now, what had caused that, what causes rifts between people who ....

Gagliano : Now, which four was that?

Martyn : It was Howard, Jim, Slow Drag, and Joe Watkins. Yeah. Neither one of them would work for George of the four of them, so that's why they got Sayles. And George ran the band. It's the funniest thing. George would tell them such and such.

Gagliano : Wait a minute. You mean George was playing?

Martyn : Yeah, George was playing.

Gagliano : Well, if they wouldn't play under him that's crazy.

Martyn : I mean, I was there. I know that that happened. I know it happened because I was there when Jaffe was talking to Sayles about being the leader. This was regular at the Preservation Hall. They wouldn't play. Neither of those four would play. I mean, Drag was the least of the protesters and he couldn't really understand.

Gagliano : I guess he was following the guys.

Martyn : Yeah.

Gagliano : So what you're telling me was there was a schism among the guys, but not big enough that they wouldn't play with him.

Martyn : Oh, no, they'd play with him. They just didn't want to be the George Lewis Band. So don't ask why. I don't know why, and George never—well, of all the people, George was the one I knew. I spent more hours in George's company, but in a way I knew him least. I don't know whether you found this at all about him. He was very hard to get to know.

Gagliano : Yeah, I guess I would be in the same position. You know, I talked to George on a limited basis, but, you know, I can tell you this, the last time that I remember seeing George was when he came back from some trip. I met him at the train station. This was probably after Jeanette had died and that was when he introduced me to Valetta.

Martyn : That was his third wife?

Gagliano : His third wife. And I'm taken aback, because I'm not aware of it.

Martyn : She was at the station with you, but you didn't know each other.

Gagliano : My recollection is that we were going in and meet George Lewis, but I don't know. It's a meeting. And I put it in the context of one of the railroad stations, and I'm meeting George and I'm meeting Valetta. Now, it had to be in the early part of '55. That seems to me to be the last time that I really saw George and had any conversation with him. And then after that, that was it. He never did call me. I never did call him. I'm deep in law school. Dorothy Tait is now doing the stuff. She don't communicate with me, and that's it. By this time, this would be my last involvement with the George Lewis Band.

And you know, you talk about how our relationship was, what I thought it was, how good and all of that? Yet I think back and I have one artifact remaining. It's a Christmas card I got from Lawrence Marrero, 1957. I don't have anything from George. The only other thing I had was I still had the banjo that Lawrence had sold, and I had Drag's homemade bass, which I decided to donate to the Jazz Museum.

Chapter 6
"CHANGE OF MANAGEMENT"

Martyn : We ought to talk about Dorothy Tait. She took over from you. Was it a transfer of power or transfer of work or transfer of pain-in-the-ass bookings? Was it a friendly one?

Gagliano : Yeah. Well, basically, what really happened, as best as I can remember and reconstruct from my notes, was that Dorothy heard the band for the first time at the Beverly Garden engagement in October, 1953, and probably went to hear them at our engagement at the Hangover Club which extended into December. She talked to George about doing a concert in Bakersfield, California where she lived, before returning home after the Hangover engagement. George gave her my phone number and told her to call me to see if something could be worked out, and he would be agreeable to whatever we could work out. She did call me, told me she loved the band and wanted to help in getting additional engagements for the band, starting with a concert in Bakersfield, and she would handle the details. She described herself as a newspaper journalist and felt she had the necessary connections to make the arrangements and also the enthusiasm to pull it off. She couldn't pull it off within the time frame, but wanted to work out something with me in 1954, and I encouraged her to do so. I told her that I was already working on an extended college tour for February and March in 1954, and return club engagements in Los Angeles and San Francisco for the fall. I specifically remember accompanying the band on the Feb-March '54 tour, probably using up my vacation time, and I don't remember any involvement by Dorothy Tait, either in arranging or accompanying the tour. Then, in mid-summer of 1954, important events occurred that would radically change my future involvement with the band, and ultimately bring Dorothy Tait in as my successor as business manager of the band – I decided to resign my position as a construction engineer and enter the Loyola University Law School in New Orleans for the fall semester beginning in September 1954. Now, being in law school, I'm probably stepping away and Dorothy Tait came in on a co-management arrangement, which ultimately led to an ill-fated – I call it an ill-fated tour. It had to be in 1955, which was planned almost entirely by Dorothy, using my prior contacts – it started in Bakersfield, then on to Ohio, and then New York, where George got deathly sick while playing at Childs-Paramount in New York; the tour ended in Boston, without George, but with others sitting in on clarinet. At the end of the tour, she called me and stated that she would be coming to New Orleans to see George, and talk to me about the situation. She came through New Orleans and when I met her – you know this is hazy to me. All I can remember is that she came to New Orleans, met with me to give me some of the details of the tour, and told me she was out of money, and asked me for a loan to get back to California. I recall scraping up $300.00 which she said would be a loan, but turned out to be a gift. It would be a number of years before I would again hear from Dorothy.

Martyn : But had you met her before?

Gagliano : No. I talked to her on the telephone. A lot of what I did in managing the band was on the telephone.

Martyn : How expensive was the telephone in those days to make long-distance calls?

Gagliano : You know, when you're in business this is a necessary expense.

Martyn : Who paid the telephone bills for the band? Did the band pay it? You paid it? George?

Gagliano : Well, the band didn't have any phone. I had a phone for the band at my home, but I suspect it was my family's phone. I don't recall ever having a separate phone, and I'm not sure whether my family got reimbursed or not. I don't remember.

Martyn : Nothing changes much, does it? Did you have business cards?

Gagliano : Oh yes, I had business cards.

Martyn : Did it have your number on it, and George?

Gagliano : I had stationery.

Martyn : Did it have both you and George's number, or just yours?

Gagliano : No, probably just mine.

Martyn : Getting back to Miss Tait. You hadn't met her. You talked with her on the telephone.

Gagliano : You asked me the question about the transition – it just happened. It was not any kind of a dramatic event. It was that I gradually pulled away. She was there. She wanted it and I just let her have it.

Martyn : Was she pushing to get in.

Gagliano : My friends in Ohio, who came back, you know, called me from time. And the word came back that she thought I was an Uncle Tom and that sort of thing.

Martyn : Why did she think that?

Gagliano : I'm getting this from either John Ball or I'm getting it from Reverend Kershaw or somebody that's calling me when the band went back up there, when Dorothy brought them there. And they were not at all happy with Dorothy Tait. That's all I can tell you.

Martyn : I know that lots of them didn't like her. Alton couldn't stand her.

Nick Gagliano's business card for the band

Nick Gagliano in the mid-1950s

Gagliano : Yeah, they didn't like her and they were calling me. But, you know, I had to welcome Dorothy Tait, because she was the person who was willing – I don't care what anybody might say about her, okay, but she had some smarts. Now, you've got to understand she was a newspaper person. I had to believe that she was somebody who was responsible. There's no doubt that she fell in love with the band. So what I'm getting at, though, as it related to me, this was a way in which I could gracefully pull away from it because I was now changing careers. I'm in the middle of law school. I've still got another year and a half to go, and I've got to start all over. I'm still a single man. I'm living at home with my family. I didn't have any particular amount of money that I had saved up from my work as an engineer, and thank God for my family that they were willing to keep me on and basically support me. My only income was what I could earn during the summer vacation at law school.

Martyn : When did you marry Marilyn?

Gagliano : I married Marilyn in 1958 after I had graduated from law school and while I was on the law school faculty at Rutgers University Law School in Newark, New York; and co-incidentally learned that the George Lewis Jazz Band would be playing a short-term engagement at the Stuyvesant Casino in New York City in the early part of 1959, and I made a surprise and very pleasant visit with George and the other regulars in the band and introduced them to Marilyn and Marilyn to the band, it was most enjoyable. That was the last time that I heard the George Lewis jazz Band in person, and it was especially memorable because it was at the Stuyvesant Casino, which was really a legendary place for me, as well as for the band.

103

Martyn : Who was in the band then? Howard, Jim Crow, George?

Gagliano : Yeah. I'm not sure whether Lawrence had recovered or not.

Martyn : Because the funny thing but Lawrence, in '59, I believe it was, took a band under his name to Cincinnati with Ernie Cagnolatti. Remember little Cag? McNeil Breaux and him, Cié Frazier I think.

Gagliano : They didn't want to use George Lewis. As far as I'm concerned, all of the band was there with Kid Howard, Alton and probably Lawrence was there.

Martyn : So then Miss Tait kind of inched her way in or blundered her way in?

Gagliano : No, basically she took over on the 1955 concert tour, which was the one which turned out bad. This was her idea. She was going to start in Bakersfield, and she was going to work her way – she was going to go up to Ohio and play the areas that we had already played, and then ultimately wind up in New York and in Boston. She just apparently was not able to book enough and I wasn't actually involved in it at all. I had sort of turned it over to her. George was willing to do that. I says, "George, it's all right to let her ....?"

Martyn : Do you think George sort of could see you, by your own choice, let's say, trying to pull away from it? Do you think George sensed that?

Gagliano : I would suppose so, because he had to realize that now that I'm in a different position than I was before, that I think he could probably see that I had to pull away.

Martyn : So he was probably glad of somebody stepping in.

Gagliano : Oh, yeah. And as I'm saying, it made it a lot easier for me to pull back because I couldn't have done it anymore. There was no doubt I could not have done and survived law school. It was impossible.

Martyn : She just came and heard the band, to your recollection, somewhere? How did she get involved with it?

Gagliano : No. What happened was, she did first hear the band and I think it was in San Francisco in 1953. This was right before I went to law school. I entered law school in '55, which would be in September of '55. I'm still in my same situation with George in the early part of '55. She had probably contacted me by telephone offering to help. "Can I help? I live here in California." She says, "I'm sure I can help the band." And I said, "Miss Tait," I said, "if you would, that would be very good." I said, "If you want to work with me, that's fine." And I'm sure that we worked together plotting that '55 campaign. All I can tell you at the moment is that I know that she took over the actual shepherding – let's call it shepherding the band, taking care of the day-to-day stuff in the field. And it started with that 1955 concert tour that she says, "Man, we're really going to make it." See, she's acting together with – and I'm saying, "I hope you're right."

Martyn : Do you think she thought there was a bigger, a better chance at the big time than you did for the band.

Gagliano : No, I thought she thought she could bring it to a higher level because she was in a position to devote 100 percent of her time, or I'm assuming that, but maybe I'm wrong. Maybe that's not what she did. But you know, there are a lot of gaps in here I can't fill in. And I don't know, I assume that she accompanied the band all the way on that 1955 tour. I can remember, at the end of it, I think George got sick sometime in 1955.

Martyn : Okay, so you thought that Dorothy sort of maybe had a little more hope that it would go national, the George Lewis Band, than you?

Gagliano : Yeah, she knew that I was limited in what I can do. The only time I was with the band in California was the first time we played the Bull/Norman concert in 1952 and we had that two-week engagement at the Beverly Cavern. That was the only trip that I made with the band to California. But I was still booking the band. I made contact with Doc Daugherty on the telephone and eventually got them the gig at the Club Hangover. That was my goal, to get them into the Hangover, and I think that that's where Dorothy Tait, who lived in Bakersfield, first saw the band in 1953.

Martyn : I know she got them up to Bakersfield to do that concert. Blue Note recorded the concert, didn't they?

Gagliano : What I think happened is, this tour, I'm not sure about it, but the tour must have been put together by her for the latter part of '55. And now by this time I'm starting law school in September of '54. My recollection is that George got sick somewhere either in Boston or New York, and it would have been in the wintertime of '55.

Martyn : When was it Tony Parenti took his place?

Gagliano : Well, that's what I'm thinking about. That's when that happened. And my recollection of it is, it was in the winter of 1955, and I got a telephone call. I'm sure I got a telephone call from her that George was ill, and then she was keeping me abreast of what was going on. As far as engaging Tony Parenti, I had nothing to do with any of that. I'm sure that she and the band got together. I don't know how that happened, but Parenti came in and played.

Martyn : I mean, Parenti was a white guy. He was a New Orleans guy.

Gagliano : Apparently, from what I've read, he knew George from New Orleans. He appreciated George's talent. George apparently appreciated his talent as one of the few white guys that played like he does.

Martyn : Well, I knew Tony and I don't remember him being racially prejudiced, you know. I mean, when I knew him, he was playing in a little trio with Cliff Jackson, who was black, and Zutty Singleton, who we know was black. I don't remember him being so – some of them from here were.

Gagliano : And it may be that he volunteered to take George's place to help the band stay and finish up the engagement. This could have been something that he did. I don't know. And then, of course, after that, when that was all over and they were coming home, that's when Dorothy Tait called me. She says, "Nick, I'm coming home with the rest of the band. Can you see me to talk about things?" I said, "Sure." Basically, she met me – I don't know whether I picked her up, brought her to my family's house, or she came out there in a taxi. I don't know. But I remember talking to her at my family's home, and she was telling me about all of the different things that happened, good and bad, about the tour. She was very much chastened, I think, that the tour didn't meet her expectations financially. And that's when she hit me. She says, "You know, I don't have any money to get back home." She says, "Can you lend me $300?"

Martyn : Well, did you think that was a peculiar request to hit you up for money.

Gagliano : No, I thought she was severely in distress and needed help. That's what I thought, and I didn't hesitate scraping up the money and giving her the money. You know, it was done as a loan, but, you know, I don't know that I had her sign any papers or anything like that.

Martyn : Do you think that she had any more influence on the band than you did? I'm talking about performance-wise. Do she put her take into any of it, said, "George, you really ought to do this," or, "You really ought not to do that"?

Gagliano : I have no way of knowing that. I really don't know. If you want my opinion, based on everything, I would think that she would not have had any more influence. But on the other hand, I have to acknowledge the fact that, where I'm managing the band from afar, she's now doing whatever she's doing in the context of being with the band.

Martyn : She traveled with them.

Gagliano : She traveled with them, and so I've got to believe that maybe she might have attempted to exert more influence, and, you know, it was becoming necessary with guys getting sick and ill and needing replacements. Now, I don't understand what happened when Lawrence got sick. They brought in John Lucas – the trumpet player.

Martyn : Yeah, Johnny Lucas. That was in '55, I think.

Gagliano : But I remember meeting Lucas, Johnny Lucas, at the Bull/Norman concert, and I think he might have played with the band as a guest.

Martyn : You couldn't forget meeting him. He was in a wheelchair and had a little trumpet specially made. He was a fabulous guy. He was a good friend of mine, Johnny, and till the day he died, he loved George and the band.

Gagliano : Let me tell you. As things ultimately turned out, during George's last days, Dorothy was here for him. She tried her best, as far as I could see, to set up some kind of financial security for George and his family. Out of the clear blue, you know, I don't know when it was, I guess it was in the mid-sixties, she's calling me on the telephone, "Nick, this is Dorothy Tait." I said, "Well, hello, Dorothy."

By this time, I'm practicing law here in New Orleans and she apparently knows that. So she says, "Nick, I would like to ask you, would you be willing to be a trustee on a trust that I'm setting up for George and his family?" I said, "Well, yeah. I mean, does George want me to be a trustee?" "Well, yeah". She says, "What I'm trying to do," she says, "you know I wrote this novel, *Five Smooth Stones*." I've read parts of it. They said George Lewis is the inspiration, but I mean, it's so far out, so far different from George's lifestyle. But in any event, she said, "I'm trying to sell the movie rights to *Five Smooth Stones*, and if I do, I will have the money to set up this trust. But in the meantime, I'm going to set it up with a minimum amount of cash, just to get it going. Your co-trustee would be my lawyer," or the bank, I forget, "out here in California, and you would be the trustee in Louisiana." So this is coming to me out of the clear blue. I hadn't heard from this woman in ten years, okay, and I hadn't heard from George in ten years. Then when she came to town, she actually – I seem to think it was her who instigated me meeting with George to write his will.

Martyn : Why did she sort of take over all these personal things?

Gagliano : Well, I think, by this time she had tried to do her best to get the band – I thought she was instrumental in the getting the band to Europe, but maybe she wasn't.

Martyn : Oh, I think she was. Let me see. He did, first, a solo tour but then that was in '57. Then in '59, he came back with the six-piece band, which was Howard, Jim, George, Joe Robichaux, Slow Drag, and Joe Watkins, and then he came back in '65 to work a tour with my band. And then he came back the year before he died, which might have been '68. I can't remember.

Dorothy Tait, was not instrumental in the latter two, because they called me from this organization, the Manchester Sports, managed by L.C. Jenkins, and they said they would like to tour George Lewis and they would like to put him with my band. Well, I was overjoyed, you know. It was great. But they said, "How would we do this?" I said, "Well, I know you have to call Miss Tait." I said, "I'll call George." I knew he would be at home at that time. George said "Well, man, well, you got to talk to Miss Tait. No sense me telling you nothing. You got to talk to Miss Tait." So I said, "All right. have you got her number?" He said, "Yeah, just a minute," and he gave me the number. And then I thought, well, let them talk to Miss Tait. I mean, I didn't know her from the tour. She came in '59, she came with the band. I know that. But I didn't get to talk to her. '59, I was seventeen, see? But when it came in '65 to tour with my band, I was twenty-four and I've got more of a business head on me and all this. So I know she was not instrumental in bringing him for the last two tours of Europe, but I think she must have been – I'm trying to think. They did it in Denmark with Anders Dyrup, I think his name was. That may be a booking agency.

Gagliano : But be that as it may, I would think that she had to make the arrangements. I'm certain, because George wouldn't do that.

Martyn : The "Call him George" book. Oh, just let me look and see when it would be published.

Okay, here, 1961. I don't remember this being copyrighted in '61, but I don't remember – I'd say it would have been '64 when this book came out, but it says "Copyrighted in '61 and '69, books by Call Him George and Five Smooth Stones." Why she used a nickname, I don't know. I really don't.

Gagliano : I think Fairbairn was her middle name.

Dorothy Tait with George Lewis

Martyn : Might be. I never thought about that.

Gagliano : It could have been that Tait was a married name and Fairbairn was her family name.

Martyn : And then she used another one, Jay Allison Stewart. Who in the heck was that?

Gagliano : Yeah, but that was in England. That was the English publication.

Martyn : Who asked you to do the will? George or Miss Tait?

Gagliano : Miss Tait. She said, "I would like to have you have a reunion with George and I would like for him to talk to you, and I'd like for you to do a will for him." I said, "Fine, Dorothy." I mean, I didn't have any rancor toward anybody. And as far as a reunion, I guess neither one of us had made any effort to contact the other when we drifted apart. It's unfortunate, but that's the way it was. I guess it's as much my fault as it was George's, but George didn't make any effort to contact me and I didn't make any effort to contact him once Mrs. Tait came in and took over most of the stuff.

Martyn : Would she pick your brains at all?

Gagliano : No. No, no, no. Well, maybe in that first thing, but after that, no, never did. No, she took over, and basically this is what the people that were writing me from Ohio says, "She's going to take over the band." I said, "That's fine."

Let her do it. I mean, if George wants her to do it, that's fine with me. That gives me a clean out.

Martyn : Well, let me ask you this. When you were managing the band's affairs, did you push George in any way to say, "You're the leader and they're just side men"? Did you say, "George, you've got to remember it's you that's drawing the people, not the band," or anything like that?

106

Gagliano : No, I don't remember that, and I don't remember George ever trying to say that. And as I told you, we had set up the band as a cooperative group.

Martyn : But I do know Miss Tait put ideas in George's head ....

Gagliano : Oh, I don't doubt that.

Martyn : .... ideas of grandeur that say, "Well, George, it's you the people are coming to see. The band is only a secondary thing," and the band begrudges that because Alton told me that. I mean, Jim, you couldn't – well, you know Jim. He made no sense.

Gagliano : I'll give you my opinion. George could have ultimately made it with any other group of musicians, probably. I don't know that he could have done it as well without his homegrown buddies, okay? And as far as I was concerned, I was managing the band. Now, my contact was George, my principal was George, but I never did in any way, shape, or form undercut the importance of the other guys. And I can only say the fact that I talked George into making this group a cooperative group when I had it and everybody was going to share if we ever hit it big, that's the way we were going to do it. Now, maybe that was the wrong way because maybe that did undercut George's influence, or certainly would have undercut his options, you know. But George and the band, they were so on the same page, for the most part, while I was with them. Maybe later on when Miss Tait had it, maybe she tried to alienate some of the guys.

Martyn : I don't think it was so much alienated them, from talking to the ones I talked to. It was more like she was telling George, "Well, don't forget, it's your band. You're the one the people come to see. They don't come to see the band. They don't care who plays in the band."

Gagliano : Well, you know, there is some truth to that.

Martyn : I wonder when the idea came to her to do that book, which was great, because it was just what he needed..

Gagliano : Yes. I don't have any idea. She never called me. She never told me anything about this book. She never talked to me about what my role was. She knew it, I guess. She must have figured out that she knew everything that I would have known.

Martyn : A lot of that book is devoted to the African stuff. That's the part I don't particularly go for that much in the book.

Gagliano : Well, you know, let me tell you. I'm very indebted to her for doing that. I liked that part. She was overdramatic with it. I will admit that.

Martyn : I mean, what black people in New Orleans can tell you about their people in Africa? I met very few of them.

Gagliano : Well, apparently Alice Zenon was a very unique woman. All of this stuff had to come from Alice. I've got to believe that all of the genealogical stuff she has in here had to come from Alice. Now, maybe she did some individual research while she was here, but I don't have any idea of what she did in creating this book. She never talked to me. So I know nothing about how she did it, when she did it, but evidently she had to spend a lot of time here in New Orleans interviewing, talking to George, talking to Jeanette, talking to, primarily, Alice Zenon, because she would be the only link to Urania and Zaire. She's the only link. As a New Orleans native, I think it sounds pretty believable the way it came out. If you asked me, I would say perhaps at first she was in love with the music of the band, but then I think she got, like a lot of women I know, to fall in love with George. Because George represents something that, to an average woman, he's like something that brings out their mothering instinct. You know, he's so little and you've got to take care of him, but he's very kind and very thoughtful.

Martyn : I mean, and he was very well dressed that I can remember. If you went into his room an hour before the show started, not the dressing room, but before we left the hotel, he was generally cleaning his shoes, you know, and you never saw him take off his tie and let it hang down or anything like that. He just never took it off. Once he took off his jacket. It was so hot in this place. I saw him take off his jacket once, but that was all.

Gagliano : Her takeover was total after 1955, okay? So I'm saying I'm reading about all this stuff, George Lewis going to Europe, George Lewis going to Denmark, George Lewis going to Japan. I said, "Jeez, man, Dorothy Tait must have really done a job."

Martyn : I was trying to think – yeah, it was still the original band, without Lawrence, I should think, when she took over, because Howard was still there.

Gagliano : Oh, yeah, when she took over. No, no. Lawrence got ill on that 1954 tour. He came ill. That's when I think he had a stroke. He did recover from the stroke and eventually went back, and then George began to be concerned about Lawrence, as I understood, and he didn't want Lawrence to travel. I think she makes reference to it in her book.

Martyn : What was your impression of her? Was she a smartly dressed woman to you?

Gagliano : I only saw her once, but yeah, she was a reasonably dressed woman. I thought she was not a very attractive lady.

Martyn : She always looked to me like she had a little Indian in her or something. She's here in this picture. She had long hair, but when she came back to tour with us, she had much shorter hair, you know, much shorter hair than that.

Gagliano : Well, I have very little personal recollection of all of that. I thought she was an unremarkable-looking woman. Pleasant, but certainly not physically over-attractive, not ugly.

Martyn : Was she an intelligent woman, do you think?

Gagliano : Oh, of course. She had to be intelligent. You know, she was a newspaperwoman.

Martyn : You said that earlier and I should have asked the question then. Do you know what she actually did as a newspaperwoman?

Gagliano : When she was in Bakersfield and she called me and said, "Look, I work for the newspaper." She was a newspaper journalist. On the other hand, there's not much of a big newspaper in Bakersfield. But that's where she lived. It's sort of like fifty thousand people?

Martyn : Yeah, if you lived in Bakersfield it meant something. Do you think she took the band to another step?

Gagliano : I had to believe that, yes.

Martyn : I think she did. I mean, with all due respect, I think she did, you know. Because as I was saying earlier, I think it was her that got the band to Europe.

Gagliano : All right, but the first time, was it George that went over by himself?

Martyn : Yes.

Gagliano : And she arranged that?

Martyn : I think so. Paddy McKiernan, the guy in Manchester, he's dead now, so we can't ask him, so I've got no way of telling who, but I think that it was her that asked him.

Gagliano : Well, let me modify my opinion of what Dorothy brought to the band. I admired her for bringing them to Europe, broadening their influence, but I had never ever understood her to have made them a lot of money, okay? So if you measure success – and, of course, a true manager of a band would measure the success by how financially successful your work is – then I would have to say she probably didn't help them very much, any more than I did. But at least she got them more notoriety and maybe did set up – maybe did create a little bit of financial independence for George.

Martyn : Well, I will say, having been there all four times George Lewis came to England, which is just the one country, I also went to Belgium; he went to Denmark; he went to Germany, but England, naturally I was there. The last two tours he did was with my band, so obviously I was there. But the first tour, I was there as a customer, if you will, and it was extremely well – they sold out every performance that George made. And when he came back with the band, they sold out every performance.

Gagliano : But you're talking about smaller venues, right?

Martyn : No, The Free Trade Hall in Manchester was over 3,000 seats as were some of the other halls. Most of the others, like the Stoll Theater in London were over 2,000 seats.

We were waiting. We, as young kids, were waiting for George Lewis. It's sort of like when the Beatles came to United States. The young kids were waiting for the Beatles. Well, juxtaposing the situation, it wasn't as big, but it was something like that. We were all waiting for George to come there, waiting. I mean, I was at the reception they had. I think I told you this. Two brass bands played, you know, for George's band, for the whole band, and it was unbelievable.

Gagliano : But did it translate into money?

Martyn : For somebody. I don't think probably for George and the band. I wouldn't know what they got. In the actual tours that George did with me, it was a deal where he worked, let's say, for two nights and a night off, two nights and a night off, that kind of thing. And Miss Tait was absolutely adamant in that, and she was right.

Gagliano : You mean for health reasons?

Martyn : Yeah, for health reasons, because he eventually collapsed on the last tour. He collapsed, and that's another story. But the one thing I'll say about him, he always gave his all, you know. He wasn't any kind of entertainer.

Gagliano : It all came out in his horn.

Martyn : Yeah, absolutely all. Everything, you know. But he worked hard. I mean, he would call numbers. He'd just say, "Breeze E flat." And we'd just come in, and when that ended, "Say Si Si, B flat." You know, I mean, it was just one after the other.

Gagliano : Yeah, every one of our concerts had at least twenty numbers and they weren't three-minute numbers. We talking seven, eight, ten minutes sometimes.

Martyn : Who worked hardest on the bandstand when you were with them? Who worked the hardest, do you think?

Gagliano : I didn't pay that much attention to who did. I would think they all worked hard. Everybody worked. I couldn't pick out, other than George himself, but George was so cool. You know, you didn't get the impression he was overexerting himself. Of course, Drag pulling on his bass would give you the impression. Joe Watkins was never turned loose on the drums. Of course, Jim Robinson, man, he was flailing those big arms, he would do this with the people, and all the people would begin to clap with him. And, of course, Alton was banging away on the piano. But, you know, he was like in the shadows. But he kept going.

Martyn : Well, I don't think I asked you this, Did you ever see George Lewis sweat, perspiration?

Gagliano : Well, can't say that I did.

Martyn : Joe Watkins said, "That little son of a bitch. He never sweats, man. I don't care how hot it gets out in that damn concert hall, he don't ever sweat." That's what Joe said, exactly that. It's almost verbatim. "That little son of a bitch." I mean, I remember when he played with us. I was conscious of what Joe told me, and I'm sitting where Joe sat and I'm looking at him a lot of times and never saw even a bead of sweat on his – and he was blowing like crazy, but I never saw any sweat. Maybe there's a what-do-you-call-it for that, a term, medical term, perhaps, for people who don't sweat. I don't know, but –

Gagliano : Yeah, there is a term for it, but I'm not familiar with it.

Martyn : Well, I never saw that. I mean, I've got to say I never saw it, and no matter what – but I told you I saw him once take off his jacket, once. I've got a picture of him with my band with no jacket on in Belgium.

Gagliano : Yeah, but was his shirt wet?

Martyn : No

Gagliano : He maybe didn't have sweat glands. I can't say that I made an effort to observe that.

Martyn : Well, I wouldn't have done, except Joe was –

Gagliano : He called your attention to it.

Martyn : Being drummers, Joe and I were very friendly, and I loved him anyway. He was fabulous, a fabulous drummer.

Gagliano : But since you asked me my recollection, I can't remember ever seeing George sweat. I tell you, I've seen Howard sweat.

Martyn : Joe would. It would be running down his face.

Gagliano : And I think even Purnell.

Martyn : Yeah, Alton too. It's a weird thing to be talking about, but it's just an interesting thing. I mean, I never saw that, you know, and see, Joe and I had become friends, and then he would tell me a lot of inside stories about George. In fact, I've still got those interviews. I'm going to go back and listen to Joe's interviews because I interviewed him a lot about playing in George's band, naturally, you know.

But I was going to ask you, did Miss Tait, do you think, did it for the same reasons as you? She wasn't stupid enough to think there was any money to be made in it, was she?

Gagliano : Well, she had more grandiose ideas than I did, and, of course, you have to also understand the difference in our experience and in our training. She was a journalist, a newspaper person, and eventually she became a novelist, or maybe she was a novelist before. So her horizons were a lot broader than mine. Her contacts were a lot broader than mine. I'm a little guy here. When I started with George, I'm working with a plumbing company. I'm an estimator and a project manager. We were building small buildings and small commercial buildings. That's what I did and that's the context in which I spent my spare time, managing George Lewis and doing what little I was doing as *Down Beat* correspondent for New Orleans.

Martyn : Were you – how's a way to put it? Did you feel, when Miss Tait took over the band, it was a step up for them, or did you feel, well, "I don't know what she's going to do"?

Gagliano : No, I thought it was – I didn't have any exaggerated notion as to what she could do, and maybe at this point maybe I have a misunderstanding as to how important she was in connection with the European trips. I will acknowledge the fact that, all in all, Dorothy Tait was a positive influence on the band. As for the transition, I was relieved of my part. My personal problem is, I am in the midst of changing my career from one which was, you know, low key in the construction industry, you know, a non-entity, so to speak, now going into law school to become a lawyer and to take advantage of all of the additional things that lawyering can afford a person. But I'm also recognizing the fact that I'm going to be struggling, as it turned out, for two or three years, trying to get established. I had the native intelligence to feel that I could not carry on with the band, doing them justice and, at the same time, try to do what I'm trying to do with regard to my own career. So when Dorothy Tait came on the scene, she came on with my welcome. With my welcome and my cooperation. The 1955 tour was primarily planned by her. She had mapped it out with me over the telephone and all that kind of stuff, and she had a much more grandiose idea as to what could happen, as opposed to what did happen. And, of course, as we all know, the 1955 tour that began in Bakersfield and wound its way up to Boston through Ohio, she was able to take advantage of the contacts that we had made in Ohio. That gave us a mid-country way station between the West Coast and the East Coast. I'm not sure who arranged the Paramount. I think I was involved in setting up the Paramount thing and whatever was in Boston.

Martyn : You mean Childs' Paramount in New York.

Gagliano : Yeah, in New York. She's working from the California end, Bakersfield and supposedly other places she was supposed to get concerts. But she never did, so that, from what I understand, she went Bakersfield, may have gone to L.A. or Frisco. Let's see what the timeline tells us. I'm saying here, "1955, March, extended tour beginning in California, back to the colleges in Ohio, and then on to Childs' restaurant in New York, and then on to Boston."

"This tour was my first plan in conjunction with Dorothy Tait and turned out to be a disaster for a number of reasons, with George nearly dying in New York, Lawrence Marrero getting sick and had to return home until he returned to carry on in the Boston gig. At the end of the tour, Dorothy called me to say she was returning to California via New Orleans and had to talk to me about the tour and future plans. I have some kind of a recollection that I might have met George at the railroad station on his return., I know he had to come back home.

Martyn : He got sick when he was at Childs' Paramount, didn't he?

Gagliano : Yes, yes. Tony Parenti took his place for a while, yeah I think Tony took his place.

Martyn : What was Childs' Paramount? What kind of a place was it?

Gagliano : It was a restaurant. I understand it was a rather large restaurant, and beyond that, that's all I can tell you because I didn't go. I wasn't up there. I did the stuff that I did on the phone.

Martyn : Well, I've seen pictures from Childs' Paramount when Louis Armstrong went there, but George is not in the pictures. They've got Howard, Louis, and Purnell, the three of them, in tuxedos. So they must have worn tuxedos.

Gagliano : I wouldn't doubt that.

Martyn : But I wonder who would have run the band when George was taken sick. Howard?

Gagliano : Couldn't tell you. Because at this point, Tait was with them on the trip. She was basically running the show to whatever extent she could. I remember one of the things that stands out in my mind was the death of Jeanette. I had arranged for the band to be playing on the West Coast. I don't know, I think they were playing in Hollywood, probably either at the Royal Room or at the Beverly Cavern. I don't recall where. And I get a call from Shirley. Well, I say it was Shirley. It could have been from somebody else. But somebody called me, like, after midnight, as I recall.

Martyn : You were here in New Orleans?

Gagliano : In October 1954, I was living with my parents in Lakeview, and I got this call and they said, "You should get in touch with George right away that Jeanette has died." I got whatever information I needed, and I immediately put in a call to the club. I called Joe Watkins. I told Joe, "Break the news to George that Jeanette died." I said, "He should make whatever arrangements he wants to make, come over here, basically to take over the funeral arrangements and all that."

Because at this time in George's life, Shirley was still a young girl. George's mother, Alice Zenon, was still living in the French Quarter, and it was only a couple of years before that they, George and Jeanette and Shirley, had moved over to their house on De Armas Street across the river in Algiers. So at that time, the only people that were living in the house when George would be on tour or playing out of state would be Shirley and Jeanette. I really don't recall all of the details about Jeanette's death, whether it was quick – I got the impression it was quick and unexpected, and apparently, other elements of the family had to come in and help out.

Martyn : What did she die of?

Gagliano : I think it was heart. So George immediately, I guess, made arrangements to come to town and take over.

Martyn : Maybe that was when what's his name took over playing, Clem Raymond took over for a little while playing clarinet. He was a New Orleans guy that lived down the coast. Maybe they played without a clarinet player.

Gagliano : I said that would be October of '54, and what this also is that I'm only now maybe three months into law school. According to my timing of it, Dorothy Tait didn't come into the picture until around 1953 and only because she had seen the band at the Beverly Caverns. She was very much taken up with them and she wanted to bring them to play a concert in Bakersfield. She contacted me by telephone around this time. This was around October of '53, and I noted we could not work out anything in time to extend the California tour. The band returned home with the understanding that she would try to work out something in 1954.

So then we did work out – or I did. I worked out all the details of the 1954 tour, which started in St. Louis at the Blue Note and then we went to University of Indiana, DePauw University, played Chicago, and we didn't play Miami on that occasion, but we did then play at Ohio State.

Martyn : What did George think of being on the road? I mean, what was his general impression of it?

Gagliano : It's hard for me to say. I think he liked it. I think he saw it as an economic opportunity. I don't think he liked the idea – I'm sure it was stressful to him to be away from home, because his mother was frail and Jeanette was by herself with the little girl. So he felt uncomfortable from a family perspective, but this was his work and he had to do it. If you want to improve your financial condition in life, you do what you've got to do. They all felt the same way. They all had a good time getting away from their drudgery daytime jobs, you know. Being out on the road was the big time for them, and they would be meeting new people or they would be seeing new things that they never saw before. I mean, like, the living arrangements with the Ohio people was a revelation to them. I mean, being hosted by these white folks, man, it sort of blew their minds. So I would say their attitude on it was pretty much positive.

Martyn : Was there any one of them that stuck out that they didn't like being on the road or complaining?

Gagliano : Not to me. Not to me, no. But, you know, at that time we weren't going out on the road that often.

Martyn : Then there was a great long period, you told me, where you had no contact with anybody.

Gagliano : Well, I did mention to you that the next time I saw George was in February or sometime in the winter of 1958 when the band went back to the Stuyvesant Casino in New York.

By this time I've graduated from law school, which I graduated from in May of '57.

Martyn : You were married, too?

Gagliano : I was married and I took my first law position as a member of the faculty at Rutgers University law school in Newark, New Jersey. By this time, my wife and I were married on the day after Christmas on the Christmas break, when I was able to come home. Colleges always had the Christmas break, so I used the Christmas break to come home and get married day after Christmas. Got married in the morning. We were on a plane at three o'clock to New York and then we established our first matrimonial home in a sublet apartment in Newark. That put us right across the river from New York, and so we spent a lot of our time going from Newark to New York because Marilyn's brother was a professional dancer. He was on TV as part of the dance ensemble for the Hit Parade program. He was also an understudy on Broadway.

Martyn : What was his name?

Gagliano : Lenny Claret. So Lenny was our conduit for tickets. So we would be going over there, and I remember we had a great Broadway season. I know we went to at least eighteen shows. But the one thing that's important here is that we had this opportunity to go see the band at the Stuyvesant Casino, where they initially had their first brush with fame as part of the Bunk Johnson band in 1945. It was on Twelfth and Second. So this was a great thing for me to tell Marilyn, "Let's go. We're going to go to New York, see the band." And we went to see the band and they were surprised. They didn't know we were up north.

Martyn : Oh, you just walked in?

Gagliano : Just walked in. Man, they were floored, you know, I think. I went over to the band and, "Man, look at Nick, I said, "This is my wife." Met my wife and she met them. We stayed for the evening, and then when it ended we visited.

Martyn : Was Miss Tait there? Did she travel with the band?

Gagliano : Well, she did later on. Well, she was with the band on that '55 tour. Oh, yeah, she traveled, because this was supposed to be her baptism with running the tour.

Chapter 7

"THE TEACHERS IN THE BAND"

Martyn : Did any of the guys in the band have students that you know of?

Gagliano : The only one that I knew about was Lawrence with John Chaffe. I'm sure there were others. Maybe Bill Huntington might have been in that group. But I don't ever remember meeting Bill at this time, and the only reason I remember meeting Chaffe is because later on in life he installed my audio system here in this house, and I have a cousin, a lady cousin, who learned banjo from John Chaffe. I guess in all of these discussions that John indicated to me that he got lessons or whatever would constitute lessons from Lawrence.

Martyn : Well, he told me that Lawrence was a good teacher. Bill Huntington told me the same thing. He said Lawrence wasn't a very technical banjo player, but he would teach you chord progressions and how to achieve a good beat and stuff, whereas in my wildest dreams I can't imagine Slow Drag teaching anybody anything or Jim.

Gagliano : The only one that I knew had, shall we say, protégés would be Lawrence. Now, of course, George developed a whole hell of a lot of protégés, as we know, but I don't remember any of them at that time.

John Chaffe said in April 1960:

I was born in New Orleans March 29th, 1938. None of my family were musicians. I started piano at age eight. The only real teacher I had was Lawrence Marrero. He taught me mostly jazz style and the rudiments of the banjo. He played a straight four beat. Lawrence used this with the George Lewis Band and the whole Rhythm section came together. Lawrence is responsible for any beat I have today. (End of quote)

John Chaffe in the 1950s

Martyn : Well, for instance, just to jump back a minute to when we were talking about Lawrence and John Chaffe taking lessons with Lawrence. When I asked John Chaffe about all this, I said, "Did you feel strange going back to Lawrence's place?" John told me when he went to Lawrence's house, he didn't feel anything amiss going into this completely black neighborhood and sitting there all afternoon playing, he said, but he knew Lawrence felt uneasy about it because he would sort of get up and draw the blinds and stuff, you know, which is kind of strange, really. You'd think, if anything, it would be the white one, the white guy that felt the thing and the black guy who didn't give a hoot. But it was the opposite, what John said.

Gagliano : The blacks were being defensive. They were being defensive. And I think that's part of the reason why – I think John, if he told you this, he put his finger on it.

Martyn : Yeah, he did say this. This is exactly what he said.

Gagliano : The reticence was more from the black than from the white who tried to integrate with black.

Well, I'm a product of my culture. I don't remember any occasion when George ever asked me to come over to his house and have dinner, and there was certainly no occasion when I ever asked George to come to my house for dinner. That would have been – you know – it wouldn't work. So it seems like George and me and the rest of the band sort of followed the time-honored tradition that was operating in Louisiana.

Bill Huntington – Interviewed by Barry Martyn 7/27/00

I only saw Lawrence play live one time before I started taking lessons from him. I really started on the banjo when I met Lawrence. When I first started playing I took piano lessons then my parents, my sister and I moved to Lakeview; to 431 Harrison Avenue which was an upstairs apartment and they couldn't get our piano up the stairs so I had to give up piano. I was always attracted to rhythm. I love listening to drummers and such. I started to play ukulele. My parents were very supportive of my music, especially my sister. She had a job at a music store that was right next to the Jesuit Church and she brought home the Bunk Johnson Victors for me. I was hooked completely. She loved jazz and she told me "You've got to hear this. This is the real thing". I was hooked on the way the rhythm section danced and that's when I fell in love with Lawrence. I said "Man, I've got to find a way to meet this guy." The George Lewis Band had a concert at Congo Square. It was a cool day and we all had overcoats on, I was enthralled. I was completely knocked out. I guess I was around eleven years old. We were leaving the concert and I could see Lawrence walking. I remember breaking with my folks and just running after him and I grabbed him and said, "Please will you teach me? ' He just looked down at me and smiled and said "OK".

My parents loved jazz and once I started playing sessions and going around, my dad would chaperone me. So I first played piano, then ukulele, then I played the banjo for years. I really started on banjo when I met Lawrence. When I asked him about lessons he said, "Yeah, I'll come out". We lived way out in Lakeview and he lived in the ninth ward over on Humanity. He'd have to take numerous buses but he'd come out every Sunday dressed in a three piece suit. It probably took him at least an hour and a half to get there but he'd come out and teach me. I'll never forget, it seemed like a lot of times it was winter or fall he'd wear an overcoat. My mom would take his overcoat, put it on a hangar and he would take his overcoat down, fold it and put it on the floor. I guess it was a racial thing. When we'd have Sunday dinner, it was a family affair. Right after the lessons, we'd have dinner and Lawrence agreed to have dinner but he wouldn't sit at the table with us. Finally after several of these Sundays we all agreed I'd go and sit with him at a little table my mother had fixed for him. I've forgotten what he got paid

for all this, probably five bucks. I got the feeling he felt he was passing something on. With those musicians, even though they loved the music, they probably felt very neglected and hopeless about passing this music on.

Everyone accepted segregation. It was a way of life, but my parents didn't like it and especially my sister didn't like it. There must have been pocket of people who felt the way we did but there was a kind of hopelessness about how we could go about changing it. My dad and me, we got stopped by the cops for being out at Mile´ Barnes house "What the hell you doing out here in this black neighborhood". That was their attitude. My dad and me we weren't trying to organize a movement. Weren't trying to get people to vote; we were just enjoying music. I guess the cops thought these are just some kooks. I mean I had the banjo with me. Lawrence was a super humble sort of guy. When I called him he said, "Oh I can't teach you nothing". But he came out and we first played some blues then we went through a method. I think it was the Nick Melanoff method. I think he never would have called me if I hadn't called him. I don't think he got that many requests for lessons. He was playing the epiphone banjo then, short neck. I borrowed that banjo a few times. See, a lot of times he wasn't working at music. He was moving furniture. He was a very quiet man. He never talked about current affairs; only music. He was a very happy guy but in all those guys there was an undercurrent of sadness. We finally got him to sit at the table with us. I imagine a black guy taking numerous buses out to us with his banjo then walking three blocks from the bus stop to our house. A black man on a Sunday afternoon in the late 1940's. Our neighbors asked us why he was at the house. We told them, "He's a wonderful musician and I'm taking lessons from him." We told them "he's travelled, made recordings and stuff" and that eased some of the tension. Our landlord wanted to evict us. Nobody

Bill Huntington

realized how important this music was and my parents, they and Lawrence, were actually heroic. They said, "Bill is doing something that someday is going to be important to people." I was the only young kid that I saw interested in this music. I would go to Manny's, Luthgens and all the joints. I felt kind of lonely. I had nobody to communicate with.

I'd keep asking Lawrence, "Where's the band going to be?" Reluctantly he finally told me they were playing at Manny's on Benefit and St. Roch. I used to go over there and finally I got up enough courage to sit in. I think I was twelve about then. I remember the place being dingy and I had to go a long way to get there with my dad. We weren't rich folks, we didn't even have an automobile. I remember the first time I sat in. The force of that rhythm section. There was only Drag and Joe Watkins, but to sit there and be a part of that! I felt that I was both on the sidelines of that force and yet a part of it. After I sat in three or four times I really felt part of it.

Later I remember when I saw the band with Alton. He and Lawrence got into it about chords. Alton played a lot of passing chords. Lawrence was calling them "Chinese chords." I tried to learn what Alton was doing so I could play those along and I think Alton kind of liked that. My feeling is what Lawrence did rhythmically transcended all this other stuff. I always thought of the banjo as a rhythm instrument. If you look back at the great rhythm players like Freddie Green with Basie's Band. That was what attracted me to Basie's rhythm section. It had the same pulse as the Lewis band. It was different of course but I think Lawrence will go down as one of the great rhythm men of all time. It's relaxed, his rhythmic stuff was just what he did. His sound meshed with the rhythm section.

Lawrence used a regulator, which is often called a mute, and he put it all the ways up to the top, right underneath the bridge. Also, his wrist was always relaxed, it wasn't a movement from the shoulder it was the wrist. He hit pretty close to the bridge too. It was mostly chords like the C7 the F, the F7, and minor chords. Now and then I think he used a diminished cord. I never saw him play an augmented chord. Lawrence had much bigger hands than mine. At the time, it was in my mind to copy him then later when I heard other banjo players; I realized I didn't have to copy him verbatim. I could do some other things. Lawrence could read simple chords, say the ones he knew, but I think he would have had trouble reading the chords to a song like, say, "Tea For Two". Lawrence, like all these guys was very impressed with technique. He also loved the blues … guitarists like B.B. King and a guy he called "Big Black". I remember George talking about Artie Shaw and people like that and how much he respected them. This whole thing of technical proficiency gets very involved. To me technical proficiency has also something to do with what you're trying to express. See something that's great; what can speed or velocity add to that. Look at Lester Young or Pops, for instance. Never a whole bunch of notes but what they played had such great feeling. Bill Russell said when someone pointed out that George Lewis was not nailing all the chord changes, Bill said "Well I like the dissonance." When I first started playing I just played straight four beats, today I'll listen to where the rhythm sections is. If I feel they're more in two I'll accent beat two and four sometimes. My

Lawrence Marrero

mind is in four/four though. Occasionally at Manny's they'd ask for waltzes, Lawrence would play three equal beats, not boom-ching-ching; boom ching-ching. In a way he was still playing quarter notes. Manny's was a dance hall but I don't remember them playing rumbas and tangos much. On jazz numbers, as soon as that drum and bass got going and it would take them anything between two and three bars to get going – it was great. They locked in, just like a juggernaught. Lawrence was not dexterous in other dance rhythms but if you'd have sat down with him and said, "Play this particular rhythm", he could have learned it, but I don't think there was ever a need in George's band for him to do anything than what he did. I think George's band basically felt they were playing dance music to make people happy.

I remember going to Lawrence's house on Burgundy and he would have Drag play with us. I got Lawrence and Drag to make a recording session with Charlie Merriweather and me. We went up to the old WSMB studio in the Maison Blanche building. We played a blues and "When you were young Maggie." On "Maggie", I kept playing the lead over and over. Here I am doing this and these two rhythm icons just kept on going, I was 13 and Charlie was 12.

It is important to point out the misconceptions about the Lewis band. Critics feel that is was rough, loose, out of tune, etc. The band was an expression of its time .... Joe Watkins played on the ride cymbal (George liked it) Lawrence used a mute on the banjo. Alton interjected comped chords. George, himself, sounded to me like he listened to Goodman and Shaw. That is all came together, was what gave it such a uniqueness. The guys played out of a love for George and the music, not out of illusions of what it ought to be or re-creation of something else. If you thought of jazz as repertory music you hated this band. It was a blues-based and it swung. (End of quote)

Martyn : Bill always understood what the band was about. What they were trying to do.
Gagliano : Yeah, it seems so.
Martyn : All of the band members, through the years gave pointers or tips to young musicians but it seems only Lawrence and George gave actual lessons and got paid for it.

Samuel Charters – December 1950 – "A Reminiscence of George Lewis" Written for this book 2009
What can I say about this gentle, serious, careful, responsive man-who was also one of the most sensitive and gifted musicians I have ever met? A man who certainly as much as anyone else set me on the path that I still am following so many years later? I've written often about him, repeating the same stories I've told many times, about nervously knocking on his door on St Philip Street in New Orleans on a gray December morning in 1950. But I think this time it could be helpful if I filled in a little of the background of the story. What I always say, when I'm asked about that knock on his door, was that I had come for a clarinet lesson.

I had come to New Orleans to find George Lewis and to ask him to give me clarinet lessons, but not in the way that sounds. I wasn't a beginner who needed to have help placing my fingers on the clarinet keys. My uncle, in Pittsburgh, Pennsylvania, had been leading a jazz/dance orchestra since the mid-1920's (my father played the banjo and violin in the band) and when I was nine or ten he passed his first clarinet on to me – a shiny metal instrument that never sounded very good, no matter how hard I practiced on it. I took lessons from the clerk in my grade school, who was a trained musician, and went through the usual series of high school marching bands and classical orchestras. Jazz began early, a better clarinet turned up in Paris in 1948, and the summer before I journeyed to new Orleans I'd led my own traditional band on a summer-long job at a hotel in the California mountains.

But what kind of jazz? And what brought me to St. Philip Street? When I first began listening to jazz in the 1930's there was a small band just with its fluid clarinet style, and there was swing, and first Larry Shields, then Johnny Dodds were immediate models. After World War II, when my family moved to Sacramento, California, I began taking the bus down to Berkeley to hear the most thunderous jazz group I would ever encounter – Lu Watters' Yerba Buena Jazz Band. The band's clarinetist, Bob Helm, became the new model, as well as a friend, and I spent two or three years trying to play as loudly as he was forced to do on their noisy bandstand.

At the same time, I was becoming increasingly dissatisfied with the struggle to sound loud and still play something with more musical sensitivity, and I was conscious there were other ways of playing. It doesn't mean what it would mean today to say that I was listening to everything that was being released on those old 78rpm singles, since so little jazz was being released that it wasn't difficult to hear it all. On the radio I had to be satisfied with half an hour of jazz from San Francisco on Saturday morning, usually devoted to Duke Ellington.

Along with the Eddie Condon sessions, and the Commodore releases, and the reissues of Jelly Roll Morton and Louis Armstrong's Hot Five, I'd also heard the recordings by Bunk Johnson's New Orleans Band made in New York at the time of their engagement at the Stuyvesant Casino in the winter of 1945. It was George's playing that stayed in my ear. I'd listened to the earlier recordings made in New Orleans, but I was put off by the sound quality, and except for the Climax sessions with George and Kid Howard I had problems with the limitations of some of the musicians. It was on the New York recordings that I began to hear George for the first time. One of the advantages of the old 78s was that you could lift up the needle and play anything on the record again, and it was his solo on "Tishomingo Blues" that I listened to over and over again, leaning over the little phonograph in my upstairs bedroom, using a rose thorn from our back garden as a record stylus so I wouldn't wear out the grooves.

What I wanted, when I knocked on George's door, was to learn his way of playing jazz. I didn't think of imitating him – I was hungry to know how to play a melody as he played it. When he came to the door he looked at me quietly and waited for me to say something. By this time a number of people like me had knocked on his door, and I wasn't the first clarinetist who had turned up. Yes, he answered seriously, he could show me some things. If I brought my clarinet the next morning he would see what he could do.

He is still working as a stevedore in the early mornings, and he had to have a nap in the afternoons, but the $5 dollars I would pay him would be useful. I immediately understood what everyone else learned about George – it wasn't only the $5 that mattered to him. George welcomed us because of his belief in the music he was creating and the importance of other people learning what it meant to the story of jazz.

When I returned the next morning he led me to the kitchen, where he'd pulled out two chairs from the table. The room was in shadows but there was a kerosene lamp burning on the table beside us, since at that time there wasn't electricity in the house. He sat us down facing each other in the two chairs, so close that our instruments were only a foot or two from each other. I played a little and told him what I hoped I would learn from him – about melody – about his gift for making a melody sing in a way I'd never heard from another clarinetist. He nodded thoughtfully. We could do that. I always remember his voice as low and softly modulated. I didn't hear anyone else in the house anytime I came for a lesson. Perhaps his wife was working, I didn't think it was my place to ask.

What George suggested was that we should pick some jazz

George Lewis publicity montage

116

pieces that I knew, and I would play the melody in the low register. He would play along with me at first, then he would improvise. I was to play the melody over and over, without improvising myself, listening to what he was playing. For the first few measures, when we began with a familiar piece, I was playing too loudly. His playing, like his voice when he spoke, was quiet, thoughtful, but not introspective. He wasn't playing for himself, he was leaving himself enough space to alter the dynamics of the melody and to make room for any subtle points of emphasis and lyrical shaping that distinguished his style. In a moment I could almost forget I was playing myself, without feeling any concern to change the background I was providing, since there was such a flow of melody from his instrument. It felt as though we were having a quiet conversation, only we were speaking in notes, and we were understanding each other in ways we never could have put into words.

I think it was the third or fourth time that I came to his door that he asked if I would like to try "High Society". Certainly. Like every other clarinetist playing classic jazz I knew the Alphonse Picou chorus. George played the familiar low-register accompaniment melody to the chorus with me, then as I repeated the melody he began his variations. What I heard, to my surprise, was that he didn't begin with Picou's chorus. He began with a different way of phrasing that had the feel of the old standby, but was distinctly his own. He went on for chorus after chorus, the melodies spilling out in a shining cascade in the small shadowy room. I lost count of the number of times I played the chorus melody over and over, but his inspiration never flagged, and I don't remember that he ever repeated himself. I had never heard anything like it, and I realized when he finally signaled me that we were on the last chorus that I would never play anything like it. It was at that moment I stopped thinking of myself as a clarinetist. After a final engagement with my band the night before I was inducted into the Army a few months later, I didn't play the clarinet again.

We sat laughing together as I shook my head at what he'd shown me. Then, as I was leaving, to my surprise he asked me if I would like to sit in with his band at Manny's Tavern the next Friday night. It was the usual restaurant dance job he played on weekends, there was no jazz show, just the ordinary songs the dancers liked to hear. Although I was now thoroughly dismayed at my obvious lack of aptitude as a clarinetist, there was no way I would say no.

The essence of the band I found setting up when I came to the restaurant was the same band that had made the recordings that had brought me to New Orleans, and I had another moment of asking myself what I was doing there. There was a different drummer, Joe Watkins instead of Baby Dodds, and the trumpeter, instead of Bunk, was Lawrence Toca, who wasn't a great jazz lead, but knew hundreds of songs. It was the band I had listened to over and over on those records. Most nights the restaurant only hired the two lead horns, George and either Toca or Coo Coo Talbert on trumpet, but if it looked like there would be a good crowd or if someone would help with the extra salary, the restaurant would also add Jim Robinson, who was already sitting in his chair oiling his trombone slide. The rhythm sections was Slow Drag Pavageau and Lawrence Marrero, with Alton Purnell on the other end of the small bandstand. I sat behind George, between Slow Drag and Joe Watkins. Lawrence was on George's left and I could look over his shoulder. Toca and Jim Robinson were on George's right.

The hours on the bandstand flew past. The dance floor was filled from the first notes to the last, and along the row of tables across the dance floor from us there was continual laughter and jokes from the family parties who came from the neighborhood. I was used to the sound of the band on those 78s, which had been recorded with microphones hovering close, and I hadn't understood that their playing was as softly understated as George's playing in his kitchen. There were no microphones setup on the stage, and the sound of the eight instruments together was no louder than the conversations at the tables near us. It was also, as George had said, just a neighborhood dance night. There were no jazz Standards, no solos, no one in the band stood up to play anything. Unlike Tocca I didn't know all the popular dance tunes but I found that in the comfortable embrace of that rhythm section it wouldn't have mattered if all I played were simple scales. With each piece I felt I was being carried along with them on a yielding cushion of that wonderfully flowing rhythmic pulse. I don't recall much of what we played. I remember the dancers liked "Putting All My Eggs in One Basket" and I seem to remember a somewhat unsteady version of "Song of the Islands." I noticed quickly that Slow Drag was following Lawrence's fingers on the chord changes, and I also noticed that occasionally Lawrence would give a small, sly smile and deliberately play the wrong chords to throw Slow Drag off. George sat with one *leg crossed over the other, listening for requests, the understated lyricism I had found in his playing in my "lessons" filling the small room with its gentle sound.*

If I had only sat with George in his kitchen and then experienced his music on a neighborhood bandstand I would have left New Orleans and sat up in the day coach on the train back to California a somewhat chastened, but satisfied musician. George, however, had much more to give me. I was staying with Dick Allen in his apartment in the back of the house at 1111 Bourbon Street, and one night

Samuel Charters carrying Red Clark's sousaphone – Mardi Gras 1954

a very tired and grimy David Wycoff and Alden Ashforth arrived, having run off from their prep school in New England. They had been drawn to New Orleans by the playing of Emile Barnes, and we sat up nights listening to the piles of 78s Dick had in every corner of the cluttered space. One Sunday afternoon as I was walking along Royal Street I encountered George and Jim in front of the "skyscraper," the old building at 638 Royal Street that for a time had been the French Quarter's tallest building. They were in their best suits, with snap brim hats and handkerchiefs in the jacket pockets. I asked them where they'd been and George said that they were returning from a funeral. Who was it? "It was a trumpet player, Big Bama," George answered. "He was a great trumpet player," Jim added.

Trying not to look confused I nodded and told George that I would be coming by his house the next afternoon. He nodded and said that he was going to be working on the docks early in the morning and he'd have to take a nap, but I could see him later, and with a quiet wave they continued down Royal Street. I was confused because along with listening to every jazz 78-single I could find, I had also read every book there was about the history of jazz – I remember four books were all that we had then – and none of them had mentioned a trumpeter called "Big Bama."

The next afternoon his wife answered the door and told me that George was still in bed, but that he would be glad to see me anyway and she led me to their bedroom. George was sitting up in bed, still in his pajamas, and he gestured to a chair beside the bed. He just was resting a little, since he had a small playing job that night and he didn't like to get too tired. A little hesitantly I said that I had thought I knew a lot about New Orleans jazz history but I'd never heard of Big Bama. Were there other people I didn't know about? George looked over at me and began to talk, and as he talked his stories brought to life a whole panorama of New Orleans music, and beyond it a world of African American culture that I knew nothing about. As the hours passed I felt like a door was swinging open for me, and I knew that somehow I had to go through that door and find what was on the other side. Years later I am still finding a world there that needs to be described and written about, and understood.

Would I have had a different life if I hadn't spent those hours sitting beside George's bed, listening to him talk? I think so. Do I have any regrets that this was the path I followed instead of so many other ways that were open then? None at all. I still think of what those moments of sitting with our two clarinets almost touching in the kitchen on St. Philip Street meant to me as he showed me how a melody could sound and what a song could mean. I wouldn't give up a moment of it. (End of quote)

Martyn : I did a tour with George Lewis. I got paid fairly, but not over-fairly, if you know what I mean.

Gagliano : Well, what kind of money did George actually get, now, for instance, when he was playing with your band?

Martyn : I think it was something like two hundred dollars a night, solo, you know, but that was about the equivalent of six hundred dollars a night now, you know. I forget. I did know once. George never ever spoke about anything much with me. He never spoke much about music, let alone about money. He told me a few things – he was funny. This is quite interesting too, I never thought we'd put it down in the record that much, but he was very hard on drummers.

Gagliano : He really sat on Joe a lot of times.

Martyn : He did me too. It was my band, but I had so much respect for him. I mean, Joe probably would have said, "Stick it up your ...." But he needed the money. I didn't so much need the money, but I just had so much respect for him.

Gagliano : From what I gather, it's very, very – to an instrumentalist, tempo and the technique of the drummer is very significant in what they can do as a soloist. And I suppose that George probably is trying to get the drummer to play in a mode that accentuates his ability.

Martyn : I'll tell you what he wanted from me – cymbals, just cymbals – nothing else. He hated woodblocks. And I even said to him – that was the nearest I came to rebellion – I said, "All the time you were with Baby Dodds ...." He said, "Yeah, Baby Dodds was Baby Dodds. That was then – this is now. You play on the cymbal." So I played the cymbal.

Gagliano : You recall my characterization of the band when they were playing the at these college concerts? Well, you know, everybody – this is one of those rare numbers in our repertoire where every man in the band gets a solo, and that included Drag and it included Joe Watkins. And these college kids are waiting, and here comes Joe. It's his turn. So Joe stays the same. Nothing in the way of deviation.

Martyn : No, Joe wouldn't – I mean, look. I knew Joe very well. Of all of them, Alton was one I knew best. Jim – well, everybody knows Jim. How could you be angry with him? And Drag, well, you couldn't understand anything he said anyway. But I loved the way he played, you know. It was fantastic. I played a Mardi Gras date with Drag once 1961, fourteen hours with him. Enjoyed every minute. I would have still been playing it if I'd had an option.

But Joe was the one I knew the best. Joe was not any kind of technician on the drums. Joe could play – he could get through a waltz, you know, as they played that "Over the Waves" most of the time. But Joe couldn't play a tango or maybe he might stretch it with a rumba because it's not very hard, but he couldn't play a samba or anything like that. I mean, I can play all those things, you know. Cie, he was my teacher. He taught me all those. He said, "You learn all that. It will come in handy," But Joe, no. Joe was strictly – Joe told me George hired him and he said, "I want autentic." Joe called it autenic. "Autenic drumming," and I didn't know what he was talking about at first. Then I realized he meant authentic. He said, "I want to you to play autenic all the time," and that meant Joe was playing on the snare drum with two choruses, then going on the cymbal, not varied at all, you know.

Gagliano : What about the bass drum?

Martyn : Well, always he wanted four-four, George, with me. Well, I knew that's what he wanted from being friends with Joe. I mean, he didn't want the New Orleans way—he didn't want nothing like that. Just straight four to the bar. That's what he wanted. But he was hard on drummers. But I don't know if he was hard on anybody else because he wasn't with my band, perhaps because he could see that I wasn't going to get angry with him and his comments. Perhaps he directed a lot of them at me, or perhaps he had the sense that if he directed them at me, I'd direct them to the rest of the band and then he wouldn't be – I don't know. Don't know what the answer is to that.

Gagliano : Well, when you were on this tour, he definitely regarded you as the leader of the band, didn't he?

Martyn : I told all my band, with any musician we toured with, Andrew Morgan, Percy Humphrey, whoever the hell it would be, I said, "Listen, if he works out as a good leader, leave him do it. If he don't, I'll get in there and take up the slack." I'm talking about the entertainment of the people. But with George, I guess that all I could say is George was a natural leader, as far as I was concerned. He, without saying anything much you knew what he wanted.

Gagliano : There were periods when Kid Howard just couldn't hit the notes and it was occasionally disruptive. I don't ever remember George taking Kid alongside, you know, chastising him or anything. I think the only guy that he ever got on, if he ever got on at all, would have been Joe Watkins, because I guess he had a certain feel for his drummers that he had to keep in line.

Martyn : Well, he liked Joe's playing very much, you know.

Gagliano : I'm sure he did. As long as he played autentic.

Martyn : I never discussed running a band with him. The only thing he said, and it's in my book, even – I remember writing it. He said, "Always keep your band dressed nice." He said, "You do." Well, we wore tuxedos for his tour on every job. He said, "I can see you like to keep your band dressed nice." He said, "Always do that." He said, "Then when you go to work for somebody, you don't look like you need their money."

Chapter 8

"George Lewis' genealogy"

Martyn : So Nick, in Dorothy Tait's book, half that book is going on, it's kind of like 'Roots' by Alex Haley, it's going on about Africa, and I don't know how she could have found all that out, whether it's true, whether it's not true, I don't know. But what did George ever tell you about his mother or his grandmother or his grandfather? Did he ever mention them?

Gagliano : Well, he certainly told me about his mother and, in fact, encouraged me to go visit her. I made several visits to her upstairs apartment, I think on St. Philip Street and found her to be a very delightful person.

Martyn : Could she speak English?

Gagliano : Oh, beautiful. Yeah. She had no problem speaking any English, and understand that she also spoke French very fluently. My situation at the time, I would have been twenty, twenty-one years old, and I think the common ground between me and Miss Alice was the fact that we were both reasonably devout Catholics. That always made me wonder, you know, about George, but at this point I really didn't know anything about George's family history. Oh, I met George first, of course, and then eventually as our relationship grew, and probably at a time when maybe I had already

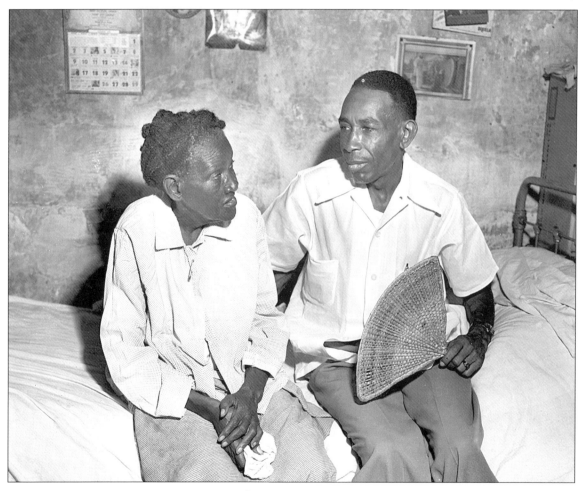

1951 George's mother's room

started working with George trying to help him get bookings, and I think at that point he thought that he'd like to have me meet his mother. He didn't come with me. I don't remember whether he brought me there or told me where it was. There's no way to call because there's no phone or anything. You just had to go.

Think about it. When I went up to visit Miss Alice – I called her Miss Alice – and she had a certain dignity about her that really sort of made me wonder about the physical conditions in which she was living. She had to be at that time – she had to be seventies, or about that. For instance, she had no bathroom facilities. She had to go to an outhouse outside, or she had to do what she had to do in a slop bucket and then have to go out. I

Alice Zeno lived in rear of this house

remember she had a little one of these kerosene stoves that was a source of heat, and I don't remember what she cooked on. But I was appalled at the conditions that she was living in.

Martyn : But George didn't live with her?

Gagliano : No. She had this one-room walkup apartment in the slave quarters of a house.

Martyn : Who lived in the house?

Gagliano : Oh, I have no idea. I just walked down the alley.

Martyn : Did you ring a bell?

Gagliano : Ain't no bell. The only way I could make an appointment with Miss Alice was I said, "George, will you tell your mom I might come up to visit her on Saturday afternoon at such and such a time?" And then he'd say, "Okay, I'll tell her." And I'd go up there, and she'd be waiting on me. I must have visited her maybe, I don't know, three or four or five times, and we would just simply chat. And she apparently worked for many years, although at the time of my visits she may have stopped working – she liked to tell about her relationship with Grace King, one of our renowned educators, and, of course, you know we have Grace King High School in Metairie named after Grace King.

Martyn : Who actually was Grace King? What did she do?

Gagliano : She was a lady who, my understanding was that she was higher up. She was a very renowned educator. She was a white woman, as far as I recall, and I think she traversed in maybe literary circles. She may have been an author of some sort. Then she told me about the other family, the Judge Renshaw family that she'd worked for.

Martyn : White judges or black judges?

Gagliano : All white. As a matter of fact, I had a connection to that family through some of my friends from Tulane University, particularly a member of the Stouse Family. Pierre Stouse was one of my classmates in engineering at Tulane, and he knew Miss Alice.

Martyn : What kind of work would she do for them?

Gagliano : I suppose cooking, taking care of the children, being really part of the household. From what I understand, that's how she got her education. That's how she learned how to speak French.

Martyn : But she would live in or just come home.

Gagliano : I'm not sure about that. Probably not live-in. I don't know that any of these black servant types would have ever been live-in. This is a sociological question I can't answer. I never did ask her, but my feeling would be, no, she did not live in, that she would be a day worker, and she'd go there early and come back home late. And then all during this period, she's trying to take care of George Lewis, too, because she was a single parent at this time. I mean, something happened to her and her husband, I don't know what it was, but apparently she didn't marry well. And it seems like if I give you – this is an impression I had, not based upon any deep understanding – but my impression is that Miss Alice was treated to some of the nicer things in life by the families that she worked for. They introduced her to books, which she never had access to. I think they are the ones who probably taught her how to speak French, because her people were not French. Incidentally, and I know you've got a question coming about how did all of this information get developed about George's genealogy going back to his maternal grandmother, who was the original African who was kidnapped from the Senegal, that's what I remember, and brought up to New Orleans. Getting back to Miss Alice, I think somehow or other she married, but she didn't marry a man that really was to her ultimate liking after she got some of this – a little bit of this refinement from the French family.

Martyn : Oh, it was a French family? It wasn't an American family that taught her how to speak French?

Gagliano : No, no, they were American, but they had French roots. When you talk about New Orleans at that time, there was a French – I will call it a French aristocracy. They looked down on ordinary whites, just like the Creole blacks looked on the black blacks. Seriously. We had a class system here in New Orleans, and I think to some extent it still exists, but at that time the French influence was still very strong. For instance, there was a school down on Franklin Avenue in the city. You may have heard of it. It is an old school down on Franklin Avenue that was named after a Mr. Gayarre, and he was another one of those French people who Alice Zeno knew and she talked about it. She mentioned the fact that she met all of these people at this home where she worked. These folks were probably very caring of Alice, and they didn't treat her like a slave. They treated her more like an estranged – maybe like an orphan dog, trying to introduce her to the better things, books, speaking French, and whatever the traditions are that that family had.

So she liked to talk about all of that, and I'm sitting here listening to all of that, and, of course, I'm also talking to her. She would talk about her religious experience and how she was a devout Catholic, and she'd say, "Oh, man, I don't know about my boy George." And I'm not about to comment on that, you know.

Martyn : How big was she? How tall was she? Taller than you?

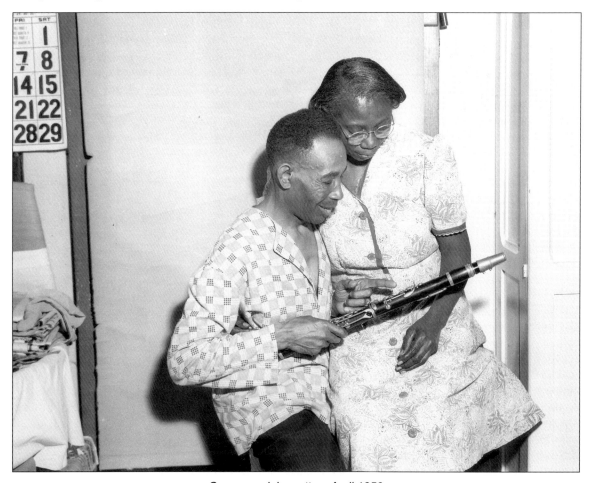

George and Jeanette – April 1950

122

Gagliano : Oh, yeah. Yeah, she would be about as tall as you, but thin.

Martyn : I'm Six-foot-one.

Gagliano : Yeah, about six – five-eight or five-nine. And at the time she looked gaunt. She was definitely a black, black. You could see no white mixture in her bloodline. Alice would be the second American born of her family; the slave lady, then Alice's mother, and then Alice. That's what I remember.

What I remember about the living arrangement with George and Alice, Alice wanted to be by herself. I say, "wanted to be by herself." I presume that. It could also be that the living accommodations of George Lewis at the time could never accommodate her. So she apparently felt it was better for her to be on her own. Of course, as she got older and older, George became, as I remember, more and more concerned about his mother. And after he finally moved into his house, I think it was in 1952, he moved over with just him, Shirley, and Jeanette. Alice is still living in her apartment on St. Philip. George was living, as I remember, on Dauphine Street, and he, Drag, and Lawrence, and whoever else in the group was helping him build his house in Algiers. And I like to think that whatever I did for George as his manager, helped him achieve enough money to allow him to buy the lot where he built his house, eventually allowed him to buy the materials, and then they started to build the house. My understanding is they got to the point where they could occupy it, and he moved over there in 1952. I would think it was in the late fifties before Alice ever moved over there, because you've got to also remember – and she may have moved over there right after Jeanette died. Now, Jeanette died, as I recall, in 19 either '54 or '55. Here it is. October the 8th or 9th, 1954, Jeanette died. So when Jeanette died, that put George in a predicament.

Martyn : Right. Well, there's no getting to Jeanette dying yet, because we haven't even mentioned Jeanette hardly. Let me just go back. So stay with the mother. Was she bent over when you knew her?

Gagliano : No, she was relatively straight, relatively. I mean, she was not really – I would say she was sort of hunched in the shoulder, but I mean she wasn't bent over. Because, remember, she had to fend for herself, and she had to walk up and down a flight of stairs just to get from her room to wherever. If she wanted to go to the grocery store or drugstore or whatever, she had to walk down those steps, she had to go walk to wherever she had to go, she had to come back, walk back, and then she had to walk up there.

Martyn : She was able to do this? Okay? Who did she rent from? Some people who owned the house in the front?

Gagliano : Yeah. I don't know whether the people that lived in the front were tenants or owners.

Martyn : Did you ever see them?

Gagliano : No. Never saw them? Well, I don't have any recollection. I had no reason to. I don't know whether they were white or black.

Martyn : So she'd be standing by the gate?

Gagliano : Not necessarily. She would probably be up in her room, and I would go up there and knock on her door, and she'd let me in.

Martyn : Oh, you could walk in the gate, or she would leave the gate open?

Gagliano : Oh, yeah. Basically you walked down an alley. Probably this would be a situation where there would be a side alley running down the sideline of the house, and you'd open up the gate, you go down the alley, and then you'd go upstairs, knock on her door, and then she'd open it, and I'd go in.

Martyn : You say George wanted you to meet his mother? Why would he want you to do that? Just to be sociable?

Gagliano : I guess to be sociable and maybe to have his mother tell me something about him. I don't know that I would have initiated it, because unless he told me, I wouldn't know that his mother was alive. So somewhere along the line, I found out that his mother was living, and he told me a little bit about her, and somehow or other we came to the conclusion that I'd like to visit her or that maybe George would like me to visit. I'm not sure which.

Martyn : Did she like you?

Gagliano : I thought she did. Well, you know, in talking to her, I'm finding out what her beliefs are and what interests her, so I decided at one point in time before whenever the next visit would be I'd go out and buy her something that would be reminiscent of what we had talked about last time.

Martyn : What did she call you? I know you said George called you Nick. Did she call you Mr. Nick or Nick or what?

Gagliano : I don't really remember. I would presume that she would call me Mr. Nick, but I don't know.

Martyn : Well, did she ever sort of say to you, "Mr. Nick, try and get my boy straight because he's been transgressing"? What was her attitude towards that?

Gagliano : No, I don't think she did. I think when we started talking about religion, I think she would sort of apologize for George, but that was it.

Martyn : "That little devil."

Gagliano : But, no, she dearly loved George, and there was no question in my mind that they were very close.

Martyn : Well, one thing, I'd just like to tell you this, and it doesn't matter if it goes in here because I'm not going to mention who it was. But I remember George saying to me, and I won't mention which one of the band it was, but one of the band's mother was sick, and George said, "Man, that boy deserves everything he get. He doesn't take care of his mother proper." He says, "He doesn't go see his mother enough. He doesn't take care of his mother."

Gagliano : Oh, their relationship was always close, and I think the fact that they lived apart, even though Alice was aged and single, I think it was economic things that kept them apart.

Martyn : Well, wait a minute, before I forget this, you know how we got back together again here, because the lady called from the Library of Congress and those two kids had recorded George's mother singing – do you know who those kids were, or you just know from the same as I do?

Gagliano : Probably the same as you do.

Martyn : So you've never heard the recording or anything?

Gagliano : No. What kind of recording did they make?

Martyn : Well, how this came about was the Library of Congress called me, and they said, "Mr. Martyn, we're trying to locate George Lewis' grandsons." I said, "Well, what is it concerning? What do you want with them?" So they said, "Well, these two boys ...." Not boys. Men, I guess. This is two white boys who when they were young come down and, I don't know, doing a, what the hell they were doing, I don't know, but they went and recorded George's mother singing two, from what I understand, two Creole songs. Now they're old men and they want to donate this to the Library of Congress, you know. Well, there's no pot of gold they are sitting on; I mean nobody cares. You and I are probably the only people that would want to listen to it. Well, I don't know, I shouldn't say that, but anyway. Then the lady says, "So we're trying to locate the two guys who are the grandsons to sign off on the donation." I said, "I don't know how you'd get in touch with them, Graylon and David."

Gagliano : Well, they finally called me.

Martyn : Yeah. Well, then they said – and this is how I came to be back in touch with you because I'd heard you went away for the hurricane and never came back. You know, you can't keep up with everybody.

So she said, the lady from the Library of Congress said, "Mr. Gagliano told us." I said, "What Mr. Gagliano ?" She said, "Nicholas Gagliano ." I said, "Nick Gagliano ? – You know Nick Gagliano ?" She said, "Well, we were in touch with him because of all this." I said, "Well, where is he now?" I said, "He's a friend of mine. I heard he went to – " I don't know where I heard you went. Somebody told me you went to Pittsburgh or somewhere. She said, "He's back." She didn't say he's back. She said, "He lives on Metairie Heights." I said, "Well, I know where he lives."

Gagliano : She called me at my law office. She didn't call me at home.

Martyn : Well, the point was, that's how you and I got back together, and that's where this business of George Lewis' book started. So you never heard the recording

Gagliano : No, she just told me that she needed some kind of a permission and that she needed to get in touch – or she asked me about George Lewis' estate, and I told her that I had handled George Lewis' estate and that I had probated his will, and had the court recognize Shirley as his sole legatee. In essence, in legal language, we put her into possession of George's entire estate, and in the descriptive list of assets, I put in a variety of royalty rights and various recordings. I could not never ever be able to put in there everything that George did, and I would have no idea whether any of them had royalty arrangements or not, but apparently a number of them did.

So I told her that Shirley was George's direct heir, and I said, "Shirley died. I did not handle her estate, but I have seen some of her estate documents. I have dealt partially with the lawyer who handled her estate because he wanted information from me to tell him how to do the judgment of possession in regard to something so I just sent him what I had, and it was at that point that I remembered that the four grandchildren became the heirs of Shirley.

Martyn : Well, we're jumping ahead. Did George's mother ever tell you she recorded a couple of songs?

Gagliano : No.

Martyn : That was later, then.

Gagliano : Yeah. This is something that probably would have happened after Alice moved in with George in Algiers.

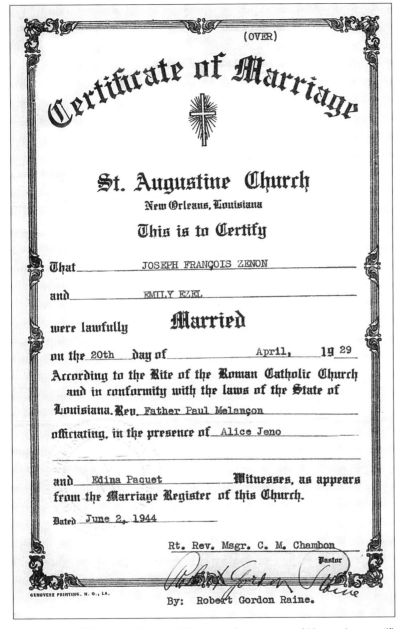

Certificate of Marriage

St. Augustine Church

New Orleans, Louisiana

This is to Certify

That JOSEPH FRANÇOIS ZENON

and EMILY EZEL

were lawfully **Married**

on the 20th day of April, 19 29

According to the Rite of the Roman Catholic Church and in conformity with the laws of the State of Louisiana. Rev. Father Paul Melançon

officiating, in the presence of Alice Jeno

and Edina Paquet Witnesses, as appears from the Marriage Register of this Church.

Dated June 2, 1944

Rt. Rev. Msgr. C. M. Chambon

Pastor

By: Robert Gordon Raine.

GENOVESE PRINTING. N. O., LA.

Martyn : So Alice's name was Alice Zeno?

Gagliano : That was her married name. She married some gentleman named Zenon, spelled it out Z-e-n-o-n. Somewhere along the line, the last N got dropped.

Martyn : Where was he from, New Orleans? Do you know?

Gagliano : I don't know for sure, But I have read that he was from Mandeville, Louisiana, which is directly across Lake Ponchartrain and about 30 miles from New Orleans; at that time there was a ferry that crossed the lake from New Orleans to Mandeville.

Martyn : But, so George at this point he changed his name from Zenon or Zeno to Lewis.

Gagliano : I have a copy of the judgment of court changing his name in my files. I'll make a copy of it. I'll give it to you.

Martyn : That'd be great, yeah, because that would pinpoint the exact time that he changed his name. But Alice never was called Alice Lewis then?

Gagliano : Oh, no. She was always Alice Zeno, and I don't know when she dropped the—or when the N was dropped, when it went from Zenon to Zeno. I have a copy of George Lewis' birth certificate when he was baptized at St. Augustine Church in Treme, and he was baptized Joseph François Zenon.

And if I'm not mistaken, I think I also have a copy of his marriage certificate to Emma Ezele.

Martyn : That's his first wife?

Gagliano : His first wife.

Martyn : Okay, here it is. April 20, 1929. Joseph François Zenon married Emily Ezele. St. Augustine Catholic Church with Alice Zenon – that's his mother – and Adina Paquit as witnesses. Who was Adina Paquit, I don't know?

Gagliano : Not anybody I would know. Probably a friend of some sort. No, he said he had children. Remember I told you about Mildred? Mildred was the one who used to kind of sing with him occasionally.

Martyn : Mary died at five months. William Zeno living. George Zeno living. Joseph Zeno living. The first Mildred died at nineteen days. Emily died at birth.

Gagliano : Well, according to this, there was seven children, three of them died really early.

I found out later reading through my stuff Mildred's married name was Major. She appeared as George brought her on

Form 7—5M—36955

STATE OF LOUISIANA
Civil District Court for the Parish of Orleans

No. 256,565   DIVISION " D "   DOCKET #   5

JOSEPH FRANCOIS ZENO,

versus

EMILY EZEB ZENO.

JUDGMENT

On motion of_____I.S.GAUTREAUX_____, attorney for

plaintiff, and on producing to the Court due proof in support of the plaintiff's demands,

the Court considering the law and the evidence to be in favor of the plaintiff, for the reasons

orally assigned.

IT IS ORDERED, ADJUDGED, AND DECREED, that the default herein

entered on_____July 5th, 1944_____, be now confirmed and made final and,

accordingly, let there be judgment herein in favor of the plaintiff,   Joseph Francois

Zeno, whose name has been changed by this Court to "George Lewis"

in the proceedings entitled "In Re: Joseph Francois Zeno, under

No.256,618 of the docket of this Court", and against defendant,

Emily Ezeb, his wife, decreeing a divorce "a vinculo matrimonii"

and forever dissolving the bonds of matrimony heretofore existing

between them.

JUDGMENT read and rendered in open Court on_____November 16th, 1944____
JUDGMENT read and signed in open Court on_____November 22nd, 1944.

_____(SGD) RENE A. VIOSCA_____
JUDGE

126

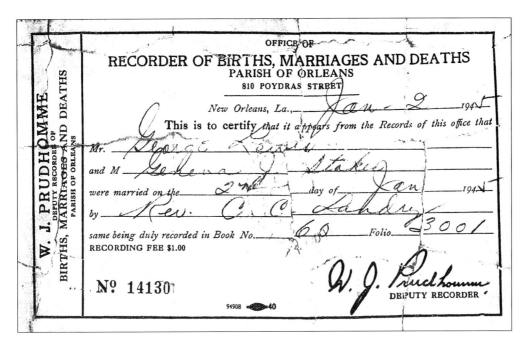

stage at the very first concert that he played, the Jazz Festival for the Jazz Club when we were invited to play one of the eight sessions. George brought Mildred to that engagement, and she sang a couple of, I think, spirituals, and that's when I met Mildred, and this was the first time I met any of George's children. First time I was aware that, you know, I guess I had some vague notion that he had been married before and that Jeanette was his second wife, but I had never met Emma, never saw her. The only one of his children that I recall meeting was Mildred. But they all went by the name Zeno, as I found out later. None of this cropped up when I was in my personal relationship with George. George didn't see any need to talk about it, and I never had any reason to talk about it.

Martyn : Well, how did George introduce you to his mother? Did he say, "This man's handling our band"?

Gagliano : I'm not sure how that happened. I really don't know.

Martyn : That's right, you said you went there and it was only her there.

Gagliano : I'm guessing that he would've probably took me there the first time.

Martyn : So you kind of went back on the four or five times.

Gagliano : I went back on my own. I'm not sure what arrangements or pre-arrangements I'd have to make. I know this, I know that in subsequent visits, I know I brought her this little statue, and not a heck of a lot long after I brought her that statue, she had a fire in her room. I think George probably told me about it. He said, "You know my mamma had a fire, and luckily everything's okay." I don't know whether they had to relocate Alice. But she made a point to show me, when I went back to visit her again, her statue, and she says, "Look. My Blessed Virgin is scorched, but still here."

I don't know that after that I paid very many visits. I don't suppose I paid more than three or four visits to Alice in this period. It's not like an everyday thing for me, and there was a little bit of awkwardness to it, given the fact that we were talking about the 1940s and fifties, with Jim Crow still intact, but it really wasn't a big concern. I guess I had a lot of other things to do.

I keep harping back on the fact that all of what I did for George Lewis was done at night and on the weekends, and I'm telling you that I'm working. I'm working full-time as an engineer, a project manager in construction, and I had to be concerned, number one, for myself.

Martyn : But you're not married yet, though, are you?

Gagliano : No, I was single, living at home with my parents. At this point in time in 1947, when I met George Lewis, we were living down on Frenchmen and Rampart Street, which was about three or four blocks from George's house.

Martyn : George was living with Jeanette.

Gagliano : George was living with Jeanette and Shirley.

IN THE INTEREST OF THE MINOR ( ) NO. A-1744

( ) JUVENILE COURT FOR THE

( ) PARISH OF ORLEANS

SHIRLEY MAE JONES (C) ( ) STATE OF LOUISIANA

J U D G M E N T

This matter having been regularly set for hearing and the Court finding that all provisions of the law have been complied with, and the State Department of Public Welfare having made proper investigation and visitation and supervision during the period of time provided by law, and the consent to the adoption having been given by the maternal grandmother, and the State Department of Public Welfare not having made recommendations against the adoption, and the law and the evidence being in favor of petitioners and the Court considering it to be to the best interest of the child that a final decree of adoption be entered:

IT IS, THEREFORE, ORDERED, ADJUDGED AND DECREED that the child, Shirley Mae Jones, be and she is hereby given in adoption, in accordance with the laws of this State, to the adoptive parents, and the said child, to all intents and purposes, is hereby declared to be the child of petitioners, George Lewis and Geneva Stokes, wife of George Lewis, residents of the Parish of Orleans, State of Louisiana.

IT IS FURTHER ORDERED, ADJUDGED AND DECREED that the name of the said adopted child be and it is hereby changed from Shirley
MARY
Mae Jones to Shirley/Lewis.

JUDGMENT READ, RENDERED AND SIGNED, this **3rd** day of __JULY__, 1952.

/s/ JOHN J. WINGRAVE.
J U D G E .

Martyn : You told me the date that they adopted Shirley.

Gagliano : I have, yes. It's in here somewhere. Yes. I have an adoption document because I needed that for her – I guess first I needed it for Jeanette's succession. I had to handle it after Jeanette died. Well, Geneva Stokes was Jeanette's real name. Jeanette would be a nickname, or her middle name, because her middle initial was "J".

And they married. Her and George married in 1945, January the second. The earliest I would have visited George at his house on Dauphine Street would be like 1947. So that tells me that they were living there for about two years. I know George lived on St. Philip Street near his mother, and I know that at some point in time they moved to Dauphine Street. I don't know any of the circumstances of that. I just have it in my mind that that's what happened.

Martyn : Well, did anybody, for instance, call her Geneva, or did they all call her Jeanette?

Gagliano : No, I didn't know her name was Geneva until I legally found out later.

Martyn : I wonder why she'd call herself that?

Gagliano : Why did George get called George? George is not in his name at all.

Martyn : You're saying here October 27, 1944, he changed his name from Joseph François Zeno to George Lewis. So most the time he was with Bunk, he was just going under the stage name of George Lewis.

Gagliano : Yeah. He had not formally changed his name until he felt it was necessary. Maybe some lawyer told him, "Hey, man, you'd better get your name changed." My reasons for asserting that some lawyer probably told him to legally change his name to "George Lewis" are as follows: The law suite that George filed for divorce against Emily Ezel in the name of George Lewis as plaintiff was given docket No. 265,565, and the law suit that George filed in the same court for a name change from Joseph Francois Zeno to George Lewis was given Docket No. 258,618. These docket numbers are assigned in the order of the date upon which such suits were filed, and therefore this clearly indicates that George filed his name change suit after he had filed his divorce suit, and while his divorce suit was pending judgment. The judgment in the name change suit was rendered in the divorce suit on November 22, 1944. Evidently his divorce lawyer must have found out sometime after he filed the divorce suit, that George's real name was not "George Lewis" when he filed the divorce suit in that name, and apparently the judgment in the divorce suit was delayed until the lawyer could straighten out the name problem.

Martyn : In Dave Stewart's account of the first Bunk jazz band recordings, he said Bunk said something about there's a clarinet player who plays pretty good called George Stewart, and later they found out it was George Lewis.

Gagliano : The first wife she must have been a very resigned person, whatever happened, happened. Any particular reason for their separation, other than that George just didn't want to stay with her and then he left. And I – you know, maybe – maybe it was around this time he met Jeanette, I don't know, and he decided, hey, I'd rather go live with Jeanette than live with these six hollering kids. I have a feeling that the pressure of parenthood on George might have been too much for him.

Martyn : Did he really have six kids?

Gagliano : Sure.

Martyn : They couldn't have children, George and Jeannette?

Gagliano : No, Shirley was apparently put in their home as a foster child, and when I met her, when I first went and saw her when she was like five or six years old. She was probably living with George in a foster home situation. I don't know that for sure, but all I know is that she had not been adopted at that time. On the timeline – I have it somewhere – oh, here it is. Nineteen fifty-two, second page, "Adoption of Shirley by George and Geneva Lewis." Shirley's birth name was Shirley Mae Jones, and it was changed to Shirley Mary Lewis. What I'm saying is my recollection was that Shirley was already living with George and Jeannette at the time I first visited them in 1947. I have a note that says that Shirley was born in 1941.

This is a judgment date 1952 in the juvenile court for the parish of Orleans. The title of the case is "In the Interest of the Minor Shirley Mae Jones." Notice they put a C behind it. [See "Judgment of adoption" left) whereby George and Jeannette adopted Shirley May Jones, and changing her name to Shirley Mary Lewis].

Martyn : What does that mean?

Gagliano : Probably colored. Now, listen to this. Here's what it says "This matter having been regularly set for hearing and the court finding that blah-blah-blah-blah, and the consent to the adoption having been given by the maternal grandmother, and the State Department of Public Welfare not having made recommendations against the adoption and all the evidence being in favor of the petitioners and the court considering it to be in the best interest of the child that I find and condone adoption. It is therefore ordered and judged and decreed that the child Shirley Mae Jones." Now, that's probably how she was recorded on her birth certificate. "She was hereby given in adoption in accordance with the laws of this state to the adoptive parents, and the said child for all intents and purposes is hereby declared to be the child of the petitioners George Lewis and Geneva Stokes, wife of George Lewis." This couldn't have been Geneva or Jeanette's natural child, and so she is actually one of the petitioners for adoption, just like George is. Then, of course, this is probably some child that was born out of wedlock.

Martyn : Put in a home or something.

Gagliano : And, you know, it's unusual for the consent to be given by the maternal grandmother, usually.

Martyn : Yeah. I wonder why the grandmother didn't adopt her?

Gagliano : On my notes, I have her being born in 1941.

Martyn : So she'd be eleven when they adopted her.

Gagliano : She would have been eleven when they adopted her. And if you remember when I first met George and went to visit him at his home, which would have been in 1947, I saw Shirley in the backyard with her mother. This is on Dauphine Street. I just presumed she would be somewhere around five years old. Now, that would be 1947. So if she was born in '41, according to the notes I have here, then she would have been six years old when I first saw her, which ties in with my recollection.

So I've got to tell you that now I'm not suggesting that there is not some kind of a distant family relationship between Shirley and maybe George or Jeanette, it's possible, but there is nothing in the records that would indicate that.

Martyn : But strange thing, I always thought that Shirley was Jeanette's daughter and then George adopted her.

Gagliano : That's not what the papers say. Not only that, but I'm not too sure that George and Jeanette could have – well, let's see, George would've been – in 1941 when Shirley was born, well, George would have been forty-one. I've got to believe that Jeanette couldn't have been that much younger than George, she would have been – in 1940 she probably would have been in her late thirties. She could have possibly had – but to me, that's not what happened. Clearly this child was birthed under the name of Jones, and we have this clear court document that says that George and Jeanette adopted her, not George alone.

Martyn : I wonder where did they know her from?

Gagliano : Now that's a good question, and I don't really know, and all I can tell you is that in Dorothy Tait's book this is their natural child. Now, it may be that our law does not want to publicize adoption. In fact, I cannot go to the court house as a third party and try to find out anything at all about any adoption. However, in this case, Shirley disclosed the fact of her adoption in an affidavit filed in the succession of her father George Lewis, which is a public record.

Martyn : Well, I guess that's good because, I mean, a lot of people who adopt these kids, they think as their regular parents.

Gagliano : That's correct. That's their business only, and maybe that's the way Dorothy played it. But I'm telling you, if you're looking for the truth, I'm simply telling you the truth here.

Martyn : Well, let me ask you, how was Jeannette to get along with?

Gagliano : Very, very easy. No, Jeannette was very friendly.

Martyn : Did you like her?

Gagliano : Oh, very much so. She was a very outgoing person, very neat. She was short like George, sort of plump

Martyn : How was Jeannette – you know, colored people who would say, well, this one was high yellow or this one was brown-skinned.

Gagliano : Oh, no. Jeannette was a dark. I would say not as dark as George's mother. George's mother, Alice, was really black. I would say that Jeannette was more the dark café-au-lait coloration.

Martyn : Not as dark as George?

Gagliano : I would say just a shade maybe, maybe a shade lighter than George. Maybe not. Maybe they were the same color. I would say they were a good affectionate pair. I don't know about Emily. His first wife. But the only member of his first family I ever met was Mildred.

And Mildred was his birth daughter of his first marriage. Now, incidentally, about two or three months ago, I checked the death notices and I ran across a Joseph Zeno. I looked at it, and this was George's son, who died about two or three months ago. And the unique thing about it is that he had something like almost a hundred grandchildren. Maybe twenty-five or thirty great-grandchildren. But I never did meet any of those kids, any of the Zenos. He never used

130

the name Zeno. I think when he started playing music he was – I'm not sure what the derivation of the Lewis part of it is.

Martyn : Quite the sort of mysterious character, really, isn't he? I mean, I didn't know. As good as I knew him, I didn't know he had three wives until talking to you.

Gagliano : Well, he had a third wife. And I remember her name was Valetta Gremillion.

Martyn : Well, then when did he marry this third woman?

Gagliano : I have a recollection that I met George at the railroad station sometime on his return from a tour in either 1954, or 1955, and he surprised me with an introduction to a nice middle-aged black lady as his new wife. I believe her name was Valetta, giving me the impression that this marriage was to solve the problem of help at home intended to Shirley and his mother when he would have to leave town in the future.

Martyn : Oh, they were married up until the day he died.

Gagliano : That's correct. I think they were living together for only a year or two, after which Valetta moved out to live separately from George. Then I have an address here, twenty-five something here in town, separated for the past thirteen years. They were married 7/28/55, this was shortly after Jeanette died, and I'm trying to tell you it was a marriage of convenience. George wanted somebody, needed somebody to take care of his mother – to help take care of his mother and his child while he goes on his trips. But they were separated for thirteen years past. So they apparently couldn't have been married but less than a year.

What I think happened is that they started this living arrangement where Valetta came over there to D'Armas Street to the house, and I think she put up with it for maybe a year and then decided no, actually had enough of it. She was a very nice looking lady, and had a little spunk to her, but I've only met her one time.

Martyn : This says here Jeanette was never married before, there were no other children, and lists Shirley as the only heir. So Jeanette dies, leaving George and Shirley. Then George married this one, Valetta, but what happened to Valetta? Anybody know?

Gagliano : No, I don't know. I'd suggest she's dead by now, because as I remember if I was looking at her and looking at George – now in 1955 – George was fifty-five. I wouldn't have any doubt in my mind this woman could have been at least fifty years old. So I would guess that she's dead now, or she'd be 108 or something.

So what my notation here is, George's will says "Leave all to Shirley." Now this is where I had to make some compromises. Okay? Under Louisiana law, at the time, there is a requirement that a parent must leave his children a certain percent of the estate. For the most part this is abolished, not totally but partially abolished, about ten years ago, and now the only clause there is in Louisiana law are children under twenty-three or children that have been seriously impaired and are unable to take care of themselves. So if a person today dies at the age of – let's say a gentleman dies and he has two children, one fifteen and one seventeen. All right? And let's say he has another one that's thirty years old that's retarded. Under the law today, one half of his estate would have to be left to those three kids. Now, that doesn't mean that the man can't write a will leaving it all to one child. That's legal. It may not be enforceable, and if you have other children that have been left out in a situation like this then those other children have to come forward and challenge the will and say that the will is in excess of what the law allows him to leave to that one child.

Now, I'm telling George that you can leave everything to Shirley but any one of your children could come in and challenge it. Not all of it, but cut it down. Then I would say, "However, if we go ahead and process your will once we process the will, get it recognized, then that starts a five-year period for anybody to come back in and upset the will."

So what happened was we made out the will to Shirley, I filed – eventually filed the succession explaining everything to Shirley. I didn't explain it to the Zeno kids, and then I had nothing to do with it because I'm not representing them, I'm representing – in this case I'm representing Shirley, George and Shirley. So after I went ahead and processed it, five years passed, then these kids can't contest it. So that's what's allowed Shirley then to have undisputed possession in the house, and then when she died, then it went to her four children.

Martyn : Well, Shirley didn't have any brothers or sisters, did she?

Gagliano : No. Well, wait a minute. Wait. That depends on who is Shirley's natural parents then. We don't even know who her true mother is. We don't know who her true father is.

Martyn : What a situation.

Gagliano : Now, you may, and really and truly I think I'm not sure what happens when a child is born, say, out of wedlock, there is going to be a birth certificate that's going to identify certainly the mother and it's going to be optional whether the mother is going to name who the father is. Okay?

Now, that's going to be the public record, in the name of that child as she was named at the time of her birth. Now when she goes through a divorce – I mean, when she goes through an adoption, I have a feeling that when the records come in to the bureau of whatever it is that they might pull the old original birth certificate out and replace it with the judgment. I don't know. So therefore we would have no way of finding out who – whether Shirley had any siblings. Before you can do that, you've got to know who her mother is and you've got to know who her daddy is.

Martyn : Well, you knew who the grandmother was.

Gagliano : No, I don't know who it was. This doesn't tell me. It just said that the grandmother was giving her consent. We don't know who the consent – the only thing we know is that the child was birthed formally under the name Shirley Mae Jones.

Martyn : Right, but we don't even know if Jones was the mother's name or the father's name or anything.

Gagliano : Most likely it would be in the mother's name on the assumption that this was maybe even a teenage, non-wed mother.

Martyn : Then after Jeanette died, so that left Shirley, right?

Gagliano : That left Shirley.

Martyn : Shirley married ....

Gagliano : Watkins, Gilbert – I think his name was Gilbert Watkins.

Martyn : .... Right, and they had the two kids, the two boys.

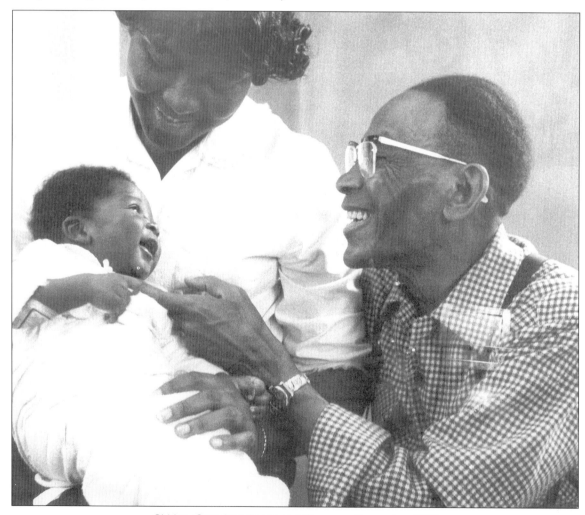

Shirley, Grandson David and George – December 1960

Gagliano : The two boys, and then later on she had twins, Barry and Berry.

Martyn : So the two boys are called Graylon and David. You have to admit it's kind of a complicated family. It's not very big, but it's quite complicated.

Gagliano : Yeah. Here's one of my documents I've run across. This is the adoption of Shirley Mae Jones. This is a judgment rendered on July 3, 1952, by a juvenile Judge, Wingerter, and it says "It's ordered, adjudged, and decreed that the child Shirley Mae Jones be and she is hereby given in adoption to the adoptive parents, and the identification of the adoptive parents are George Lewis and Geneva Stokes, wife of George Lewis." "It is further ordered, adjudged, and decreed that the name of the child is hereby changed from Shirley Mae Jones to Shirley Mary Lewis."

So 1952 was the official adoption, but as I have told you before, when I first visited George and Jeanette in 1947, I estimated Shirley to be somewhere between five and seven years old. So what I think happened is that George and Jeanette took Shirley in as a foster child, and she lived with them for a number of years before they filed the formal petition to adopt her. So at the time then that I visited George in 1947, Shirley had not been adopted. This document says that she was adopted in 1952. And you know what I think? George now is beginning to have enough money to pay for this stuff. Because it would have cost him at least a couple of hundred dollars by 1950 standards, or '49, '50 standards, to pay for this, and he probably didn't have it. So, anyway, in 1952 they were able to do the adoption.

Martyn : Well, you haven't told me much about Jeanette yet.

Gagliano : Okay. I'm going to tell you what I know. Let's go back in my documentation, and I have the act of sale where George and Jeanette bought the property in Algiers. Now, this is 1950, July 21. There's a cash sale to Geneva Stokes, wife of, and George Lewis.

Martyn : So that was just about seven weeks after the recording for Doc Souchon.

Gagliano : That's correct. I started my management with George in 1949. I don't know how much George was able to save from his New York trip in 1945 with Bunk. Evidently, he must have been able to save some money from that.

Martyn : I would have thought so. But George, to my knowledge, I mean – well, no, you've been on the road with him – he was pretty frugal, as I remember him. I mean, he wasn't drinking or anything to speak of.

Gagliano : No, never. When I was with him, he was dry.

Martyn : And he ate like a bird.

Gagliano : That's true.

Martyn : So what else did he spend his money on?

Gagliano : He had to pay rent.

Martyn : No, I mean when he was on the road, what would he spend money on? It seemed to me he was always impeccably dressed. Would you have said that?

Gagliano : Yeah, Yeah.

Martyn : I've seen him take off a pair of pants after work. He'd take off his pants and he'd hold the leg of his pants and line them up exactly and run his finger down the two creases and hang them over a chair.

Gagliano : Yeah. And I'll never forget his cigarette holder. He'd smoke his cigarettes with this cigarette holder that was about six inches long.

Martyn : Did he always smoke cigarettes?

Gagliano : He wasn't a notorious smoker, but apparently he was concerned about the effects of cigarette smoke. That's why I think he was using the holder. It might have been a filter, as far as I know. No, I don't remember that much about it, except that I do remember his cigarette holder and he'd smoke his cigarette through the holder.

Martyn : You never saw him without a cigarette holder early on, then? He wasn't smoking that in the forties, fifties?

Gagliano : I have no idea. It wouldn't surprise me that he was.

Martyn : But let me ask you this. This is really not concerned with this, but I said to him, "Did you ever fool with any kind of dope, marijuana or anything?" And he said "no indeed".

Gagliano : Oh, I wouldn't think so.

Martyn : And he just said, "No." I mean, if you asked me, I would say, no, it's not my generation. I mean, I didn't know anything about that, and I don't think that George did. He said he didn't, but, I mean, that we were friendly enough that he wouldn't have lied.

Gagliano : Okay. You want another certificate? This is January 2, 1945. Mr. George Lewis and Miss Geneva J. Stokes. Geneva J. J could be Jeanette. That's where the Jeanette may have come from. Okay? And they were married on

January 2, 1945. Let's see what else I've got here. I have a note that says Jeannette was born in Phoenix, Louisiana, which would make her a country girl.

Now, when I'm laying out my information for handling his succession, George Lewis, name legally adopted in the 1940s. At that time, I didn't know. I have since got a copy of it, and he was legally married – I said twice. Legally married to Emma Ezel, and they were married in April 20, 1929, and they were divorced in New Orleans in 1940. They had seven children. Mildred Zeno married to somebody named Major, at this time she was forty-seven years old.

So I would have made these notes after George had died. He died in '68. I have another file here that would pin down the dates a little bit better, because now I have a judgment of possession in George Lewis' estate, and it's dated May 30, 1978. That's ten years after George had died.

Martyn : After he died, yeah. Well, he died on New Year's Eve, didn't he?

Gagliano : New Year's Eve – so that would be about ten years after. Dorothy Tait called me from California years later.

Martyn : Oh, about the setting up the trust?

Gagliano : Setting up the trust, and so I said, "Sure, Dorothy. If you want me. Does George want me to be?" "Oh, yeah", she said, "George wants you to be the trustee." I said, "Okay, I'll be the trustee." And she said, "You will be acting as co-trustee with the bank that I'm going to have in California, and I can assure you that this is not going to overburden you with detail." She said, "It may never come to fruition anyway because the money that I need to really set it up right would come from my sale of the movie rights to Fox for the *Five Smooth Stones*." She says, "I'm in negotiation right now on it," she says, "It looks pretty good and I think it's going to happen but I want to set up the trust in advance."

Martyn : Well, it was nice of her to do it, though, no?

Gagliano : And then she said, "I want to set up something primarily for George and Shirley and the grandchildren so that when I die ...."

Martyn : When were those grandchildren born?

Gagliano : I'm sure they were all in existence at this time.

Martyn : Okay, yeah, I don't know. I never knew that.

Gagliano : But I don't really know. But, and I don't know that I had a copy of the trust and probably that I have, this is my file on it. Establishment of the trust ....

Martyn : You had to do all that work for that trust?

Gagliano : Now here's an amendment. This amendment was entered the 24th day of July 1968 between Dorothy Fairbairn Tait. So the pseudonym that she used on the second edition of the book. Fairbairn.

Martyn : That was her middle name?

Gagliano : Well, it could have been her maiden name. Tait could have been her married name.

Martyn : I don't know if she was married. I don't know that she was ever married.

Gagliano : I don't know she wasn't, but I don't know that she was. I do recall getting a copy of Dorothy's will, as part of the trust, where she identifies herself as Dorothy Fairbairn Tait, a 'widow'. That would suggest to me that Fairbairn would be her maiden name, and Tait would be her married name.

This is what she's saying. Paragraph B2 of that agreement is provided in part as follows. Upon the death of the trustor, the trustee shall divide the trust estate as follows: two-thirds of the trust estate shall be set aside for the benefit of David Watkins, Graylin Watkins, Barry Watkins and Berry Watkins – there they are, those are the names.

Martyn : So Barry and Berry were the two twins?

Gagliano : Barry and Berry, they were the twins. B-e-r-r-y and B-a-r-r-y. And she's identifying them as the children of Shirley, and then she said, "One-third of the trust estate shall be distributed to the NAACP." Now, that's what was in the original. Then she says she desires to amend the trust agreement to say that, "Upon the death the trust shall be set aside for the benefit of David Watkins, Graylin Watkins and or their survivors." In other words, taking the one-third away from the NAACP and making the grandchildren the sole trustees of this trust.

Martyn : Well, were the twins by the same father as the first two.

Gagliano : I don't know. There's some indication they might not be. So here is the original trust, which was set up in 1968, and so now remember 1968 is after I wrote George's will. My recollection then now is that probably Dorothy called me in 1967 to tell me, "George is in bad shape. He's in Tulane Hospital. He says he needs to write a will. Can you handle that for him?" I said, "Sure. Where is he?" So I remember going to the hospital and talking to George, and he was under a tent, as I remember. Now evidently, he must have survived that situation because he didn't die that year.

Martyn : Yeah, yeah, for sure.

Gagliano : That's when I wrote the will, in '67, and apparently it was shortly – it was after that – in other words, I think then that Dorothy renewed her relationship with me by calling me to get me to go to the hospital and set up George's will. Well, he was in a terminal state almost at that time, so I went over to the hospital and it was somewhat awkward because, you know, George can't talk very well and he's getting oxygen and we talked. He tells me – basically, he tells me, "I want to leave everything to Shirley."

I got to believe that all of his family information that I have on those notes must have come from Shirley, because I don't think George could have – was in a position to give me all that stuff. And I remember I didn't notarize George's will, because I had my law partner notarize it, but I served as a witness on the will, so meaning that my colleague went with me to the hospital, and we probably went to the hospital, and we had, I think, Louis Nelson, the trombone player was the other witness. He came to the hospital.

Martyn : Why did they pick him? Was he a good friend?

Gagliano : Apparently, he was playing with George at time. The date that I did his will was July 28, 1967.

Martyn : Sixty-seven. So he lived about two years after that will was done then.

Chapter 9
"RECORDINGS AND BROADCASTS"

Martyn : I wanted to talk to you about the recording sessions they made just to get your reaction on various sessions.

Gagliano : Let me make a general comment that might alter your plan. I was not really involved deeply in any of the recording sessions. As a matter of fact, the only one that I can recall ever being present on was the one that Doc Souchon did. It was a great session. I remember it was one of the last that we had with Elmer Talbert. But afterward, everybody stood around and went and listened to some of the tapes, and they were just very delighted with it. But that is the only one that I remember. Good Time Jazz came in right after that. I wasn't involved. My recollection is it was done on the second floor of some place on Baronne Street, and I think it was Filiberto's. I think it was a music shop or something. Upstairs they had, apparently, a studio.

Martyn : Must have been some studio. It's one of those things, it's such a legendary session, you think you're going to find pictures of it which are colossal works of art, but they're just snapshots, the three. They've got all busted radios and televisions and what all around it.

Gagliano : At that time, I had nothing to compare it with. The only other studio I ever remember being in was Cosimo's, and I might have been at some sessions there with George. But I did very little. In fact, I don't recall doing any of the negotiations for them. The only time I really got involved in that aspect of it was when we did the Ohio Union concerts when Bob Clark tracked me down at the auditorium before we set up and made a deal. George made all the arrangements himself, apparently, with whatever union officials he needed. That's how it got done.

Martyn : George, was he a very big union man? Did he go through the union or not?

Gagliano : I don't know that he did, but all I can tell you is I'm not sure what George used as a measure for whatever he was going to charge for the session. I mean, I can tell you from my experience that George did receive royalties, miniscule, as far as I was concerned, for various recordings. In order to get royalties, I presume you had to have some sort of a contract that provided for a royalty. Well, I remember it as having been there at the Souchon session. It was more like a party. It wasn't a full-blown recording session. I guess his idea of a party was maybe to have some booze up there for the guys. I think he did that in order to loosen them up, would be my thought, and maybe it did the trick. Let's see. The band was Elmer Talbert, George Lewis, Jim Robinson, Lawrence, Alton , Slow Drag, and Joe Watkins, the normal band. The normal band with Talbert, that's how the band started. If I go back to the 1949 Jazz Festival Concert put on by the New Orleans Jazz Club, Talbert was the sole trumpet, and then the rest of the band, as it went down through the years.

The second set of concerts, either the second or the third, I'm not sure which, George brought in Albert Walters as the second trumpet at this time with Percy. My recollection is that the first guy that apparently replaced Talbert after he died was probably Percy Humphrey.

Martyn : Let's get back to the recording session, which you say you have a few mental pictures of. What Souchon said is that he put a tub with ice in it of soft drinks and beers and water.

Gagliano : I imagine that, and then some hard liquor.

Martyn : Who would have drunk most of that in the band?

Gagliano : If you want my opinion, I could tell you it would probably been Jim Robinson and maybe Drag.

Martyn : Did Drag drink?

Gagliano : I think he did, but he didn't necessarily show it. But I think he drank. I know George didn't. George was a reformed drinker, so for the most part in our relationship George didn't drink. So he was very conscious about his sidemen getting overloaded. So his main concern, as I recall, would have been Jim, in drinking. So I guess Joe Watkins must have tipped a little. Alton and Lawrence, to me, no, I don't think Lawrence drank at that time. Drag, I know, and, of course, I think that Talbert probably drank a little. But when he said it was a party, what I think he meant was he had invited a few people, probably Jazz Club people, to come in and listen. I happened to be one of those, plus I had another reason to be there, being George Lewis', quote, "manager," unquote.

Martyn : Well, would you have been there officially to see that nothing harmful happened to the band or would you ....

Gagliano : No.

Martyn : Or did you trust the people that were running the recording session? You knew them.

Gagliano : Yes, I trusted them.

George Lewis / Red Allen recording session, WDSU studios, August 6, 1951.
Lawrence Marrero, George Lewis, Lester Santiago, Bill Matthews, Jim Robinson, Red Allen, Alton Purnell,
Slow Drag Pavageau, Alvin Alcorn, Joe Mares, Armand Hug, Paul Barbarin and Nick Gagliano

Martyn : We found from this picture that you were at the session with George's band with Red Allen.

Gagliano : I see that, but I don't remember it, but evidently I was there, and this is typical of a lot of things that didn't stay in my memory bank; but there is no doubt that I was there, and I was sitting right next to Paul Barbarin. Yeah well, I can say I recognize most of the guys, starting from the left, it looks to me like, we start out with Lawrence Marrero, then Jim, George, and Lester Santiago, and you said Bill Matthews...

Martyn : Yeh, that's Bill Matthews

Gagliano : Oh, yeah that's Alvin, then Purnell, Slow Drag, Joe Mares, Armand Hug.

Martyn : Why was Armand Hug there do you think?

Gagliano : He was a friend of Joe Mares, and just probably a spectator like me.

Martyn : Well, do you think George was impressed with making a recording with Red Allen.

Gagliano : He was pleased to be able to record with Red Allen, Ah Red Allen, Jr.; for one thing they both lived in Algiers, and he had a high regard for him, and I think it was something he looked forward to. I don't know how the session was arranged, how it was that Red Allen would be playing trumpet rather than the regular guys.

Martyn : Well, the session was actually done by Joe Mares for Rudi Blesh's Circle label.

Gagliano : Who was the leader on our side, was it George?

Martyn : It was George Lewis as the leader. Red Allen had special billing, because I worked on the Circle re-issue with

137

George Lewis recording session, WDSU Studios – August 6, 1951. Jim Robinson, Henry "Red" Allen

George Lewis recording session, WDSU Studios – August 6, 1951
Bill Matthews, Alvin Alcorn, George Lewis

Recording session, WDSU Studios – August 6, 1951
Joe Mares, Lester Santiago, Slow Drag Pavageau, Bill Matthews, Paul Barbarin, Lawrence Marrero, Union
delegate Alton Purnell, Jim Robinson, Alvin Alcorn, George Lewis

the George Buck label, so there was no question of it, it was George Lewis's session. But Red was living in New York.

Gagliano : I think George held Red Allen in high regard, figures out that he was a rather successful jazz player, great national reputation; whether or not Red would share that with George; you know the guys who stayed in New Orleans and didn't go to New York may have held the other fellows in a sort of esteem.

Martyn : Well, I imagine, I don't know, I never heard it mentioned, but I imagine that when Bunk's band was playing at the Stuyvesant Casino that Red must have gone over to see them because he knew most of the people, but there was never much of a mention of Red Allen having anything to do with Bunk.

Gagliano : If he had anything really to do with him, other than maybe being a spectator or maybe even sat in.

Martyn : I wonder if Red thought he was going back in time playing with a band like George's.

Gagliano : I would suspect he would think he was going back in time, you realize he had left the New Orleans area for many, many years. Now he was in the New York environment with an entirely different environment than what George and the boys maintained, and I think the fact that the George Lewis Jazz Band stayed here on the ground all those years gave them, shall we say, the reputation of being the original unadulterated traditional New Orleans jazz, mostly ensemble work, very little solo work; and of course Red Allen being in New York in the situation he was used to in the Dixieland thing, it would have been a typical opening ensemble, a bunch of solos, and a closing ensemble, and then this way he would have to work a lot harder with this band.

Martyn : To give Red credit, he certainly did phenomenally well, you know, I mean they say that old New Orleans

George Lewis recording session, WDSU Studios – August 20, 1951
Bill Matthews, Alvin Alcorn, George Lewis

musicians never forget, and you can put them together in China and they still gonna fit together. But he fit in very well with this – but I don't know – I talked to Rudi Blesh but never asked him 'did he want to bring Red Allen to play with George Lewis' band because he thought it might do some good for his label or did he think about Red coming back here to play some old style antique music – or was Red in town visiting his dad, his daddy was probably still alive when this record was made, or was he just in town and somebody thought it would be a good idea?

Gagliano : Can't offer you any suggestions of any of those things.

Martyn : Here's another peculiar thing, you see these guys were here, looka here, Purnell was here but he wasn't playing, there were two sessions recorded on this job, on August 6th, 1951, there were two sessions recorded by Joe Mares, the one with Red Allen which was only for, five or six numbers, whatever it was, and then the session with the other gang, which Allen sat out, and Alvin Alcorn came in, which is this session, you see, this is the same day.

Gagliano : That's with Bill Matthews. Why the WDSU mikes?

Martyn : Well, it was recorded at the WDSU studios, that what I wanted to ask you if you knew why it was recorded at WDSU.

Gagliano : No, I can offer nothing on that.

Martyn : There was a recording that they made in 1953, September 25, 1953. It was done – the address is given here as 1410 Jena Street. It's never mentioned much.

Gagliano : That's uptown.

Martyn : Uptown, right. They made "Dallas Blues," "Redwing, Louisiana," and "Careless Love, " "St. Philip Street Breakdown", "Salty Dog," with Doc Souchon singing, "Corinne, Corinna," and "Old Rugged Cross." Now, then this session, was recorded for a guy named Pete, I can't think of his second name. Pete somehow, he was a member of the New Orleans Jazz Club. He was one of the past presidents, I think.

Gagliano : Peter Miller. Peter Miller was the first president after Doc Souchon. Long dead, as far as I know.

140

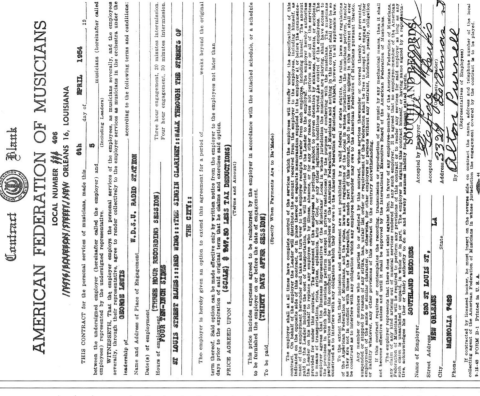

Martyn : Do you know any of his people or any of his kids or anything like that? Do you ever hear of them?

Gagliano : No. I know that both he and his wife were members of the club. I knew him at the time. This would have been in he became president, my guess is, around 1950, '51, something like that.

Martyn : Well, he recorded the band in '53, but it wasn't a band. It was just George and the whole rhythm section.

Gagliano : This must have been one of these. I really don't know but as I wasn't invited and I know nothing about it.

Martyn : It said 1410 Jena Street, and it's been issued many times.

Gagliano : Well, 1410 would mean it would be right around in the vicinity of Magazine – no, Prytania.

Martyn : Probably at his house, I would have thought, wouldn't you?

Gagliano : Probably, yeah. If it's an issue, we could go back into the city directories and see who lived there.

Martyn : You see, they issued two-thirds of the session, but there's still unissued numbers from the session, and I wondered how we could get hold of them.

Gagliano : Gee, I would have no way of knowing how to do that.

Martyn : But I'll try and find .... because if we can find it, if it was down at this man's house, Pete Miller's house, we might find there's still somebody called Miller lives at the house, and I could call them and say, "Look, I'm trying to locate Peter Miller, who was president." And then they might say, "Well, that was my grandpa, my granddaddy." So then I would say, "I know that George Lewis' band recorded in your house. Do you have any idea where the rest of the tapes are?" Who knows maybe one day we'll find the unissued stuff. What about the Broadcasts? I know the band did several over the early years.

Gagliano : I remember taking a train to go to Mobile to play a gig for Regal Brewery, I think. We played the WTPS Radio show once a week, Sunday night. It was live. Ed Hart was the announcer, and we had a blues singer, a male blues singer. That was the other part of the program. It was George Lewis traditional music, and I think it was a guy named Earl King, but it could be different, who was the rhythm and blues component. And that was the show, lasted, I don't know, six months or nine months or whatever. Then it was discontinued.

Martyn : You were telling me that at around this time a lot of black – the audience I'm talking about – were into rhythm and blues.

Gagliano : I can give you an incident that will explain that. Ed Hart and I, through these broadcasts, we became friendly. Ed was not very schooled in traditional jazz, but he appreciated George Lewis Band. I don't know whether it was my idea, his idea, or it just hatched, but, "Man, we ought to put this show live." This is what we were thinking. He said, "Yeah, man," he said, "let's try to do that." Then we made our biggest mistake. "Where we gonna do it?" "Well, how about Booker T. Washington High School Auditorium in the black community?"

Okay, so we set out to promote this thing and we died. We didn't get anybody there. Not too many of the people that went to hear the R&B guy, but nobody of any consequence, you know. We didn't have any major budget to advertise this thing. We were counting on some of the people who heard the show, assuming there ought to be a couple of followers out there who'd listened to it, and maybe they'll come and see it live. And nothing ever happened.

Martyn : I think, in a way, though, that black audiences never really supported black traditional jazz too much.

Gagliano : No, because it was part of their oppressive era. They thought it was Uncle Tom? If you study the history of this music, if you take Jim Robinson's story, he grew up on a plantation. Supposedly, he may have learned from Percy Humphrey or Willie Humphrey. We're talking about their grandfather, James Brown Humphrey, going down and teaching music to the farmhands on the plantations, and they surmised that Jim Robinson might have gotten the beginning of his in that situation, and when he got in the army in World War I, then maybe that formalized him. So actually I think the younger blacks coming up would associate this music with the era of oppression of the blacks. I was deeply involved in them. I just don't remember all the detail. The detail that I do remember is that it was at WTPS, that it was on a Sunday night. My recollection is that WTPS wanted to satisfy both the contemporary camp, which was represented by – well, you take like – I don't know. Would you characterize, say, Irma Thomas today? Would you put her in a rhythm and blues classification? In the Second Line, there is a reference in the 1950's, that one of the reasons that the Jazz Club considered George's band at that time to be one of the busiest in New Orleans was that it had the El Morocco gig and it had the Sunday night broadcast on WTPS.

What I remember is I don't even know whether it was an hour show or a half hour. All I know is that Ed Hart was the announcer. We became sort of friendly, and I find out going through the minutes that Ed Hart had been one of the announcers on the first set of concerts, and he shared the announcing with Dick Bruce of WDSU.

Martyn : Did they get paid for the broadcasts?

Gagliano : Sure that was a gig. And I would thing that probably the band played maybe as many as maybe three, possibly four at the most tunes, and then the singer would have two or three songs, sponsored by Regal Beer. I remember that Regal Beer-sponsored train trip to, I think, to Mobile, which may have been some sort of a tie-in with the radio show.

Martyn : And George and the band were playing on this?

Gagliano : Oh, yeah. We took a train and there was a dedication of something in Mobile. I remember we played even at the railroad depot. In Mobile. I remember it as part of my deep memory about all of this. The other thing that I would remember at the time, WTPS' studios were that beautiful building on Lee Circle, where we now have – well, it was the building that was purchased by this oil man, Taylor, I believe, Museum of Southern Oil.

Martyn : Oh, to the left of the Confederate Museum on Lee Circle?

Gagliano : The building I'm talking about was on the corner. You know the building with turrets and beautiful brickwork? Well, that was the studio of WTPS. And I remember that we would somehow meet, and I would pile in my car and we'd go there.

Martyn : Did they give you a dressing room to go to at the radio station?

Gagliano : No.

Martyn : I've never seen any pictures from the radio station broadcast and stuff.

Gagliano : No. I don't know that anybody ever took them.

Martyn : Did they wear their band uniforms?

Gagliano : Oh, no. It's a radio thing. You know, we all dressed casually for this. It's not TV, man. It's radio. No I would think that probably the band played maybe as many as maybe three, possibly four at the most, tunes, and then the singer would have two or three songs. That would be Earl King. He was a very cordial guy. We all got along well.

Martyn : None of those broadcasts have ever surfaced.

Gagliano : Maybe someday they will. This is something interesting, I began to think in terms of the first concerts we played in Cincinnati and Miami University in Oxford, Ohio, and I'm thinking to myself, you know, these might be the very first jazz concerts played by a jazz band on a college campus, in the United States. So I did a little Googling on my computer, and I came up with one hit and it was from Oberlin College in, Ohio, which, in a sense, is coincidental, because what I thought were our first concerts were in Ohio. I have a copy of the article. It was talking about the history of music at Oberlin, and they touted a 1953 concert where they featured Dave Brubeck and his trio. I'm not sure whether Dave, at that point, had reached the kind of fame he ultimately did.

Martyn : I don't think so. Not in '53.

Gagliano : So I guess he was out there hustling in the bushes at that time, and he played this concert, which they took great pride in. Then they conjectured in the piece that this could very well be the very first jazz concert at a college or university, and they expressed their whatever little bit of scrutiny they did and made that suggestion. They didn't come out and claim it. So I'm saying to myself, gee, well, I got that beat right here.

I went to the Hogan Archive, and went through the George Lewis what they call vertical file, and I went through a file by Bob Greenwood, whom you knew. Now, in one of those files I came across a printed sheet of paper. Bob is making a memorandum – this is typewritten. He's making a memorandum of a jazz concert by the George Lewis Jazz Band at McAlister Auditorium at Tulane University on November 4, 1949. Which predates Dave Brubeck by four years. By four years and predates the Ohio concerts by three years. So I'm kind of scratching my head. 1949, I've only been out of Tulane – I got my degree in engineering in 1948 – which would have been June of '48. November of '49 would be a year and a few months later than that. I still had a lot of my connections at the university, and as I indicated to you – I'm saying this by way of braggadocio, but at the time, I was one of the personalities on the campus. So you'll see my picture throughout the yearbook, being a member of the Student Council, president of the engineering student body, all that kind of stuff. So I had some notoriety and I met a lot of the people at the university, students and faculty that I never would have met otherwise.

So I said to myself, well, yeah – and I'm also looking at the timing. In my previous interviews with you, I pegged my formal beginning, if you will, as manager of the George Lewis Jazz Band, with the concert that the band played in the very first series of jazz concerts sponsored by the New Orleans Jazz Club out on Beauregard Square, or Congo Square, in New Orleans. They put on four weeks of concerts and George Lewis' band was in the first three or four, so that marked when I started my active work, if you will. Forty-nine. According to the date of the Jazz Club concerts, I think it was in May. So, in other words, the band had already played a concert out at Beauregard Square under the auspices of the Jazz Club. That was in May. Come November, the band is playing another concert, this time at Tulane University at McAlister Auditorium, which is a big auditorium.

Then I also saw a very cryptic reference to this in my review in the Second Line, which were published by the New Orleans Jazz Club. In one of their retrospectives, when they were going back talking about the early days of the Jazz Club, because the Jazz Club's Second Line was not being published in '49, but in one or two or three years later, they were rehashing what the club did in its period from its forming in 1948 to '50, when the Second Line first came out, and they had a very short cryptic statement in there, with no description other than that they had co-sponsored a concert at Tulane's McAlister Auditorium on that day in November of '49. So I'm saying, hey, this thing is a reality.

Martyn : But you don't remember booking it.

Gagliano : Well, no, this is what I'm saying. I'm thinking back on it, and I have no recollection of it, but my instincts are telling me, with the timing in all of this, that I had to be involved. So the net result is that I made a contact over at the Tulane University Archives. Last week at Tulane University, as distinguished from the Hogan Archives at Tulane University. Tulane has its own archives.

Martyn : Right. Apart from the Jazz Archive.

Gagliano : Apart from the Jazz Archive. In fact, it's on the second floor right below the Jazz Archive. Bruce Raeburn gave me the name of a lady, very helpful. Her name is Ann Case. I told her what I was looking for, and I said, "I was hoping that maybe we could find some kind of reference to this in your archive." I said, "The first we've got to do, while I'm here, let's get the 1950 Tulane yearbook." Now, the 1950 Tulane yearbook would cover the period from, say, August of 1949 through graduation, August of '50. I said, "Let's see what we can find." After about ten minutes, I'm going through and I see there's a series of photographs on the homecoming activities.

Martyn : What is a homecoming? I played them, but I don't know. I never asked.

Gagliano : Every year, universities have what they call an annual homecoming for the alumni to come back to the college, to visit the college.

Martyn : Oh, like the class of '57, class of '59.

Gagliano : Yeah, and then they have special notations for the ten-year class or twenty-year class. Well, I was in the fifty-year class, and for some reason or other, I didn't go to the sixty-year class, which was last year. But anyway, that's what homecoming is.

Martyn : All right. I've got it now.

Gagliano : And I wasn't looking for that. I'm just looking for something in the yearbook, and sure enough, in a collage of pictures for the homecoming celebration in November of 1949 was this picture of the George Lewis Jazz Band. This is just a picture. So I take that and I go to Miss Case, and I said, "Miss Case, this confirms what I suspect or what I've been told and what I've read in little things." She says, "Sure enough. That's it." I had already sort of piqued her interest in this, because I'm telling her that what I'm thinking is that this concert is going to be the very first jazz concert played on a college campus in the United States. I said, "You know, I previously thought we did this in 1952 up in Ohio, but lo and behold, now I find out we did it at Tulane in 1949."

So I also told her that I had a reference in the Second Line that this happened. Okay. So what she did was, first thing she did was she went ahead and she looked in her schedule of activities for November 4, the official statement of activities. As I remember looking at it, it covered the whole week. So in other words, it covered the activities, say, from October 30, say, to November 5 or 6. And right there on November 4, lo and behold, there was no reference to a jazz concert at McAlister Auditorium, but there was a movie to be shown at 7:45. She showed me this. She says, "There must be something wrong here, because this is not on the official schedule." I said, "Well, that may be true. Maybe it happened before." Then she said, "Okay, I'll go see what I can find."

About a couple of weeks later, I called her. I said, "May I come and see what you have?" She had previously told me that she was able to find four negatives, one of which was used in the yearbook. She said, "I have three other ones which are different. You think you might be interested in looking at it?" I said, "By all means." So she graciously went ahead and had these negatives scanned. And sure enough, when we went there, she had these four photographs.

I asked her about the Tulane newspaper. Well, first of all, let me point out, the official schedule didn't show anything about this jazz concert. I said, "Now, what I think I would like to do would be to go back and check the records, check the student newspaper." Tulane has a student newspaper called The Hullabaloo. She says, "Yeah, we have those at the main library right across the way."

So I said, "Okay." So she sent me over there. They dug out a microfilm for the period. We looked in November, and I asked the lady to go back before November 4 because I wanted to pick up maybe some notice or advertisement. Sure enough, we came to November 3, '49, and what that article said – it had a headline. It said "Concert and Parade Tomorrow Night." So this publication date is November 3. So it says "Concert and Parade Tomorrow Night." I'll just read a little bit of it. It says, "Tulanians will have the opportunity of hearing such nationally famous jazzmen as Jim Robinson on the trombone, Lawrence Marrero on the banjo, and George Lewis on the clarinet tomorrow night from seven to nine p.m. at McAlister Auditorium, when George Lewis and his Ragtime Jazz Band give a concert jointly sponsored by Greenbackers and the New Orleans Jazz Club."

Martyn : Who are the Greenbackers?

Gagliano : Greenbackers was a group of students forming what they call a spirit organization, school spirit, and they would have been deeply involved in homecoming because the apex of homecoming is a football game. It turns out that there was a football game, and in this case, Tulane was playing Navy, at Tulane Stadium. So that confirms what the picture was doing as part of the homecoming stuff. See, and then it goes on to say – and this is what's interesting to me personally and it confirms what I thought. It says "Nicholas Gagliano , an alumnus of Tulane and a member of the New Orleans Jazz Club, is responsible for bringing the band before the student body." Then it says, "Following the concert will be a pep rally concluded by a shirttail parade."

Martyn : What the hell is a shirttail parade?

Gagliano : There again, a bunch of students parading down the street. This was interesting – it says, "which will start at Elks Place." That's in downtown New Orleans. "Go along Canal Street all the way to the St. Charles Hotel." That was the route of the parade. Now, the band had nothing to do with that. What happened here is that after the concert, which was supposed to have ended at nine o'clock, according to this schedule, according to that, they got shuttle buses to take the students from the university, from the campus to Elks Place. Bring them downtown so they could create this parade and create some kind of ruckus. So this article clearly shows that it happened. It shows that it happened from seven to nine, and obviously the notice of a movie had been put on somewhere earlier and this preempted that.

Well, I just want you to understand that I had asked Miss Case, in looking for anything, I said, "Miss Case, do you think there was any possibility that this could have been recorded?" She said, "Well, I don't know. I'll see what I can find."

Well, when I finally met her and when she gave us copies of these four photographs of the band, she gave me something else that I didn't even ask for or knew existed. *[See over page]*. It was an excerpt from a little publication, a student publication called the *Urchin*. Now, I remember as a student that the Urchin was like a scandal sheet. It's a gossip sheet. It's gossip about students, and it's unofficial. It's not a university publication, but it was apparently well enough organized by the students that they could go out and sell ads for it. There was a very little clip in it about the concert last night, how everybody enjoyed it and how they feel that the university should do this more often.

But the other thing is this tells me that Miss Case went beyond the bounds of what I asked her to look for. So she came up with that, but she says, "I can't find any kind of evidence of a recording." Now, you and I are looking at these photographs, and we were wondering whether the microphone setup would indicate that maybe it was recorded. I think your conjecture was that maybe this might have been recorded by Herbert Otto.

Martyn : It's just around the time he was there, because his party was a week later. Look, right off the bat, it confirms one thing. Here's the brass band sequence. There's a photograph of it, so it confirms they did that. Also, there's this microphone, which looks like, to me, the same microphone. It's a Shure microphone, the old Shure from the early forties or maybe even late thirties. That was the one that they used in the outside photographs of the band in Look magazine. It's the same mike. I recognize it. But that's on a little wheeled dolly thing moving around because Alton was a songster, and Joe Watkins and Elmer Talbert and Kid Howard. But this microphone here is a – I mean, this is all conjecture – but we'll check it out. You never know what you're going to find. This is not a movable microphone, because it looks like in position, straight dead ahead in front of the band. It looks to be – of course, you want things to happen, but it looks like it's put there to record. Well, we'll get to the bottom of that.

But let me ask you this. Howard is playing a trumpet, and you say you never knew him play anything but the trumpet. You never knew him play a cornet, huh?

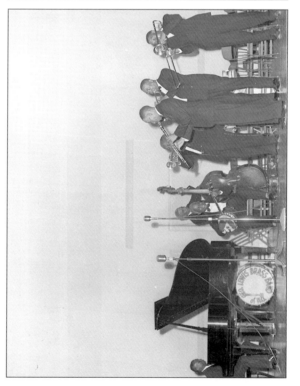

First College Concert – McAlister Auditorium, Tulane University – November 4, 1949. Elmer Talbert, Kid Howard, Jim Robinson, George Lewis, Alton Purnell, Lawrence Marrero, Slow Drag Pavageau, Joe Watkins.

146

Gagliano : That's right, and as I told you, I think that I would have really recognized and remembered if I ever saw him play a cornet.

Martyn : It's funny, because I never saw him play anything but a cornet.

Gagliano : I've never seen him play anything else but a trumpet in the years that I was associated with the band.

Martyn : But another interesting thing is about these pictures; they're all in tuxedos. I mean, it certainly was not a scrappy band, was it? I mean, you know, if you're a student, you come and see a colored band, as they were called in those days, playing and they're dressed like that. They're a pretty well-dressed band, aren't they, you know?

Gagliano : Well, I think that's pretty intentional because, as I told you, I think when we did the concerts for the New Orleans Jazz Club the first time, I'm sure we went out and somehow scraped up the money to buy some new clothes. I don't remember it being a tuxedo, though. I suspect that the band members, individually, had tuxedos from their earlier days playing gigs. The other thing you've got to remember is that we were starting, at this time, to do university fraternity parties. We were being engaged to do high-society debutante parties, and all of which sort of demanded that the band have a reasonable uniform kind of a dress, whatever it was. To me, that's why they showed up in these tuxedos. I can't say that we bought them new when I came on or whether they had them already.

Martyn : Well, George's looks like he got that from Adolphe Menjou. I mean, that's one hell of an old tuxedo he got there. That looks like the little short jacket and the draped pants. But the rest of them look modern tuxedos, if you will, for that, but George's ....

Gagliano : Yeah, I think George's is probably vintage.

Martyn : Yeah, vintage. That's a hell of a tuxedo, that. Did Celestin's band wear tuxedos at the time?

Gagliano : Yeah, my recollection is they did. Yeah, well, they were even more so than George because they played more of those social events than we did.

Martyn : Plus they were called the Tuxedo Band too. They were called that, so, you know.

Gagliano : So it was logical for them. But for us it was a matter of making a neat presentation, you know. Let me finish up, if you don't mind. In my review of the Hullabaloo records, I just commented on the notice that the concert was going to be handled. Then the next issue was November 10. Hullabaloo is a weekly. Now, on the tenth, they wrote up about – the headline is "Rally, Big Game, and Dance Make Up the Weekend." It says, "Homecoming this year provided a busy weekend. Friday night, hundreds of students turned out for the pep rally. George Lewis and his Ragtime Jazz Band began the night's festivities by playing old jazz pieces." Now, that's the end of the reference to George. Then it goes on to say, "The bonfire crowd, sparked by the cheerleaders and the band, had Coach Franka and Dick Sheffield give pep talks." Franka was a renowned football coach that was coaching Tulane at the time. Then it goes on to describe the pep rally downtown and the parade along Canal Street and all that stuff, which meant it was a pretty big thing. So it's interesting that the George Lewis Band was made an organic part of that celebration.

Martyn : Well, it must have been because of you and your connections. I mean, I can't see any other way.

Gagliano : Well, the article says it. It says it. The irony of it is that I can't dredge this up out of my memory. So what this is doing for me is this is allowing me to find out things that I've done that I just don't recall. It would seem to me that here I am, there's this concert that I'm apparently help arranging within a year after I graduated from the school. I knew probably a bunch of the students that would be there, and I've got to believe, frankly, that I was there. I've got to suggest, although I can't at this moment say it, that this might have been the very first presentation of the funeral sequence which we adopted and used in all of our concerts in Ohio. And here I am. Probably this was the prototype.

Martyn : Well, at least it's given you the idea of the whole thing that was used later on.

Gagliano : Well, you'll notice that, as you noted originally, that the bass drum that Lawrence Marrero uses is there.

Martyn : Yeah, it's his own bass drum.

Gagliano : They were using it as a prop to show the name of the band, but then when the parade sequence came on, then Lawrence – well, you can see he's wearing the drum on his chest. In this discography, Hymn to George that you showed me this morning, which talks about this concert, it specifically mentions "The funeral scene includes three titles, "Just a Little While to Stay Here," "Just a Closer Walk with Thee," and "You Rascal, You." So they are listing it as a funeral sequence setting the scene.

Martyn : A hymn to a funeral dirge to a ragtime.

Gagliano : I've got to believe that, as I did in Ohio, it was logical for me to be involved.

Martyn : To tell them what was going on.

147

Gagliano : We're doing it here for the first time. We had never done it before. So this is my conjecture.

Martyn : Well, you don't know whose idea it was, though. I can't imagine it was George's idea.

Gagliano : I have to feel that it probably was my idea to take advantage of the band members' experience as musicians by taking advantage of the curiosity that white folks have as to the jazz band funerals.

Martyn : Well, they had never seen anything in the white world like that.

Gagliano : Well, now, you've got to remember. The white world in New Orleans, we had no white world specifically in terms of neighborhood. I mean, our neighborhoods were fairly integrated. Well, let's put it this way. The lower middle class, the working-class neighborhoods were basically integrated. They may have been predominantly white, but there would always be sprinklings of black families living there, just like there would be sprinklings of white people living in predominantly black neighborhoods. So a lot of white people knew about these parades, actually saw them. My wife even tells me, when she was a girl, she lived on Washington Avenue right off of Baronne, and she said, "Man, they were having parades all the time up and down Washington Avenue."

Martyn : Parades. But funerals?

Gagliano : Well, both. Both. The brass bands were playing not only for funerals, but they were playing for fraternal parties. I mean, all of the ladies' organizations would have them, and they would have a parade and they would always have a brass band playing at their parade. So there was a lot of this going through the different neighborhoods. Now, as a boy, I don't remember ever having seen any in my particular neighborhood, but I do remember going out – when I was in the Jazz Club, we would go out and scout them, and go out and see them. But the local people here, we never saw anybody turn up, the local people, unless they were to do with the deceased, and we never saw a black band playing for a white funeral.

Martyn : It was clearly a black tradition. It's mostly Baptist, too, because Catholic very seldom had it. We always liked it when it was Baptist because the minister would go on and on and on and on and on in that church. We'd be outside talking to the musicians for sometimes an hour and a half. It was great, because they couldn't go anywhere. I mean, if they left to go to a barroom, then the preacher would finish and out would come the coffin, the casket, and then they would berate them for – "Well, man, you're supposed to be here."

Gagliano : Getting back to the planning for that funeral sequence, I specifically remember sitting down several sessions with the band and telling them to enlighten me about the process. What I got from that was that there was actually three phases to the sequence. George told me, he says, "Well, we play a different tune for each one of these sequences."

So I said, "Well, what are these sequences?" He said, well, first, the band would somehow have a place to congregate, and then at that point they would march from that point toward the funeral home or the home where the body was. They would play a tune like what they had here: "Just a Little While to Stay Here." Well, that's apropos. "A Little While to Stay Here."

Martyn : Well, it's the same today. We do the same thing. We play "Over in the Glory Land," "Lily of the Valley," "Just a Little While to Stay." Hymns. Hymns.

Gagliano : So then I said, "Okay, what happens next?" He said, "Well, then the next thing is we'd go to the church or wherever the body was, and now we've got to go to the cemetery." He said, "That's when we'd play the slow dirge."
"Flee as the Bird to the Mountain." What we played here was, we used "Just a Closer Walk with Thee." And then, of course, he said, "After the body has been put in the ground and everybody is ready to leave, then we go into the Second Line set and then we start that." They said, "Well, what should we play?" I said, "I remember a tune called "I'll be Glad When You're Dead You Rascal You." So we played that. Then we would play, "Oh, Didn't He Ramble?" So the numbers were interchangeable, as long as it fit. And that's how I learned about it. I didn't know the sequence before that from my own experience, but in sitting down with the band and finding out about this—and, of course, I thought we did all of that in preparation for the Ohio concerts in '52, but all of this information we're uncovering suggests to me that we did it for the first time at McAlister. That contained the template for what we did later.

Martyn : Yeah, exactly. You could never convince me you were rehearsing in '49 for what you were going to do in '52 in Ohio. I mean, you didn't even know you were going to Ohio then.

Gagliano : We had no idea about where we would go. In fact, the students at Tulane would be interested in this, because, you know, Tulane had a lot of out-of-state students. But even the local white kids may not have been aware of the cultural aspect of this thing. So basically what we're doing as a band, is we are explaining to them what the black funeral music was all about, giving reasons. You know, but look, it went over great because every time we did it at the

148

college, man, and especially in Ohio – and we did it at McAlister. The pictures we have here seems to look like the band might have marched around the stage. But when we did it in Ohio, actually the horns went out in the hall. The horns went out into the audience, man, and, boy, I'll tell you, these students got ripped up. Well, they had never seen anything like that. Those young white kids, they didn't know what the hell was going on. I mean, even down here, you know. But in retrospect it does not seem that this concert at McAlister was recorded. I think that's pretty definite.

Martyn : Do you think George in these years had a plan for his career?

Gagliano : I don't know that he had a plan. He may have had an ambition. He said "After that situation in New York, we're gonna do it again, but we're gonna do it right this time".

Martyn : I wonder why so many bands, or maybe I should say black bands recorded in radio stations during the fifties.

Gagliano : I don't remember too much about the ownership of WDSU. When I was working as an engineer one of my premier jobs was the air conditioning and ventilation of WDSU TV studios. It was owned by Edgar Stern and the family was a very liberal Jewish family deeply involved in black causes. Mrs. Stern was an heir of the Sears Roebuck business.

Martyn : See they recorded the Red Allen session at WDSU and then did two sessions of the band with Alvin Alcorn on two separate days. August 6th was the session with Red and the first session with Alvin was on the same day. Then they did another session with Alvin on August 20th, 1951. I wonder why?

Gagliano : I have no idea.

Martyn : Here's a photo of George doing an interview with Al Rose and Joe Mares. Did he do many interviews on the radio talking to people?

WSMB broadcast. George Lewis, Al Rose (standing), Joe Mares

149

Gagliano : Now you'll notice here this is WSMB which stands for Maison Blanche. The studio was in the Maison Blanche building up on the roof. They were probably plugging one of Joe Mare's sessions.

Martyn : Why were they all called "W", the radio stations?

Gagliano : All the way up the Mississippi every station to the east of the river carries the letter "W" and all to the west they are starting with a "K". That goes all the way to Minnesota.

Martyn : To get back to the recordings with Red and Alvin Alcorn, I'm wondering why both Purnell and Lester Santiago are in the photo. Then it struck me, Purnell must have been there a Union Man. He was a "walkin delegate" as they called it. He was sent by the Union to check that the record company didn't tape more than they were supposed to.

Gagliano : And Purnell didn't play on any of the three sessions?

Martyn : That's right. Also I wanted to ask you, you told me that station WTPS stood for the "Times Picayune States". What would they be doing with a radio station?

Gagliano : Well it's just a media. The Times Picayune was a print media and the WTPS radio station would just compliment the newspaper. The station lasted for maybe ten years or so.

Martyn : There is one bootleg session that has been around for years with "West Indies Blues" and "Climax Rag" on it. It comes from WTPS.

Gagliano : I never heard it.

Martyn : I remember there's a short announcement on it where the guy says, "and now "Jamaica", which is really "West Indies Blues". I'll have to listen to it again and see if it's Alton or Charlie Hamilton, playing piano.

Gagliano : Well the announcer is probably Ed Hart. If you play it to me I'll recognize his voice.

Martyn : It's funny, something I wanted to tell you concerning the Doc Souchon session. When it first came out there was a 10-inch LP on Paradox and then an EP on PAX. The PAX release had three second takes and one different song, "Chicken ain't Nothing but a Bird". When the record came out it said, "Chicken" with unknown female vocalist and I showed it to Alton. He hit the roof, "Goddam. Shit – 'Unknown female vocalist' – I got to live with that!" He was incensed and he went on and on about it. I guess on that little humorous note we can end this chapter.

Nick and Marilyn Gagliano – Christmas 2009

Nick Gagliano

" In terms of how I look at it and what happened, all I can tell you is my experience
with the George Lewis Band was one of the most satisfying things I have ever done.
If my work with George seems to warrant this book –
well, nobody ever wrote a book about me as a lawyer. "

Barry Martyn

" The George Lewis Ragtime Band was the most exciting jazz band I ever heard.
The seven pieces generated so much in the way of ever-shifting patterns,
both melodically and rhythmically, that it is hard to describe if you never heard it live.
The band brought nothing but joy to millions of people, all over the world.
For those who have soul and a sense of aesthetics no explanation of their music is necessary.
For those who do not, no explanation is possible. "

The George Lewis Band in Ohio

George Lewis Book CD

1.) **"Lord, Lord You Sure Been Good To Me"**: (v. Howard)
Avery Howard, (trumpet), George Lewis (clarinet), Jim Robinson (trombone), Alton Purnell (piano), Lawrence Marrero, (banjo), Gene Mayl (tuba), Joe Watkins (drums) – 1953

2.) **"Corinne Corinna"**: (v. Watkins)
Personnel as for #1 but add Gene Mayl's trumpet player – 1953

3.) **"Sheik of Araby"**: (v. Watkins)
As for #2 – 1953

4.) *Dialogue between Joe, Lawrence and Jim*
with unknown female student, Harold Apel and John Ball – 1953

5.) **"Just a Closer Walk With Thee"**: (v. Watkins)
Gene Mayl's band with guest spots by George Lewis, Alton Purnell, Joe Watkins,
Lawrence Marrero, (enters halfway through song,), Percy Humphrey, and Jim Robinson
– 1952

6.) *Dialogue between Harold Apel, John Ball with George and Alton.*
Alton Purnell plays solo on "Boogie Woogie" and "Twelfth Street Rag" – 1953

7.) **"Corinne Corinna"**: (v. Lewis)
Gene Mayl's band with George Lewis and Alton Purnell – 1952

8.) *Dialogue between Harold Apel, John Ball, and George Lewis*
Subject: New Orleans Funerals – 1953

All the music here comes from two parties at John Ball's home with George Lewis'Band and the local musicians that made up Gene Mayl's band.

The first title is the complete George Lewis band with Gene guesting on tuba. Then, as at all party/jam sessions, the personnel fluctuates somewhat. The first three titles are from the band's 1953 College Tour in Ohio, as is all the dialogue. Track #8 with George talking about funerals is the most concise explanation I have ever heard on the subject.

The remaining two tracks (#5 & #7) are issued here to give the flavor of the 1952 tour. What is interesting is Percy's magnificent two chorus solo on #5 and George's vocal on #7.

Hopefully this CD of previously unissued material will give the listener the feeling of being on tour with the George Lewis Band in those barnstorming days.

Barry Martyn: New Orleans
September 2010